Praise for *The Proverbial Woman*

Amy Chase offers a fresh reading of the Proverbial Woman in Proverbs 31 that emphasizes the ambiguities and tensions that a dialogical reading of this text in its social context(s) offers. Attending to the role of narratology, affect theory, and feminist biblical interpretation, Chase helps the reader see that it is not unimportant which narrative we tell as words indeed create worlds.

—L. Juliana Claassens, professor of Old Testament, Stellenbosch University

The Proverbial Woman, like its biblical namesake, deserves great praise. Amy Chase has written a smart, compassionate, and compelling study of Proverbs 31. She attends to the complexity and literary art of the text while also inviting us to consider which voices might be neglected or silenced. *The Proverbial Woman* is a worthy guide to a complicated and important biblical text.

—Rhiannon Graybill, Marcus M. and Carole M. Weinstein & Gilbert M. and Fannie S. Rosenthal Chair of Jewish Studies, and professor of religious studies, University of Richmond

You may not recognize the women at the end of Proverbs after reading *The Proverbial Woman*! Expertly attuned to class and gender dynamics, this analysis reveals both King Lemuel's mother and the *eshet chayil* as complicated, surprising, and even troubling figures. Many communities and commentators focus on these exceptional women, exalting especially the *eshet chayil*; Chase's reading exposes multifaceted figures more worthy of resistance than of emulation.

—Jennifer L. Koosed, professor of religious studies, Albright College

In *The Proverbial Woman*, Amy Chase artfully presents a fresh reading of Proverbs 31's poems, uncovering their multivalent meanings regarding the privileged class, vulnerable groups, dynamic dialogues between family members in their respective socioeconomic contexts, the silenced characters, and their elite counterparts. Her carefully crafted questions about the text engage the reader creatively in contemplating the implications of identity construction and deconstruction in the act of reading the text in its context.

—Chloe T. Sun, professor of Old Testament and program director of the Chinese Studies Center, Fuller Theological Seminary

Close readings of texts can produce expansive rather than restrictive meanings, and deconstructive as well as generative savvy in theorizing and interpretation. That is what Amy Chase accomplishes in *The Proverbial Woman: Class, Gender, and Power in Hebrew Poetry*. Deploying insights from the field of narratology to examine questions of genre, gender, economics, cultural context, ethics, and spirituality in the prose-poetry of Proverbs 31, Chase demonstrates how texts and textual interpretations can be damaging to marginalized subjects and, thus, are in need of new and fresh readings. By centering and decentralizing the *eshet chayil* and placing her alongside other characters, Chase successfully and brilliantly offers an interpretive gift of the values of polyvalence, polyphony, disputation, and ambiguity in the search for the Proverbial Woman. She does this in regard to the text about her as well as interpretive traditions that provoke both admiration and unpleasantness, especially when pressed up against the discrepancies and precarity of personal, communal, historical, and cultural life in the face of power imbalances, empire, and the possibilities of transgressing boundaries that marginalize. Chase's detailed analyses move beyond literary and exegetical minutiae, bringing together epistemological clarity and ambiguity, contextual specificity and nuance, identity formation and ethical/ideological struggle for the interpretation of Proverbs 31. The result is a powerful reading in the field of Proverbs studies that pushes against dominant and binary modes

of material, ideological, and male-gendered interpretations of the text—which Chase describes as distortion—to reveal readings in favor of marginalized characters in the text and the ethical work that such marginalization does in the productions of the Proverbial Woman.
—Kenneth Ngwa, John Fletcher Hurst Professor of Hebrew Bible, Drew Theological Seminary

The Proverbial Woman—who can find her? If we think we have found her neatly contained and ripe for emulation in Proverbs 31, Amy Chase suggests we think again. In both her guises—the outspoken queen mother instructing her son and the dazzlingly resourceful wife ensuring her husband's success—the contradictory and controversial Proverbial Woman has a complicated story that teems with nameless people, churns with social struggles, and spills beyond the page to capture its audience in its morally compromising currents. In Chase's expert reading, the Proverbial Woman steps firmly off her traditional pedestal and enters a messier fray that reflects, generates, and challenges the elitist impulses to survive and succeed at the expense of others. A truly remarkable study that deepens our knowledge as readers and our awareness as moral agents.
—Danna Nolan Fewell, John Fletcher Hurst Professor Emerita of Hebrew Bible, Drew University

A damaging text such as Proverbs 31, like many an androcentric and elitist text in the Hebrew Bible, has been used to "other" and damage subdued voices. In her book, *The Proverbial Woman: Class, Gender, and Power in Hebrew Poetry*, Amy J. Chase successfully enables justice-seeking readers to "hear" the multiple muted voices of the underclass in Proverbs 31 and frees them "to step into a public square, open our mouth, and be the speaker who calls for what we want and need." It is a must-read for all justice-seeking Hebrew Bible scholars and students, religious leaders in general, and clergy persons in particular.
—Madipoane Masenya (Ngwan'a Mphahlele), professor emeritus, Department of Biblical and Ancient Studies, University of South Africa (Unisa)

The Proverbial Woman

The Proverbial
WOMAN

Class, Gender, and Power
in Hebrew Poetry

Amy J. Chase

FORTRESS PRESS
MINNEAPOLIS

THE PROVERBIAL WOMAN
Class, Gender, and Power in Hebrew Poetry

Copyright © 2024 Fortress Press, an imprint of 1517 Media. All rights reserved. Except for brief quotations in critical articles or reviews, no part of this book may be reproduced in any manner without prior written permission from the publisher. Email copyright@1517.media or write to Permissions, Fortress Press, PO Box 1209, Minneapolis, MN 55440-1209.

29 28 27 26 25 24   1 2 3 4 5 6 7 8 9

Library of Congress Control Number: 2024933940 (print)

Cover image: The god-fearing wife praised by Solomon (Prov. 31) by Ephraim Moses Lilien, 1914, with collaged textures
Cover design: Kristin Miller

Print ISBN: 978-1-5064-9153-0
eBook ISBN: 978-1-5064-9154-7

Contents

	Acknowledgments	vii
	Proverbs 31	ix
1.	Bourgeois Poems and Proletariat Poets	1
2.	The Drama of Mothers and Kings: Proverbs 31:1–9	33
3.	Of Wifely Exertions: Proverbs 31:10–22	65
4.	Designing Woman: Proverbs 31:23–30	95
5.	Class and Conflict at the City Gates: Proverbs 31:31	135
6.	The Implications of Wisdom's Cry	161
	Bibliography	177
	Subject Index	187
	Scripture Index	191

Acknowledgments

I'm grateful for the encouragement and guidance extended to me by so many while producing this book. Thank you to my Fuller community conversation partners, Pamela Scalise and Beth Elness-Hanson. Thanks also to my professors at Drew University, especially those on my dissertation committee: Danna Nolan Fewell, Melanie Johnson-DeBaufre, and Kenneth Ngwa. Your insights stretched me and deepened discovery of the *eshet chayil* as gleaned from socionarratological study of Proverbs 31. I'm grateful for the companionship of Elizabeth Freese in our weekly writing sessions, as well as that of The Professor Is In's daily writing groups, with most loyal participants Tanya Walker and Rebecca Williams. I appreciate also Lisa Withrow for pointing me toward Fortress Press, and editor Ryan Hemmer for his support in transforming my PhD dissertation into a book suitable for multiple audiences. Finally, I thank my husband, Brian Loudermilk, for steadfastly serving as my rock to lean on. Your faith in me and this project has made all the difference. To our children, Ben and Jane: I hope this book makes you proud, as I am proud of you.

Proverbs 31

1. The words of Lemuel, a king, the burden [*massa*] with which she rebuked [*yasar*] him, his mother:
2. "What, my son—and what?! son of my womb; and what—? Son of my vows?!
3. Do not give to women your strength [*chayil*], or your ways to devourers [*makhoth*] of kings."
4. "Not for kings, Lemuel, not for kings the drinking of wine, or for princes, beer.
5. ... Lest he should drink and forget the decrees and change the verdict of the sons of oppression."
6. "'Give beer to the perishing, and wine to the bitter of soul'—
7. Let him drink and forget his poverty; let him not remember his toil anymore."
8. "Open your mouth for the speechless, on behalf of all who are perishing.
9. Open your mouth—judge rightly! Plead the case of the poor and oppressed."
10. *Eshet chayil*, who can find? Her value is far beyond jewels.
11. Her husband takes shelter in her, and never lacks for plunder.
12. She supplies for him good things, not bad, all the days of her life.
13. She pursues wool and flax and applies her hands with pleasure.
14. She is like trading ships; from far away she brings her food.

PROVERBS 31

15. And she rises while it is still night and provides prey to her household and assigned tasks [/portions] to her girls.
16. She schemes to get a field and seizes it; from the fruit of her hand she plants a vineyard.
17. She binds with strength her loins, and she braces her arms.
18. She knows that her trading is good, and her lamp does not go out at night.
19. Her hands thrust toward the distaff; her palms grasp the spindle-whorl.
20. Her palm she stretches toward the poor; her hands thrust toward the oppressed.
21. She does not fear snow for her household, for all her household are clothed in double layers.
22. She makes bed coverings for herself; linen and purple are her clothes.
23. Known at the gates is her husband, in his sitting with the elders of the city.
24. Fine linen wraps she makes and sells; woven belts she delivers to traders.
25. Strength and honor are her garments, and she laughs about the days to come.
26. She opens her mouth with wisdom, and the teaching of loyalty is on her tongue.
27. Watching over the actions of her household, for laziness does not eat bread.
28. Her sons arise and bless her, her husband, and he praises her.
29. "Many daughters do *chayil*, but you, you ascend above them all!"
30. 'Charm is false and beauty a vapor': a woman—fear of Yahweh—she! *She* will be praised.
31. Give to her from the fruit of her hands, and let them [/they will] praise her in the gates, her works.

CHAPTER ONE

Bourgeois Poems and Proletariat Poets

Two women speak in Proverbs 31. One speaks with her words, the other with her actions. Only a few biblical texts feature women, so naturally this text commands attention. Many read for role models, for guidance on who and how women ought to be, while others want to understand how such an influential text constructs expectations of the same. For some, the proverbial woman is assertive. For others, she is the paragon of submission.

I, as a reader, want to be friends with this text. But: "An excellent wife, who can find?" (Prov 31:10).[1] This line generates *unpleasantness* within. One part of me tries to reassure myself that it is only a setup to a perfectly innocuous litany of praise, yet the feeling nonetheless remains: a tiny cringing. "He never lacks . . ." and "She supplies him . . ." These lines, too, provoke. Why?

Emotions signal an interpretation of reality, based on bodily stimuli and past experience.[2] As I try to understand my experience of affect in relation to this poem, I recall other instances of

---

1 ESV, NASB translation. Others offer "Who can find a virtuous wife?" (KJV); "A good woman is hard to find" (The Message); "A wife of noble character, who can find?" (NIV); "A capable wife who can find?" (NRSV).

2 Lisa Feldman Barrett, *How Emotions Are Made: The Secret Life of the Brain* (New York: Houghton Mifflin, 2017), 59.

unpleasantness in similar contexts. I recall my very first reading of Genesis 2 and 3: summertime, aged fourteen, bayside on a towel with my Bible, a journal, and a snack. I read then: "It is not good for the man to be alone. I will make a helper suitable for him" (Gen 2:18 NIV). First animals, then a woman formed of the rib of a man. "'She shall be called 'woman,' for she was taken out of man" (Gen 2:23 NIV). The serpent comes, then shame and blame, pains in childbirth, and Adam names again, this time "Eve, because she would become the mother of all the living" (Gen 3:20 NIV). I remember a similar sinking feeling then, difficult to distinguish but containing surprise, confusion, sadness, and dread. This prominent story in the Bible's first pages presents the proto-woman as an afterthought, as dupe or villainess, deserving of suffering and subjugation, labeled by a man according to his vision and values. It did not seem right to me. But I did not want to be disloyal to God, to my ideas about God, or to my many family members, friends, and church mentors who encouraged me in faith. So, I shut my Bible and pushed away my unpleasant gut reaction to this biblical text.

I understand now that emotion is a type of knowing to which we all, instead of ignoring, should attend. Emotion is not an alternative to rationality or an inferior mental activity, nor does it occur after thoughts as mere reactions to them. "Emotions are meaning," writes psychologist Lisa Feldman Barrett. They are concepts formed of mental categorizations and predictions, and they are invitations to action.[3] So while biblical scholars must exercise reason and logic to study and communicate, our work ought also to include identifying emotional appeals or triggers in biblical texts as essential aspects of interpretation. What meaning does my unpleasant affect, sparked by Proverbs 31, contribute? Does it convey information about the text, or myself the reader, or both, or something else, something more?

According to Barrett, both *affect*—the general sense of pleasant or unpleasant, and calm or agitation—and *emotions*—experiences

---

3 Barrett, *How Emotions Are Made*, 126–27.

more specific and varied than affect—aid the brain in assessing the body's energy needs.[4] These internal activities in turn aid in budgeting energy outputs to meet those needs.[5] Presumably, an unpleasant experience anticipates some strain. The snippets of Proverbs 31 cited above are androcentric, projecting male interests and values, relaying what a man sees in a woman he values. I am not male; I am female, so I do not really know whether this text aligns with my interests or values or how I see the world. Perhaps that is what I know about this poem in my feeling about it.

These lines are representative of Proverbs 31's "arrogant eye" focalizing the poem. As Hilde Lindemann Nelson defines this term, an arrogant eye indicates the gaze of dominant group members who take their own "standpoint as central, their needs, opinions, and desires and projects as the salient ones, their experience and understanding as what is the case."[6] Those outside the dominant group matter only according to how they affect the dominant group; they are otherwise dismissed, degraded.[7] Such attitudes and accompanying actions shape these outsiders' identities, damaging them as the dominant group's evaluation of the other as inferior limits these others' opportunities for valuable social roles and key relationships.[8] Identity shaping can occur via direct interaction among community members or through exposure to communal master narratives, wherein readers identify with characters who have been assigned certain characteristics that imbue them with distinct functions, privileges, or constraints. Such narratives have heft because they are topically "woven around the features of people's lives that they . . . care about most."[9] A text with heft is bound to stick around, to have a lasting impact on its readers.

---

4 Barrett, *How Emotions Are Made*, 66.
5 Barrett, *How Emotions Are Made*, 73.
6 Hilde Lindemann Nelson, *Damaged Identities, Narrative Repair* (Ithaca, NY: Cornell University Press, 2001), 173.
7 Lindemann Nelson, *Damaged Identities, Narrative Repair*, 173.
8 Lindemann Nelson, *Damaged Identities, Narrative Repair*, 20.
9 Lindemann Nelson, *Damaged Identities, Narrative Repair*, 96.

Proverbs 31 may be considered just such a text. Its two poems concern relationships, power, wealth, success. David Blumenthal writes of biblical texts: "As one reads the stories, studies the laws, and ponders the images, metaphors, and figures of women, one absorbs, almost subliminally, the attitudes that these sources convey."[10] Perhaps identity construction is what my unpleasant feeling is on the lookout for. Am I in danger of being damaged by this text?

But women are central in Proverbs 31, praised and projected as strong, a loyalist might protest. How could that be bad for you—or for me? As Mikhail Bakhtin notes, no utterance occurs in isolation but rather is said in response to what has been said before while anticipating responses still to come.[11] Context contributes to meaning, not only the surrounding "what is said," but also the "what is not said but implied" and the "what is not said for a reason that itself matters." In *Letting Stories Breathe: A Socio-narratology*, Arthur Frank explains multiple ways stories can be dangerous. They can "project possible futures, and those projections affect what comes to be."[12] They can misleadingly simplify inherently complex situations, distort reality through binaries of us/them or right/wrong, cause readers to identify with, root for, and imitate people who are not actually good. Any one story's popularity prevents alternate versions from being circulated, limiting the culture's models and messages. Proverbs 31's two poems, not full narratives, are narrative-like, with inferable conflicts, characters, settings, and events, and thus resemble stories in all their identity-shaping potential, for good or for harm.

---

10 David R. Blumenthal, "Images of Women in the Hebrew Bible," in *Marriage, Sex, and Family in Judaism*, ed. M. Broyde (Lanham, MD: Rowman & Littlefield, 2005), 16.

11 Mikhail Bakhtin, "The Problem of Speech Genres," in *Speech Genres and Other Late Essays*, ed. Caryl Emerson and Michael Holquist, trans. Vern W. McGee (Austin: University of Texas Press, 1987), 69.

12 Arthur Frank, *Letting Stories Breathe: A Socio-narratology* (Chicago: University of Chicago Press, 2010), 10.

THE CONTESTED MEANINGS OF PROVERBS 31

In this history of interpretation, Proverbs 31's narrative elements shaping identity have been only minimally acknowledged. Scholars have studied the text to understand its genre and form, labeling verses 1–9 as an instruction, resembling Egyptian and other ancient Near Eastern wisdom literature.[13] They identify verses 10–31 as encomium or variation of the heroic hymn genre, one that exalts economic and domestic productivity instead of praising military exploits.[14] Scholars have analyzed the structure of Proverbs 31, seeking patterns, usually recognizing little by way of thematic development, but noting in verses 10–31 an acrostic form and a chiasm or two. Scholars, too, have tackled puzzling vocabulary and syntax to understand how these fit in their context or whether they might signal textual corruption. Albert Wolters's theory that the first word of verse 27 involves a Hebrew pun on the Greek word *sophia* (meaning "wisdom") has attracted much attention for its implications for the theme and dating of the poem.[15] Alexander Rofé examines verse 30's phrase *yir'ath yahweh*, concluding based on comparison with other texts that it is not original but a later substitution for a word meaning "intelligence," made by a copyist who believed a religious reference more suitable to themes of wisdom literature.[16]

Scholars have also explored Proverbs 31's primary themes, connecting them to messages elsewhere in Proverbs, in other wisdom literature, or in other biblical passages. Earlier treatments labeled verses 1–9 as an oracle on royal duty, while more recent studies note

---

13 E.g., James L. Crenshaw, "A Mother's Instruction to Her Son (Proverbs 31:1–9)," *PRSt* 15, no. 4 (1988): 9–22.

14 See Albert Wolters, "Proverbs 31:10–31 as Heroic Hymn: A Form-Critical Analysis," *VT* 38, no. 4 (1988): 446–57.

15 Albert Wolters, "Ṣôpiyyâ (Prov 31:27) as Hymnic Participle and Play on Sophia," *JBL* 104, no. 4 (December 1985): 577–87.

16 Alexander Rofé, "The Valiant Woman, *gynē sunetē* and the Redaction of the Book of Proverbs," in *Vergegenwartigun des Alten Testaments*, ed. Christoph Bultmann, Walter Dietrich, and Christoph Levin (Gottingen: Vandenhoeck & Ruprecht, 2002), 153.

its sympathetic portrayal of the poor, contrasting with attitudes elsewhere in biblical literature associating poverty with laziness or other moral infraction.[17] But do these sentiments genuinely represent the needs and perspectives of the poor?[18] Joanna Stiebert writes that this mother's "claims to champion the oppressed are questionable at best, sinister at worst."[19] As for the acrostic in verses 10–31, much debate has taken place concerning the nature of the *eshet chayil*, whether a real or ideal woman, an allegory or personification of wisdom, aspect of God, or incarnation of a goddess. Many build on Claudia Camp's argument for viewing the *eshet chayil* as both an ideal woman and a representation of wisdom drawn from the activities of real women.[20] Jacqueline Vayntrub's recent study highlights the poem's multiple mentions of hands as "agents of productivity" promoting "active, learned wisdom *above* passive, natural beauty."[21]

Scholars of a more historical bent analyze Proverbs 31 for indicators of the social conditions in the era producing this text. According to Ehud Ben Zvi, verses 10–31 constitute "an ideal site of memory" that enabled the Persian-era Yehudite community to explore and express its views about necessary economic activity.[22] Hans-Peter Mathys identifies several allusions to Phoenicians in Proverbs

---

17 James Crenshaw, "Poverty and Punishment in the Book of Proverbs," *QR* 9, no. 3 (1989): 30.

18 A pushback explored by such scholars as Eben Scheffler ("Poverty in the Book of Proverbs: Looking from Above?," *Scriptura* 111 [2012]: 480–96) and Makhosazana Keith Nzimande ("Postcolonial Interpretation in Post-apartheid South Africa: The Gibirah in the Hebrew Bible in the Light of Queen Jezebel and the Queen Mother of Lemuel" [PhD diss., Bright Divinity School, 2005]).

19 Johanna Stiebert, "The People's Bible, Imbokodo and the King's Mother's teaching of Proverbs 31," *BibInt* 20, no. 3 (2012): 278.

20 Claudia V. Camp, *Wisdom and the Feminine in the Book of Proverbs* (Decatur, GA: Almond, 1985), 93.

21 Jacqueline Vayntrub, "Beauty, Wisdom, and Handiwork in Proverbs 31:10–31," *HTR* 113, no. 1 (2020): 54.

22 Ehud Ben Zvi, "The 'Successful, Wise, Worthy Wife' of Proverbs 31:10–31 as a Source for Reconstructing Aspects of Thought and Economy in the Late Persian / Early Hellenistic Period," in *The Economy of Ancient Judah in Its Historical Context*, ed. Marvin Lloyd Miller et al. (Winona Lake, IN: Eisenbrauns, 2015), 28, 31.

31:10–31, explaining how the *eshet chayil*'s positive depiction as a Phoenician promotes her as an accomplished trader and particularly wise.[23] Christine Yoder also focuses on economic references to demonstrate how "woman wisdom" of Proverbs 1–9 resembles the real-life woman that is Proverbs 31's *eshet chayil*. Yoder's "socioeconomic reading" connects economic success with wisdom and piety to convince young men of the advantages of marrying well, including increased wealth, honor, security, and leisure.[24]

Much has been gleaned also about the worlds behind and within Proverbs 31 through comparison with other texts. Bernhard Lang compares the "Hebrew wife" of Proverbs 31 to the Ottoman wife described in a presumedly contemporaneous text, Xenophon's *Oeconomicus*, concluding that her activities typify the gendered division of labor prevalent in ancient societies.[25] Antje Labahn compares Proverbs 31 to a text from Elephantine in Egypt that describes the activities of a similarly wealthy woman, the Egyptian Mibtahiah, who is noted as enjoying greater juridical equality with men.[26] Scholars have also read Proverbs 31 intertextually with Ruth, in which the titular character is also named an *eshet chayil* (Ruth 3:11), and with Esther.[27]

---

23 Hans-Peter Mathys. "The Valiant Housewife of Proverbs 31:10–31: A Phoenician Business Woman," in *Foreign Women—Women in Foreign Lands*, ed. Angelika Berlejung and Marianne Grohmann (Tubingen: Mohr Siebeck, 2019), 157–74.

24 Christine Yoder, *Wisdom as a Woman of Substance: A Socioeconomic Reading of Proverbs 1–9 and 31:10–31* (Berlin: de Gruyter, 2001).

25 Bernhard Lang, "The Hebrew Wife and the Ottoman Wife: An Anthropological Essay on Proverbs 31:10–31," in *Anthropology and Biblical Studies: Avenues of Approach*, ed. Louise J. Lawrence and Mario I. Aguilar (Leiden: Brill, 2004), 149.

26 Antje Labahn, "'Wealthy Women' in Antiquity: the 'Capable Woman' of Proverbs 31:10–31 and Mibtahiah from Elephantine," *IDS* 48, no. 1 (2014): 1.

27 Elaine Goh, "An Intertextual Reading of Ruth and Proverbs 31:10–31, with a Chinese Woman's Perspective," in *Reading Ruth in Asia*, ed. Jione Havea and Peter H. W. Lau (Atlanta: SBL Press, 2016); Samuel Goh, "Ruth as a Superior Woman of חיל?: A Comparison between Ruth and the 'Capable' Woman in Proverbs 31.10–31," *JSOT* 38, no. 4 (2014): 487–500; Joel Soza, "Linking the אשת חיל ('Woman of Strength') of Proverbs and Ruth in the Leningrad Codex,"

In a recently published summary of Proverbs scholarship, Alice Ogden Bellis notes the emergence and continuing significance of readings from non-Western and gender-sensitive perspectives.[28] Sun-Ah Kang is representative of such scholarship in her essay, "Re-reading a 'Virtuous Woman' (*eshet chayil*) in Proverbs 31:10–31." Kang argues that a contemporary Korean context causes the woman described in Proverbs 31:10–31 to be frequently construed according to Confucian ideals prevalent in Korean culture. Thus the *eshet chayil* is viewed as entirely subordinate, sacrificing herself in service to her husband and children, without the companionship of friends or family. Yet, Kang writes, the influence of Confucianism can be resisted through rereading the text in light of Michel Foucault's model of panopticon, wherein a real or imagined invisible gaze of the other acts as a control. Recognizing the "anonymous gaze of the narrator" in Proverbs 31 reveals that though her agency is limited, the *eshet chayil* nonetheless remains fearless and strong.[29]

Kang's gender-sensitive reading follows the work of multiple feminist scholars studying Proverbs 31. Beatrice Lawrence applies gender theory to note in this text a canonization of a certain division of labor that enables males to embody the public face of society while women do everything else. According to Lawrence, describing the female protagonist with masculine images shows that ancient Israelite literature "demonstrates playfulness and flexibility in its use of gender."[30] Camp perceives an empowered depiction of the ideal woman in Proverbs 31, explaining the three mentions of *betah* ("her

---

ATJ 45 (2013): 21–28; David J. Zucker, "Esther: Subverting the 'Capable Wife,'" *BTB* 48, no. 4 (2018): 171–78.

28 Alice Ogden Bellis, "Proverbs in Recent Research," *CurBR* 20, no. 2 (2022): 133–64.

29 Sun-Ah Kang, "Re-reading a 'Virtuous Woman' (*eshet chayil*) in Proverbs 31:10–31," in *Landscapes of Korean and Korean American Biblical Interpretation*, ed. John Ahn (Atlanta: SBL Press, 2019), 139, 143.

30 Beatrice Lawrence, "Gender Analysis: Gender and Method in Biblical Studies," in *Method Matters: Essays on the Interpretation of the Hebrew Bible in Honor of David L. Petersen*, ed. Joel M. LeMon and Kent H. Richards (Atlanta: Society of Biblical Literature, 2009), 343.

house") as indicating that the woman depicted not only runs the household but defines it, supplying its very identity. That the poem refers to her husband as *ba'al* ("master," or "lord") Camp deems "almost ironic."[31] Madipoane Masenya understands the projection of women and men in Proverbs 31 as defense against a worry that marriages to women deemed foreign could disrupt "the socio-economic, socio-political and socio-religious lives of the 'true' Jews and ultimately of the whole nation." Although, to Masenya, the text is mainly patriarchal, it can still offer liberative possibilities to women in her South African context.[32]

Other feminist interpreters exude more skepticism toward Proverbs 31, in terms of its content, authors, and traditionally male interpreters. Cheryl Kirk-Duggan reads verses 1–9 and 10–31 as one pericope in which a queen/mother warrior is a victim of systematic oppression and exhibits multiple "pathologies" that inhibit healthy self-care or mothering.[33] Carole Fontaine writes that the mother of verses 1–9 has internalized the male fear of women prevalent throughout Proverbs.[34] Diane Bergant describes her as androcentric, discriminatory, and actively participating in cultivating the next patriarch.[35] As for the woman of verses 10–31, Esther Fuchs labels her a typical depiction of "good" wives in the Hebrew Bible, classified as good solely because of their devotion toward their husbands.[36] Single women are not empowered by the *eshet chayil*, writes Wilda

---

31 Camp, *Wisdom and the Feminine*, 91.
32 Madipoane Masenya, *How Worthy Is the Woman of Worth? Rereading Proverbs 31:10–31 in African-South Africa* (New York: Peter Lang, 2004), 99, 126.
33 Cheryl A. Kirk-Duggan, "Rethinking the 'Virtuous' Woman (Proverbs 31): A Mother in Need of Holiday," in *Mother Goose, Mother Jones, Mommie Dearest*, ed. Cheryl A. Kirk-Duggan and Tina Pippin (Leiden: Brill, 2009), 111.
34 Carole Fontaine, "Proverbs," in *The Women's Bible Commentary*, ed. Carol A. Newsom and Sharon H. Ringe (Louisville: Westminster John Knox, 1998), 159.
35 Diane Bergant, *Israel's Wisdom Literature: A Liberation-Critical Reading* (Minneapolis: Fortress, 1997), 98–99.
36 Esther Fuchs, *Sexual Politics in the Biblical Narrative: Reading the Hebrew Bible as a Woman*, JSOTSup 310 (Sheffield: Sheffield Academic, 2000), 174.

Gafney.[37] Juliana Claassens writes, "Glaringly absent from the Strong Woman's life is the right to political participation and free speech."[38] Yoder points out that these verses of tribute constitute also an objectification of women.[39]

An interesting collection of Proverbs 31 readings has emerged among African scholars who draw on perceived similarities with African culture to interpret and apply this text. Lechion Peter Kimilike views verses 1–9 as reflecting challenges similar to those faced in modern-day Tanzania, with varied mentions of the plight of the poor indicating the "multifaceted nature of poverty that subjects households, communities and society at large to a state of powerlessness, hopelessness, and a lack of self-esteem, confidence and integrity." For Kimilike, the oracle's advice to leaders models a "transformative metaphor."[40]

Many African commentators share the concerns of Western feminists as to the impact of this text on women. Ezra Chitando connects African interpretations of Proverbs 31 to the spread of HIV infection among African women, arguing that these interpretations condition wives not to advocate for needed resources, and they condition husbands to believe that they have bought their wives and thus the right to have sex with them anytime and in any manner, with no regard for the impact on their women.[41] Chitando, like Kang and Masenya,

---

37 Wilda C. M. Gafney, "Who Can Find a Militant Feminist? A Marginal(ized) Reading of Proverbs 31:1–31," *The AME Zion Quarterly Review* 112, no. 2 (2000): 29.

38 L. Juliana Claassens, "The Woman of Substance and Human Flourishing: Proverbs 31:10–31 and Martha Nussbaum's Capabilities Approach," *JFSR* 32, no. 1 (2016): 14.

39 Christine Yoder, "The Woman of Substance (*'št-Ḥyl*): A Socioeconomic Reading of Proverbs 31:10–31," *JBL* 122, no. 3 (2003): 446.

40 Legion Peter Kimilike, "Poverty Context in Proverbs 31:1–9: A Bena Tanzanian Analysis for Transformational Leadership Training," *OTE* 31, no. 1 (2018): 147, 157.

41 Ezra Chitando, "'The Good Wife': A Phenomenological Re-reading of Proverbs 31:10–31 in the Context of HIV/AIDS In Zimbabwe," *Scriptura* 86 (2004): 153.

also advocates rereading, noting that a woman compared to a jewel (v. 10) ought to be treasured, protected, and cared for.

Other African scholars lean into perceived similarities between traditional African culture and the cultures reflected in biblical texts. Emmanuel Nwaoru offers the genre of *oriki* oral poetry from Nigeria to illuminate Proverbs 31 as not a hymn but an individual recitation of praise, perhaps for a funeral.[42] Joel Biwul warns the modern woman of Nigeria not to adopt "intruding ideologies foreign to her socio-cultural and religious upbringing" but rather to imitate Proverbs 31's "submissive and respectful wife" in demonstrating traditional African respect for elders and those in authority.[43] In a second essay he engages what Masenya decries as a "hi-jacking" of the *eshet chayil* to elevate the contribution of the husband in Proverbs 31, arguing that his unimpeachable moral character is what enables the *eshet chayil's* success.[44]

APPRAISING THE APPRAISALS

Of these investigations, and others as well, much can be appreciated. My approach builds on many of them to examine the narrative elements shaping identity for individuals in community, especially the feminist lens and the recognition of economic priorities in verses 10–31. As to narrative, Ben Zvi employs terms such as "story," "villains," and "plot" in his historical analysis. Although such references for him are largely decorative, they encourage us to think of the two poems narratively. Others participate in understanding the poems as

---

[42] Emmanuel Nwaoru, "Image of the Woman of Substance in Proverbs 31:10–31 and African Context," *BN* 127 (2005): 41–66.

[43] Joel Biwul, "Reading the Virtuous Woman of Proverbs 31 as a Reflection of the Attributes of the Traditional Miship Woman of Tanzania," *OTE* 26, no. 2 (2013): 288.

[44] Madipoane Masenya, "Brief Notes: Response to Biwul," *OTE* 29, no. 2 (2016): 360; Joel Biwul, "What Is He Doing at the Gate? Understanding Proverbs 31:23 and Its Implications for Responsible Manhood in the Context of African Societies," *OTE* 29, no. 1 (2016): 33–60.

narratives when imaginatively filling out details of the text's character constructions. For example, Leo Perdue surmises that Lemuel is a newly installed king: "Perhaps his royal father has recently died."[45] Kirk-Duggan asks of the *eshet chayil*, "What are her thoughts about her life and her world?"[46] So, too, does J. J. Kimche, in considering whether the husband is a "dominant, central protagonist or an absent, uninvolved, even submissive figure."[47]

Those who acknowledge multiple ways of reading this text, multiple meanings, and the relevance of context in making meaning open opportunities for my identification and integration of gaps, contradictions, ambiguities, and multiplicities of meaning present in Proverbs 31. Fontaine's research into female proverb performance notes that women and men can tell the same story with different meanings[48] and thus that interpretation of Proverbs 31 ought to include consideration of what gender of voice speaks and how gender affects meaning. Kimche writes, "The sparse, lyrical, and multifaceted depictions of the [*eshet chayil*] provide space for the reader to cast this literary character in an array of divergent molds."[49]

Of value also are readings that query the intent of the poems' authors, either conceived as individuals or as a collective of scribes or literati. Ernst Wendland asks, "What is the rhetorical point and purpose of this ode to the noble wife? What did the original author of this poem and/or the final editor of Proverbs want to teach any potential (implied) audience through such an artistically composed discourse?"[50] Ben Zvi asks what the Proverbs 31 acrostic was *doing* for the ancient community, and he answers that its intent was to socialize

---

[45] Leo G. Perdue, *Proverbs* (Louisville: Westminster John Knox, 2000), 271.
[46] Kirk-Duggan, "Rethinking the 'Virtuous' Woman," 100.
[47] J. J. Kimche, "A Husband of Valor: Who Can Find? The Husband's Role in Proverbs 31:10–31," *JBQ* 49, no. 3 (2021): 148.
[48] Carole R. Fontaine, *Smooth Words: Women, Proverbs, and Performance in Biblical Wisdom* (London: Sheffield Academic, 2002), 151.
[49] Kimche, "Husband of Valor," 154.
[50] Ernst Wendland, "Communicating the Beauty of a Wise and 'Worthy Wife' (Prov 31:10–31): From Hebrew Acrostic Hymn to a Tonga Traditional Praise Poem," *OTE* 19, no. 3 (2006): 1252.

men and women to value trade and profit making as good for the entire community. While authorial intent can never be definitively determined, asking such questions empowers others to attend not only to the words themselves on the page but also to how these words represent interests and agendas of people forming them, which is relevant to meaning.

In addition to questions as to *intent*, observations of *impact* hold value. A plethora of scholars and laypersons have identified how the unlivable fantasy of Proverbs 31:10–31 sets up expectations of servitude compromising women's well-being. Ilze Jansen writes, "A contextual reading of Proverbs 31:10–31 indicates that the pericope was and is still being used to judge women and their conduct, not only personally but also professionally."[51] Claassens notes that the potentially damaging effect of Proverbs 31 extends beyond gender to include also class. Of the *eshet chayil* she writes, "Proverbs 31 offers a view from a socially privileged class who may be exploiting those less privileged."[52]

The Proverbial Woman considers both intentions and impacts as part of its interpretive approach to Proverbs 31. It aims to supplement—sometimes correct—prior interpretations in specific ways. It deprioritizes definitive claims in favor of accuracy in acknowledging ambiguities or polyphony. Examples abound. The term *chayil* (v. 10) is well known to possess multiple nuances and associations, several of which recur throughout the two poems: fighting, economic wealth, sexual virility. Choosing one to the exclusion of others distorts. Most commentators simply choose one, thereby dulling this multifaceted woman into "an excellent wife," "a capable wife," "a woman of valor," "a strong woman," "industrious wife," and so on.

Existing interpretations often derive claims based on assumptions about genre that are not actually indicated: not the claims, the assumptions, or the genre. Genres are imprecise, a best guess at patterns of structure, style, and content, and interpreters should

---

51 Ilze Jansen, "Proverbs 31:10–31: A Contextual Reading," *Verbum et Ecclesia* 41, no. 1 (2020): 1.

52 Claassens, "Woman of Substance," 16.

understand them as such. Otherwise, as Mieke Bal writes, "Masterful interpretations based on invisible assumptions can ... be given an authority that censors other views."[53] Proverbs 31 is classified as wisdom literature, verses 1–9 an "instruction," which has caused interpreters to filter out any suggestion of emotion or drama and to read only for somber, dignified counsel, as when James Crenshaw translates *mah* as "listen" (v. 2) instead of the literal "what."[54] Verses 10–31 are presumed to fit the genre of encomium, a praise of a virtuous wife, and this presumption filters from view any critique or contradiction in the text. Such outcome Bruce Waltke acknowledges in commenting on verse 15: "The incomplete metaphor of a predator, she provides (*wattiten*, see 1:4) *prey* for its young (*trp*) is so shocking that most translators and the LXX, which reads *brōmata*, opt to render *ṭerep* [as] 'food.'"[55] "Food" fits the expectations of an encomium.

Some approach the task of interpretation as if the social location of interpreters does not matter. In one sense, we all must know that it does, because so much effort is put into studying conditions in the ancient Near East, using this background to explain biblical references that would otherwise not be understood to people living in quite different conditions today. Yet when it comes to differences among present-day interpreters, these have traditionally been ignored or minimized, resulting in interpretations that seem natural to those that hold them but that are not to many others. Waltke claims the *eshet chayil* "is exclusively a homemaker," but, thanks to her *husband's* success, is free to "settle down and function to her maximum ideal," running a "cottage industry."[56] Such portrayal says more about the life experience and worldview of

---

53 Mieke Bal, *Narratology: Introduction to the Theory of Narrative* (Toronto: University of Toronto Press, 2009), 16–17.

54 Crenshaw, "Mother's Instruction," 11. Also, William McKane references Arabic *ma* as favoring the meanings "'listen,' 'take heed'" (*Proverbs: A New Approach* [Philadelphia: Westminster, 1970], 408).

55 Bruce Waltke, *The Book of Proverbs: Chapters 15–31* (Grand Rapids: Eerdmans, 2005), 524–25.

56 Waltke, *Book of Proverbs*, 519–20, 522.

Waltke than the content of Proverbs 31. The existence of homemakers is primarily a middle- or upper-class American conception of modern invention.

Still other interpretations exhibit fealty to authors and narrators—real, implied, or inferred. According to this interpretive commitment, whatever these figures assert, explicitly or implicitly, must be true. As applied to Proverbs 31, Lemuel and his mother must be wise and good—the ones readers should believe and root for—because they are the ones who speak. Similarly, the one praising the *eshet chayil* is assumed to be accurate in depiction and appropriate in assessment, obliging all readers to adopt for themselves this speaker's point of view. JiSeong Kwon exhibits a typical example of this practice when he writes of the *eshet chayil*, "She is not simply a wife who promotes prosperity, but she is a moral woman who possesses a heart of wisdom and Torah." And also: "All the activities which this poem undoubtedly describes are associated with genuine virtues: goodness to her husband (v. 12), delightful service (v. 13), diligence (vv. 15, 18, 27), compassion (v. 20), assurance (v. 21), self-dignity (vv. 22, 24), wisdom, loving-kindness (v. 26), and fear of Yahweh (v. 30)."[57] But such favor avoids acknowledging or pursuing any aspects of the worlds behind and within the text that are not promoted by the narrator and whoever has created "him." It is limiting and can be damaging to any who are thereby ignored or detrimentally depicted. Avoiding reference altogether to authors or narrators achieves the same outcome, influencing readers to accept that what is presented is all that needs to be considered.

Other readers overlook the harm that occurs as texts shape identities of people who see themselves or who are seen by others as depicted within them. Often those harmed are not in a position to recognize their condition, much less testify to their harm. They are excluded from the places where the rules of interpretation are

---

57 JiSeong Kwon, "Wisdom Incarnate? Identity and Role of אשת־חיל ('the Valiant Woman') in Proverbs 31:10–31," *Journal for the Evangelical Study of the Old Testament* 1, no. 2 (2012): 167, 173.

taught, where texts are discussed and interpretations applied. They are, like the poor and the *eshet chayil* of Proverbs 31, busy working and serving those who do belong in those privileged spaces.

Finally, most interpreters miss the narrative elements present in Proverbs 31 and their contribution to meaning. These include suggestions of conflict, event, developing tension, characterization, dialogue, and setting. When it is assumed, as per tradition, that the lines of Proverbs 31 have little connection to each other[58] and do not develop as a story in any way, then meaning is extracted largely by focusing on each individual line, producing moral tenets. "Women and drink are two large temptations to a man with power and money," writes Tremper Longman of Proverbs 31:3.[59] Conceiving Proverbs 31 as story-like expands meaning and significance beyond viewing Lemuel's mother and the *eshet chayil* as role models, paragons of virtue and ethical counsel.

A NEW READING OF PROVERBS 31

The Proverbial Woman conceives of these two poems narratively and dialogically to identify tensions among characters that surface issues of survival in Persian-era Yehud. It unearths the poetry's social, sexual, and political silences and silencings by highlighting forgotten or overlooked characters: the women who destroy kings, the silenced poor, displaced peasants, and foreigners. It encourages the reader to recognize the drama taking place in the world created by the text and to explore how narrative elements enabled an ancient community pondering these sapiential lines to process their cooperation with empire in an economic system that benefited some and exploited others.

---

[58] McKane, *Proverbs*, 665–66.
[59] Tremper V. Longman III, *Proverbs* (Grand Rapids: Baker, 2006), 538.

A Narrative Interpretation

Some argue that poems cannot be considered narratives.[60] Even to the extent that this may be true, as Bal points out, narratological analysis of nonnarrative texts can supply insights overlooked by traditional approaches.[61] Much of the processing involved in understanding a text as narrative occurs within the minds of readers as they pick up on textual details and fill in gaps to form a story worth following and figuring out.[62] The oracle and acrostic that comprise Proverbs 31 each contain the elements that Lindemann Nelson prioritizes in marking a text as a story: they selectively depict human experience in ways that are both interpretive and connective.[63] Verses 1–9 portray a mother's highly personal rebuke of her son concerning social expectations, while verses 10–31 use a husband-wife relationship to depict human longings, anxieties, and needs. Marie-Laure Ryan contends that narrativity can be understood as degrees along a continuum stretching from description to narrative.[64] In Proverbs 31, individuated subjects, mention of locations, the suggestion of "event," and indications of conflict warrant its classification as narrative-like, or as narratized description.[65] Therefore, this book will approach these two pericopes (vv. 1–9 and 10–31) as narratives.

---

60 Monika Fludernik, *An Introduction to Narratology* (London: Routledge, 2009), 6.

61 Bal, *Narratology*, 13.

62 See Richard J. Gerrig and Giovanna Egidi, "Cognitive Psychological Foundations of Narrative Experiences," in *Narrative Theory and the Cognitive Sciences*, ed. David Herman (Stanford, CA: CSLI Publications, 2003), 36.

63 Lindemann Nelson, *Damaged Identities, Narrative Repair*, 11–12.

64 Marie-Laure Ryan, "Toward a Definition of Narrative," in *The Cambridge Companion to Narrative*, ed. David Herman (Cambridge: Cambridge University Press, 2007), 28–31. In addition, Frank promotes the study of narrative to include "the fullest range of storytelling, from folklore to everyday conversation" (*Letting Stories Breathe*, 12).

65 Harold F. Mosher Jr., "Towards a Poetics of Descriptized Narration," *Poetics Today* 12, no. 3 (1991): 426.

Characterization

Characterization forms one especially important narrative element to explore in Proverbs 31. King Lemuel, his mother, the *eshet chayil*, and her husband: May readers understand them as characters? If so, how much depth of character may we plumb? For such explorations, David Gunn and Danna Nolan Fewell offer a persuasive argument as to why, despite commentators' historical resistance, it is acceptable, even necessary, to psychologize biblical characters. By this they mean to engage with biblical textual characters in ways that are similar to how people engage with other humans in real life: observing, analyzing, making assumptions, inferences, and conclusions about them.[66] Gunn and Fewell argue that to refuse to do so is to unfairly denigrate ancient authors as primitive, incapable of sophisticated communication via innuendo or implication.[67] But biblical texts are not unsophisticated; though notable for reticence, they can and do sustain elaborate character construction.[68] Furthermore, readers of any narrative text, ancient or modern, unavoidably engage in speculation about whatever they may categorize as a character; that is what makes a story interesting and facilitates learning. The character sketches produced in this study are based on details of the text, not extraneous flights of fancy, but also in many cases details not explicitly stated. They emerge, rather, through probing potential motives and implications of descriptions, actions, and expressions in the text.

When studying characterization, it should be noted that narrators are characters, too, worthy of being questioned and analyzed as to reliability, objectivity, and motive. Bal notes that whenever anything is expressed, *someone said it*, and that someone ought to be noticed.[69] Though rarely recognized as such, the narrator is a "fictional construct" with characteristics readers infer, perhaps of

---

66 See David Gunn and Danna Nolan Fewell, *Narrative in the Hebrew Bible* (Oxford: Oxford University Press, 1993), 46–81.
67 Gunn and Fewell, *Narrative in the Hebrew Bible*, 47–48.
68 Gunn and Fewell, *Narrative in the Hebrew Bible*, 48–49.
69 Bal, *Narratology*, 21.

being smart, competent, wise, and so on.[70] The narrator directs a reader's gaze and influences what they see.

Relatedly, focalization needs to be attended when interpreting narrative. As Bal explains, "Focalization distinguishes between the vision through which the elements are presented and the identity of the voice that is verbalizing that vision." The latter constitutes narrator, and the former, focalizer. Together, they influence what is noticed, what matters in the world of the text, and how the audience feels about those objects. Focalization, writes Bal, is "the most important, most penetrating, and most subtle means of manipulation."[71] Noticing narrators and focalization is vital for understanding the ideological timbre of a writing, for enabling characters and readers to exist independent of the will of the narrator and the narrator's creator, the author(s).

Analyzing the narrator also invites recognizing yet another character present in narrative scenes and events: narratee(s), the "intrafictional addressee[s] of the narrator's discourse."[72] For Proverbs 31, this potentially includes apprentice scribes, boys who may have been learning to read and write through using this text.[73] It also may include a general ancient community, a social network known to gather at city gates to share information. These audiences can be assumed to enjoy performance of these poems, and their assumed presence affects the narrator's choice of words and an audience's reception of them.

Attending to narrator and narratees as characters draws attention to narrative levels. As Monica Fludernik explains, two levels may be distinguished in every narrative, the "level of the world represented in the story and the level at which this representation takes place."[74]

---

70 Gunn and Fewell, *Narrative in the Hebrew Bible*, 53; see Monika Fludernik, "Identity/Alterity," in Herman, *Cambridge Companion to Narrative*, 260.
71 Bal, *Narratology*, 145, 176.
72 Fludernik, *Introduction to Narratology*, 23.
73 Acrostics may have functioned as tools for scribal instruction, writes F. W. Dobbs-Allsopp, *On Biblical Poetry* (Oxford: Oxford University Press, 2015), 304.
74 Fludernik, *Introduction to Narratology*, 21.

Proverbs 31 contains sections where the narration is ambiguous, leading to uncertainty as to whether the narrator is an actor within the scene or external to it. Bal labels this "text interference." It occurs when "narrator's text and actor's text are so closely related that a distinction into narrative levels can no longer be made."[75] Such phenomena complicate the text, multiplying options for interpreting it. This allows narrator and narratees to become actors in a given scene.

Public Performance

Factoring narrative levels into interpretation makes sense when readers bear in mind the public performance of ancient moral poems. Unlike our modern engagement with texts, members of ancient communities usually were not able to read poems privately but rather most often experienced them aurally as a communal performance.[76] Performance criticism attends to "aural, kinetic and visual aspects of performance, that is, for matters of voice and instrumentation, gesture, and setting and performer identity."[77] Interpreting Proverbs 31 in light of such considerations brings new significance to its mentions of the body and its abrupt shifts in address that could signal changing speakers and addressees. These references and changes affect communication, for example, if lines are delivered with a sarcastic tone or suggestive gesture, rendering a meaning quite the opposite of words that are interpreted independently of such context. Attention to performance is also useful for detecting humor, which can be easily overlooked when something meant to be spoken is written down. Although the visual significance of the acrostic form and chiasm show an origin in script, Proverbs 31's alliterations, repetitions, and allusions to orality indicate a context of public oral performance for this poem. Interpreting Proverbs 31 within a presumed context

---

75 Bal, *Narratology*, 56.
76 Dobbs-Allsopp, *On Biblical Poetry*, 197.
77 Robert D. Miller, "The Performance of Oral Tradition in Ancient Israel," in *Contextualizing Israel's Sacred Writings*, ed. Brian Schmidt (Atlanta: SBL Press, 2015), 183.

of public performance enhances suggestions of rebuke within the poems. An ancient convention known as "shaming speech" requires that words intended to embarrass a person into conformity "be publicly staged in order to draw on the energies and backing of a desired audience."[78]

Setting

Settings suggest stories. Several locations are mentioned in Proverbs 31: fields and vineyards, homes, foreign lands, and city gates. In verse 31, the action advocated to take place in the gates is the very action the poem itself engages: praising the *eshet chayil*. The locations mentioned are not just offhand references but places where the characters and action are visualized. When a character does something or undergoes some action, they do so from a place.

Settings contribute greatly to characterization. The activities that people engage within a given space form their identities and are reflected in their labels. Within a kitchen, the cook cooks. Within a church, a preacher preaches. Furthermore, the locations that comprise settings for a given narrative have associations, often manifold and conflicting. These could be related to the people expected to occupy that space, or to activities that normally take place there, or to particularly memorable historical events occurring at that place. The World Trade Center in Manhattan possesses associations of cityscape, of commerce, of professional workers, especially in the financial or corporate sector, but also of trauma and terrorism related to 9/11. Spaces can function as cultural, religious, or political symbols; they can evoke sentimentality and other emotions. These associations become attached to characters in narratives who are occupying the narrative's settings and contribute to their identities.

Spaces are not neutral. They can empower or constrain, elevate or demean according to who is affirmed as belonging, contributing, or

---

78 Victor Matthews, "Honor and Shame in Gender-Related Situations in the Hebrew Bible," in *Gender and Law in the Hebrew Bible and the Ancient Near East*, ed. Victor Matthews et al. (Sheffield: Sheffield Academic, 1998), 100.

valued in a given space and who is not. Such work sets up or solidifies hierarchies among actors within a location: who serves whom, who dominates. In examining the contribution of Proverbs 31's settings to constructions of gender and class identity, the work of space theorists Henri Lefebvre, Doreen Massey, and Tim Cresswell can help bring underexamined features to the surface.

Lefebvre builds on Karl Marx's insistence on noting not just what *is* but also the social relations and forms of relations that exist between what is.[79] Lefebvre's analysis of everyday life asserts that space is not merely a static and neutral aspect of nature. Rather, space should be understood as a tripartite construction of physical, mental, and social reality according to how people conceive it and use it. Approaching spaces in this way reveals a dialectical process of human social activity in which space is both socially produced and socially productive.[80] That is, human activity determines what a space is, and conversely, the limitations, intentions, and real experience of space determine what humans are and how they relate to one another in spaces.

Massey diversifies Lefebvre's Marxist interest in the role of capital shaping space and place, noting that factors such as ethnicity and gender also affect experience of place.[81] She emphasizes the artificiality of spatial boundaries. Spaces overlap and boundaries are permeable. According to Massey, the identity of a particular place forms via "the juxtaposition and co-presence there of particular sets of social interrelations, and by the effects which that juxtaposition and co-presence produce."[82] Certain social groups possess more power than others both to move and to direct mobility. Labeling this phenomenon "power geometry," Massey writes, "Mobility and control over mobility both reflect and reinforce power. It is not simply a

---

79 Henri Lefebvre, *The Production of Space* (Oxford: Blackwell, 1991), 83.
80 Lefebvre, *Production of Space*, 129.
81 Doreen Massey, "Power Geometry and a Progressive Sense of Place," in *Mapping the Futures: Local Cultures, Global Change*, ed. Jon Bird et al. (London: Routledge, 1993), 62.
82 Doreen Massey, *Space, Place and Gender* (Cambridge: Polity, 1994), 169.

question of unequal distribution, that some people move more than others, some have more control than others. It is that the mobility and control of some groups can actively weaken other people."[83]

Cresswell, like Lefebvre and Massey, also views space as "coconstitutive"[84] and as an ideological tool for those with power based on class, gender, race, sexuality, age, and other variables to define what constitutes appropriate behavior—and deviance—in a particular place. He writes, "A discussion of the role of the geographic environment—the power of place—in cultural and social processes can provide another layer in the understanding and demystifying of the forces that effect and manipulate our everyday behavior."[85] While norms of behavior in place often go unnoticed when everyone enacts their assigned-as-appropriate roles in their assigned-as-appropriate locations, "transgressive acts" call attention to the artificiality of these expectations, raising questions as to their suitability: Whom does this present practice serve? Sit-ins, for example, rely on the clash between the activity normally taking place in a space—lunch counter, financial district, freeway—and the "unsuitable" presence of those who through interrupting it object to the normative behavior, making claims as to harm. Cresswell writes, "Transgression is important because it breaks from 'normality' and causes a questioning of that which was previously considered 'natural,' 'assumed,' and 'taken for granted.'"[86] Transgressive acts can make those advantaged by the way things are feel threatened, nervous about anticipated change, and thus respond with words and deeds putting transgressors in "their place," punishing their transgression and shoring up the status quo.

Jon Berquist observes, "The Bible is obsessed with space."[87] In biblical narratives, characters fight over cities to live in, wells to

---

83 Massey, "Power Geometry," 62–63.
84 Doreen Massey, *For Space* (London: SAGE, 2005), 10.
85 Tim Cresswell, *In Place/Out of Place: Geography, Ideology, and Transgression* (Minneapolis: University of Minnesota Press, 1996), 11.
86 Cresswell, *In Place/Out of Place*, 26.
87 Jon L. Berquist, "Critical Spatiality and the Construction of the Ancient World," in *"Imagining" Biblical Worlds: Studies in Spatial, Social and Historical*

draw from, lands to journey to, to pass through. Are these space-obsessed texts challenging present occupation of ancient spaces or digging in to keep things as they are? Who decides the occupation, use, and meanings of biblical spaces? Critical spatiality studies such as those described above can assist in understanding what is at stake in the lives of ancient people developing and pondering biblical texts that sometimes reinforce boundaries, sometimes transgress them, sometimes redraw them. Reading Proverbs 31 in light of these ideas enables us to consider the work its two poems are doing in their references to fields, vineyards, homes, foreign lands, and city gates. What anxieties or needs do they reveal? *Whose* anxieties and needs do they reveal? Two societal divisions depicted in Proverbs 31 are gender and class. What does the depiction of spaces here reveal about power arrangements between these groups? How do its spaces construct identities of women and men, of wealthy and poor?

A Dialogic Interpretation

As Bal observes, simply noting literary features accomplishes little. Rather, the value of narratological scrutiny comes from gaining perspective on culture through asking such questions as, "To what is this a reply?"[88] Such a view conceives of texts as participating in communal conversations, and it leans heavily on the work of Bakhtin, who promoted texts as *dialogic*.

Writing in Soviet-era Russia, Bakhtin suffered political constraints that suppressed some of his works, clouded the authorship of others, and delayed his recognition in the West.[89] Eventually, as his work became known, it vastly expanded possibilities for understanding rhetorical activity in texts. Bakhtin described traditional scholars as picking one style present in a novel and applying it to describe the

---

Constructs in Honor of James W. Flanagan, ed. David M. Gunn and Paula M. McNutt (Sheffield: Sheffield Academic, 2002), 25.

88 Bal, *Narratology*, 227.

89 Pam Morris, "Introduction," in *The Bakhtin Reader*, ed. Pam Morris (London: Edward Arnold, 1994), 1.

novel overall, falsely promoting consistency of voice, an approach Bakhtin described as "monologic."[90] In contrast, Bakhtin understood texts as "polyphonic," containing multiple voices, perspectives, interests, and arguments. He writes, "Any concrete discourse ... is entangled, shot through with shared thoughts, points of view, alien value judgments and accents."[91] Furthermore, he pointed out, words have a history; traces of previous usages remain to influence meaning by either confirming or contesting the present utterance.[92] This makes texts dialogic not only in relation to the words in proximity on the page but also with prior uses of those words, sometimes preserved in other texts. Each utterance occurring in response to previous utterances requires recognizing that no utterance is final; each may trigger some new response.[93] Focusing primarily on Fyodor Dostoyevsky's novels, Bakhtin celebrated dialogism for resisting the hierarchy that exists in monologic texts of author/narrator over characters, instead allowing multiple perspectives to coexist.

In explaining how texts are dialogic, Bakhtin identifies patterns of words that serve rhetorical purposes. These he labels with such terms as the "sideways glance," "interruption," "juxtaposition of quotations," "change in address," "loopholes," "double-voicedness," "questions," "carnivalesque," and "intertextuality." These terms are useful for identifying the rhetorical features of a text that betray the presence of multiple voices and perspectives. Some patterns assert a "centripetal" force, and others "centrifugal" force. Both forces are always present in any text: common understandings that "unify and centralize the verbal ideological world," and differences and interruptions that disunify and decentralize. These types of patterns appear in Proverbs 31 and illustrate Bakhtin's promise: "It is possible

---

[90] Mikhail Bakhtin, "Discourse in the Novel," in *The Dialogic Imagination: Four Essays*, ed. Michael Holquist, trans. Caryl Emerson and Michael Holquist (Austin: University of Texas Press, 1981), 263–65.

[91] Bakhtin, "Discourse," 276.

[92] Sue Vice, *Introducing Bakhtin* (Manchester: Manchester University Press, 1997), 47.

[93] Carol A. Newsom, "Bakhtin, the Bible, and Dialogic Truth," *JR* 76, no. 2 (1996): 294.

to give a concrete and detailed analysis of any utterance, once having exposed it as a contradiction-ridden, tension-filled unity of two embattled tendencies in the life of language."[94]

Bakhtin and Biblical Studies

Although Bakhtin expressed reservations concerning the potential of poetry to display dialogism, scholars have applied his theory to understand biblical texts, both narrative and poetic.[95] Such an approach works well for Proverbs 31, which contains multiple ambiguities and contradictions. Whereas other critical approaches oblige these to be somehow resolved or dismissed, dialogism accepts them as legitimate communicative morsels, worthy of study and integration into the overall message of the text. As Bakhtin writes admiringly of Dostoyevsky: "In every voice he could hear two contending voices, in every expression a crack, and a tendency to go over immediately to another contradictory expression; in every gesture he detected confidence and lack of confidence simultaneously; he perceived the profound ambiguity, even multiple ambiguity of every phenomenon."[96]

Dialogism also suits biblical texts because of their intertextual nature. As Fewell notes, the Bible is itself a compilation of texts that "complement, supplement, contradict, and undermine one another."[97] Similarities of theme and vocabulary connect Proverbs 31 to other passages in Proverbs, as well as to Judges, Ruth, Esther, and Job. Bakhtin's emphasis on dialogue encourages interpreting

---

94 Bakhtin, "Discourse," 270, 272.
95 Vice, *Introducing Bakhtin*, 77. See Roland Boer, *Bakhtin and Genre Theory in Biblical Studies* (Atlanta: Society of Biblical Literature, 2007); Barbara Green, *Mikhail Bakhtin and Biblical Scholarship: An Introduction* (Atlanta: Society of Biblical Literature, 2005); Newsom, "Bakhtin, the Bible," 290–306.
96 Mikhail Bakhtin, *Problems of Dostoevsky's Poetics*, ed. and trans. Caryl Emerson (Minneapolis: University of Minnesota Press, 1984), 30.
97 Danna Nolan Fewell, "The Work of Biblical Narrative," in *The Oxford Handbook of Biblical Narrative*, ed. Danna Nolan Fewell (Oxford: Oxford University Press, 2016), 18.

and assessing Proverbs 31 as including multiple voices contributing to communal discussions.

The Role of Readers

In Proverbs 31, Lemuel's mother asks, "What, my son—?!" (v. 2), and of the *eshet chayil*, others ask, "Who can find?" (v. 10). Questions invite dialogue; they conjure not only a listening audience but also an expectation that someone or someones ought to respond. This respondent could be characters in a scene, or it could be readers who cannot help consciously or subconsciously to conjure potential replies. Both question and answer influence interpretation.

Readers contribute to meaning also through what they inject, ignore, and prioritize. Every text contains gaps that readers fill, often unknowingly, according to their experience and assumptions.[98] Texts may contain contradictions or loose ends that readers resolve or decide to ignore in order to form for themselves the story that makes sense to them. Mere morsels of text can matter greatly, as in Proverbs 31:31, a *mem* and *hireq* attached to *peri* ("fruit"). These signal the presence of the word *min*, meaning "of" or "from." Does this word modify the speaker's exhortation to give not "*the* fruit of her hands," her entire produce or profit, but "*of* the fruit of her hands," that is, a mere portion of that profit? Perhaps it is the same thing, really, or not a significant difference, a reader of certain disposition may wish to reason, in order to preserve conceiving the speaker as generous, as benevolent. Or perhaps *min* indeed *is* significant, betraying in one tiny syllable a more reserved, dominating attitude or impulse. The reader decides.

Bakhtin scholar David Lodge describes the benefits of dialogism as understanding meaning not as a fixed object needing to be discovered but as concepts that come into existence through interaction between "many subjects, between texts and readers and between

---

98 Luc Herman and Bart Vervaeck, "Ideology," in Herman, *Cambridge Companion to Narrative*, 218.

texts."[99] Rather than one fixed meaning, we can adopt Jeannine K. Brown's image of meaning as a sphere, "a complex entity that still may rightly be described as having boundaries."[100] A sphere looks differently according to how it is turned. Frank describes stories as being "out of control." They are "tricksters," saying one thing one moment, and another the next, depending on the position of the reader and where focus is directed.[101] Stories, Frank argues, must be allowed to breathe.

Rather than tying them up, readers can "improve the quality of companionship between humans and stories"[102] through an interpretive approach he labels socionarratology. This method combines narratology's appreciation for the world-making capacity of narratives with a sociological interest in the function and impact of narratives on communities developing and reading them.[103] Socionarratology examines (1) how stories give people the resources to figure out who they are, (2) how they both connect and disconnect people, (3) how they inspire toward good, (4) how they create and play with boundaries, and (5) how they make life dangerous, especially by casting others as objects of aggression.[104]

Probing Proverbs 31 with these notions in mind exposes a fuller picture of the world generated by this text. *The Proverbial Woman* excavates the power dynamics that promote elite ideologies even as

---

99 David Lodge, *After Bakhtin* (London: Routledge, 1990), 86.

100 Jeannine K. Brown, *Scripture as Communication: Introducing Biblical Hermeneutics* (Grand Rapids: Baker Academic, 2007), 85.

101 Frank, *Letting Stories Breathe*, 35–36.

102 Frank, *Letting Stories Breathe*, 19.

103 Thus my approach resists Norman Whybray's assertion that Proverbs is more concerned with individuals than community. See Whybray, *The Good Life in the Old Testament* (London: T&T Clark, 2002), 161. All narratives have world-creating power, writes David Herman, *Story Logic: Problems and Possibilities of Narrative* (Lincoln: University of Nebraska Press, 2002), 16.

104 Frank, *Letting Stories Breathe*, 71. For a critique, see Jarmila Mildorf: "This open-endedness of the proposed research method, where everything seems to be at the discretion of the researcher, is problematic, as it may well lead to arbitrariness." Mildorf, review of *Letting Stories Breathe: Socio-narratology*, *Biography* 34, no. 4 (2011): 835.

gaps, ambiguities, and contradictions enable marginalized perspectives within the text to resist them. Expanding options for meaning and recognizing multiple voices enables Proverbs 31 to be conceived as not only a "master narrative" summarizing and justifying a society's common understandings of how the world works.[105] Rather, it may serve also as a "counterstory,"[106] resisting the damaging identities of master narratives, liberating those demeaned to contribute to communal identity constructions and decision making, to see themselves represented in crucial communal texts, and to advance their own interests in conference with others.

CONCLUSION

This book is written for anyone damaged by texts in their identity constructions, especially biblical texts. It demonstrates an approach to interpretation that acknowledges and attempts to avoid hermeneutical practices that limit and exclude marginalized members of society, instead facilitating those damaged to see themselves and hear their own voices present in a damaging text. *The Proverbial Woman* accomplishes this through a devoutly close scrutiny of that text. This approach is different from extracting one monologic message, to which readers respond with either objection or defense, resistance or acquiescence. It understands the text itself as a cacophony of disparate utterances all weighing in with various interests on what is needed for this community to survive and thrive.

This book is written also for those readers who contribute to the damage of others through their use of biblical texts. Whether the damaged are women, the poor, or any potential "others," many a well-intentioned Bible teacher has reinforced marginalization through participation in the traditional hermeneutical game. This book, I hope, shows how arbitrary, even unfair, are its rules.

---

105 Lindemann Nelson, *Damaged Identities, Narrative Repair*, 106.
106 Lindemann Nelson, *Damaged Identities, Narrative Repair*, 150.

THE PROVERBIAL WOMAN

On whichever side readers find themselves with regard to common social divides, they will benefit from learning through this book how language and locations can be deployed to control and harm. Understanding how this happens can check the instincts of those with power to grab more and can enable those without power to understand these mechanisms happening and resist them, claiming their own desired places, telling their own counterstories. The intent is to dilute those textual voices that dominate—include them still but have them sit on the elders' bench while others stand to speak. "An *eshet chayil*, who can find?" (v. 10). We will find her, all right.

Proverbs 31:1–9

1 The words of Lemuel, a king, the burden [*massa*] with which she rebuked [*yasar*] him, his mother:
2 "What, my son—and what?! son of my womb; and what—? Son of my vows?!
3 Do not give to women your strength [*chayil*], or your ways to devourers [*makhoth*] of kings."
4 "Not for kings, Lemuel, not for kings the drinking of wine, or for princes, beer.
5 ... Lest he should drink and forget the decrees and change the verdict of the sons of oppression."
6 " 'Give beer to the perishing,
   and wine to the bitter of soul—
7 Let him drink and forget his poverty;
   let him not remember his toil anymore."
8 "Open your mouth for the speechless,
   on behalf of all who are perishing.
9 Open your mouth—judge rightly!
   Plead the case of the poor and oppressed."

CHAPTER TWO

The Drama of Mothers and Kings
Proverbs 31:1–9

"What, my son—?!" Proverbs covets our attention. The book hooks readers' interest here through repetition and questioning, through suspense evoked by withholding detail amid signals of emotion and tension. Proverbs 31:1 draws us into a dramatic scene and leaves us wondering just what is happening in it. Who is this ruler? Where is this kingdom? What is happening to prompt a mother's rebuke?

Assertive, emoting, she has strong words for her son, the king. Such postures are not unusual among depictions of females in the few biblical scenes where they appear. Abigail, Achsah, Deborah, Job's wife, Michal, Miriam, Tamar, and Woman Wisdom: all admonish the men in their lives, whether husband, father, brother, or others. A mother who speaks and acts to ensure her son's success also appears elsewhere in the Bible; think Sarah, Rebekah, Hannah, Bathsheba. But these women are foils or tropes to support an androcentric agenda. They are secondary characters known and valued through their connection to the males that are so central to the plots in which they appear. As such, they project damaged identities that circulate within master narratives to promote social values that benefit some while limiting agency and opportunity for others.

When readers cooperate with such staging, they overlook or limit the options for meaning and significance in the text that can be discerned by pressing against its subordination of women and other marginalized characters. Gaps, ambiguities, and contradictions: attending to these reveals worlds of subtensions and subplots. No person exists as an island; nor does any text. Behind, within, and in front exist communities composed of individuals who affect one another, for good or for ill. Fuller and more responsible readings can emerge by bearing in mind these communal dynamics, especially where power is deployed. There are no original utterances, writes Mikhail Bakhtin. Every word is put forth as a response anticipating another's hearing and response.[1] But what is the question to which this mother in Proverbs 31 is an answer? What is the agenda driving the text, what is its impact—should readers cooperate or resist? Rebekah's intervention in her sons' affairs (Gen 27) matters for the fate of the nation, Israel, as does Bathsheba's (1 Kgs 1). What about here in Proverbs 31? Does this mother's intervention matter? How does she reinforce postexilic Israel's communal stakes?

Our aim in this chapter is to become more savvy readers of the full drama of this text, a text perhaps not obviously a drama in light of its affinity with other genres—oracle, instruction, poetry—but one that, due to its characters and conflict, we can deem *narrative-like*. Attention to narrative details reveals Proverbs 31:1–9 as expressing postexilic anxieties concerning social organization, class conflict, distribution of resources, and cooperation with empire. The drama of mothers and kings is a drama of civilizational precarity.

A DIALOGIC TEXT

Traditionally scholars have been more inclined to highlight Proverbs 31:1–9's affinities with ancient Near Eastern wisdom literature than to dwell on narrative details. "These verses present no internal compositional problems," writes Norman Whybray.[2] More recent, feminist

---

1 Bakhtin, "Problem of Speech Genres," 69.
2 Norman Whybray, *The Composition of the Book of Proverbs* (Sheffield: JSOT Press, 2009), 153.

interpreters have begun to engage the dramatic elements of the poem. Yoder depicts the mother as attempting to snap her son out of a stupor. "One imagines the mother scolding Lemuel . . . seizing a bottle from him . . . and waving it toward the masses whose plight she depicts without mincing words."[3] Kirk-Duggan asks whether she might be fostering dysfunction by violating boundaries needed for proper child development.[4] To these I aim to add Bakhtinian-based recognition of the text as inherently polyphonic, many voices present and speaking.

"The words of Lemuel, a king, the burden with which she rebuked him, his mother" (Prov 31:1). Whose words are these, exactly? Lemuel's or his mother's? The Hebrew phrase *divre Lemuel* has comparable parallels in biblical texts, including *divre Agur* (Prov 30:1), *divre rivqah* (Gen 24:30), and *divray Yahweh* (Num 11:24), where it is presumed the person mentioned is the speaker of the words to come. So it would seem noncontroversial to attribute Proverbs 31:2–9 to Lemuel.

Yet the text also says that with these words his *mother* rebuked *him*. So were they first *her* words? Is Lemuel quoting her? Is he summarizing or merely incorporating some of her thoughts? Who really is the speaker here? Some commentators argue that in this context these are not words spoken *by* Lemuel but *to* Lemuel. "The 'words of Lemuel' are really those of his mother," writes Roland Murphy.[5] Yoder insists, "These are the instructions of his mother."[6] Crenshaw offers a syntactical clarification: "The genitive relationship in Prov. 31:1 (words of Lemuel) is an objective one (words directed to Lemuel)."[7] Michael Fox straddles the options: "Lemuel received them from his mother and spoke them in his own teaching."[8]

---

3 Christine Yoder, *Proverbs* (Nashville: Abingdon, 2009), 292.

4 Kirk-Duggan, "Rethinking the 'Virtuous' Woman," 102.

5 Roland E. Murphy, *Proverbs*, WBC 22 (Nashville: Thomas Nelson, 1998), 26.

6 Yoder, *Proverbs*, 290.

7 Crenshaw, "Mother's Instruction," 14. This view contradicts the guidance in *Introduction to Biblical Hebrew Syntax*, which lists v. 1 as an example of genitive of agency, in which the second word does the action of the first, translating the phrase "words by Lemuel" (*IBHS*, 143).

8 Michael V. Fox, *Proverbs 10–31: A New Translation with Introduction and Commentary* (New Haven, CT: Yale University Press, 2009), 884.

Each interpretation follows a traditional, monologic approach to the meaning of texts, wherein only one voice could be speaking at a time, and one is enough to express this text's truth. But Bakhtin offers an alternative. He understands truth and meaning as attained not through resolving ambiguity into one correct and static expression but rather through recognizing and giving full voice to the assortment of interpretive options that ambiguities allow. Proverbs 31:1–9 could have been introduced precisely as "The words of Lemuel," or alternatively as "The words of the queen, mother of Lemuel." As it is written, the ambiguity of the speaker's identity fulfills Bakhtin's description of a polyphonic text, in which an author gives up control of perspective and projects several consciousnesses with equal and independent points of view.[9]

Readers may approach Proverbs 31 without needing to settle on one voice. Instead, we can recognize that the peculiar phrasing of the verse sets up two simultaneous voices: both Lemuel and his mother. This approach resembles that of Athalya Brenner and Fokkelien van Dijk-Hemmes, who conceive of biblical texts as "dual gendered."[10] By this they mean, instead of traditional readings assuming a male orientation, that texts can be read with both a male and female voice and a male and female "readerly attention" in mind.[11] "In many cases, two parallel readings are possible," they write.[12] Entertaining both readings enables the mother's portrayal of her son to be responded to in readers' own minds through her son's concurrent portrayal of her speaking (and vice versa). The mother speaks, and the son relays a *memory* of her speaking, we could say. Adult themes of sex, drinking, oppression, and suffering, delivered as a scolding fit for a child, received with silence by the son, suggest influence of the

---

9 See Newsom, "Bakhtin, the Bible," 295. See also Green, *Mikhail Bakhtin and Biblical Scholarship*, 48.

10 Athalya Brenner and Fokkelien van Dijk-Hemmes, *On Gendering Texts, Male and Female Voices in the Hebrew Bible* (Leiden: Brill, 1996), 9.

11 Athalya Brenner, "Figurations of Women in Wisdom Literature," in *A Feminist Companion to Wisdom Literature*, ed. Athalya Brenner (Sheffield: Sheffield Academic, 1995), 56.

12 Brenner and Van Dijk-Hemmes, *On Gendering Texts*, 9.

present on the remembered past. Conceiving of Proverbs 31:2–9 as a memory fits its structure; the abrupt shifts in topic (from women, to drinking, to the plight of the poor) can be understood as several corrections having occurred at different times but here compiled into one, or they could distill a lengthy tongue-lashing. They could be the stream-of-consciousness recall of a son mid-crisis, drawing on this memory, however inexact, to process his current circumstances. Some studies have shown traumatic recall narratives to be dominated by sensory and emotional details, as Proverbs 31:1–9 contains, described below.[13]

How shall we then characterize the interaction of these two simultaneous voices? Two aspects suggest mother and son engaged in a dispute. The first is the vocabulary employed in verse 1, the words *massa* and *yasar*. Some render *massa* as a place name, but Fox convincingly explains that the grammatical construction argues against doing so.[14] *Massa* literally means "burden," as in Exodus 23:5: "If you see the donkey of one who hates you lying down under its burden [*massa*]..." (ESV). It is a term that elsewhere introduces prophecy (Isa 13:1; 14:28; 15:1; 17:1; 19:1; 21:1, 11, 13; 22:1; 23:1; 30:1, Ezek 12:10; Nah 1:1; Hab 1:1; Zech 9:1; 12:1; Mal 1:1), metaphorically appropriate to such context in that prophetic utterances are often unwelcome and unpleasant, hence a burden. *Massa* is usually translated into English as "oracle," losing the nuance of "burden" within the primary meaning of "oracle" as oral speech. The prophetic signal of the term *massa* preps readers' expectation of the words to come as confrontational, as is common not just in biblical prophetic literature but also in narratives involving prophetic figures, such as the rebukes of David by Nathan (2 Sam 12:1–4) and the wise woman of Tekoa (2 Sam 14). Additionally, *massa* (מַשָּׂא) forms a homophone with another word, *massah* (מסה), meaning "quarrel"—notable as the name given to mark the location of the Hebrews' grumbling in the wilderness (Exod 17:7).

---

13 Maria Crespo and Violeta Fernandez-Lansac, "Memory and Narrative of Traumatic Events: A Literature Review," *Psychological Trauma: Theory, Research, Practice, and Policy* 8, no. 2 (2016): 149.

14 Fox, *Proverbs 10–31*, 884.

An ancient listening audience would have understood either word or both as being spoken: burden *and* quarrel.

As for *yasar*, most translations render it as "taught." Yet elsewhere it usually appears as "discipline," or "punishment," including physical violence. For example, 1 Kings 12:11 and 2 Chronicles 10:14 both read, "My father disciplined [*yasar*] you with whips, but I will discipline [*yasar*] you with scorpions" (ESV). Deuteronomy 21:18 says, "If a man has a stubborn and rebellious son who . . . will not heed his parents when they discipline (*yasar*) him . . ." It could be that in Proverbs 31 the gender of the speaker, or assumptions as to genre, or inferred identification with doting Hannah (1 Sam 1)[15] influence the choice to translate it in Proverbs 31:1 as "taught." But what effect on translation and interpretation results from hearing in verse 1 not Hannah tenderly clothing Samuel but these parents in Deuteronomy who are instructed to bring their "stubborn and rebellious" son to the city gate to be stoned? I translate *yasar* as "rebuke."

Second, the presence of emotion in Proverbs 31:1–9 suggests dispute. Such is communicated via repetition and syntax: the threefold "*mah*- . . . *mah*- . . . *mah*-" (v. 2), which translates, "What . . . what . . . what?!" Or as some render, "no! . . . No! . . . NO!"[16] Readers must imagine how tone and inflection change across the repetition but can easily infer the crescendo of intensifying emotion this pattern expresses. As Fox points out concerning the larger context of verses 1–9, "The tone of urgency here gives the impression that Lemuel has already done wrong and his mother is imploring him to cease."[17] Reference to her womb (v. 2) also, with its associations of intimacy, connection, and compassion, communicates emotion.[18] Throughout verses 1–9, self-interruption occurs, as when this

---

15 E.g., Crenshaw, "Mother's Instruction," 15; Yoder, *Proverbs*, 291; Perdue, *Proverbs*, 272.

16 Fox, *Proverbs 10–31*, 882.

17 Fox, *Proverbs 10–31*, 885.

18 Amy J. Chase, "Feeling Womb-ey: The Presence and Significance of Emotion in Proverbs 31:1–9," *Bible and Critical Theory* 18, no. 2 (2022), www.bible-andcriticaltheory.com/issues/vol-18-no-2-2022/vol-18-no-2-2022-amy-j-chase/.

speaking mother moves from correcting her son's company with women to his excessive drinking (vv. 3–4), and then from her son drinking to poor people drinking (vv. 4–7), and then from the poor drinking to her son's obligation to enact justice (vv. 8–9). In the midst of this is inserted a likely communal proverb, as if to bolster the speaker's view: "Give beer to the perishing, and wine to the bitter of soul" (v. 6). It all contributes to the impression of emotional outburst, akin to Reuben's heart-wrenched stuttering in Genesis 37:30b when he realizes that his brothers have sold Joseph into slavery in Egypt. Francoise Mirguet writes similarly about the style of David's lament over Absalom in 2 Samuel 19:4, "Repetition, the staccato rhythm, and syntactical discontinuity convey emotional intensity."[19]

Recognizing the quarrel portrayed in these opening lines is vital to grasp the text's full meaning and significance. In one sense, the Bakhtinian notion of every utterance being a response that anticipates response makes every utterance a vector in some quarrel. Each literary volley intends an effect, a change to the status quo, while silence supports and preserves it. Such is an understanding of communication that applies to any text. Here in Proverbs 31 we are recognizing that the text itself, in its blurring of speaker and suggestions of quarrel, is testifying to "unfinalizability" (another Bakhtinian concept). Whereas a monologic text "pretends to be the ultimate word,"[20] polyphonic texts signify that in dialogue there is always more to say about *what is being said* about the situations and persons concerned. In recognizing this quality of Proverbs 31:1–9, we thereby do not have to pledge allegiance to the dominant message as it informs and forms its audience. We are instead free to explore additional meanings also present. Attending to this dialogic quarrel in Proverbs 31:1–9 allows counterpoints to be recognized, tangling what would otherwise seem a mother's straightforward priorities and natural, obvious, commonsense, and universal instructions on what to value and how to act.

---

19 Francoise Mirguet, "What Is an 'Emotion' in the Hebrew Bible?," *BibInt* 24, nos. 4–5 (2016): 453.

20 Bakhtin, *Problems of Dostoevsky's Poetics*, 293.

Accusations and Insinuations

Women, sex, alcohol, travesties of justice, the plight of the poor. This royal mother's focus shifts across utterances from personal behavior to social responsibility. Her rebuke resembles Victor Matthews's description of "shaming speech," where a woman speaks to defend her household (or, that is, the household of her father, husband, or son) when its honor is threatened or diminished.[21] Matthews writes, "If a member of the household performs or is about to perform some action that would reflect badly on the household, it is the responsibility of every other member to attempt to prevent a repetition of this dishonorable action or to convince the deviant to reconsider his or her actions and come back into compliance with honorable behavior."[22]

But does Lemuel deserve the characterization implied? Is he wayward, intemperate, irresponsible, unqualified, or, in other insinuated ways, deficient? Or are these words a reflection of this mother's own state of mind, a projection based on her circumstances and limited agency? If we take up the text as reflecting Lemuel's memory of his mother, we can ask whether his recollection is reliable. Cognitive theorists note that memory is not a "carbon copy of the original experience" but a version of the past reconstructed according to current needs of the one remembering.[23] Literarily, too, critic Mieke Bal describes memory as a particular type of focalization consisting of "a 'vision' of the past but, as an act, situated in the present of the memory."[24]

As memory, Lemuel's mother may function more as symbol than actor. Massey points out that males commonly idealize a mother figure "not as herself a living person engaged in the toils and troubles and pleasures of life, not actively engaged in her own and others'

---

21 Victor H. Matthews, "Female Voices: Upholding the Honor of the Household," *BTB* 24, no. 1 (1994): 8.
22 Matthews, "Honor and Shame," 98.
23 Kitty Klein, "Narrative Construction, Cognitive Processing, and Health," in Herman, *Narrative Theory and the Cognitive Sciences*, 65.
24 Bal, *Narratology*, 150.

history, but a stable symbolic centre—functioning as an anchor for others."[25] Any crisis could provoke recall of a mother because of the manifold associations attached to them. These include feelings of soothing and security but also, due to inevitable separation over time, exposure and loss. In verses 2–4, Lemuel records his mother three times referring to him as "son" and also three times as mentioning kings. These are both significant identity labels. Is some crisis causing confusion or conflict between identities, loyalties, duties?

CASTS AND CHARACTERS

Readers learn from and are shaped by such psychological subtleties. To the extent that characters are relatable and able to offer a persuasive perspective about how the world is or should be, a story's cast communicates meaning. These meanings can include "damaged identities," which develop as "master narratives" project derogatory ideas about types of people that limit agency and opportunities for those people.[26] Readers absorb as much and adopt those identities for themselves or project them onto others. It is therefore worth our time to read closely to understand, in any given drama, how characters are constructed, what their identities are, and how such characterization potentially shapes the identities of readers.

So, who are Lemuel and his mother? For readers, they are teachers of wisdom, as indicated by their location in Proverbs, a wisdom text, and their subject matter: warnings about sex and alcohol, common topics in the wisdom tradition. Hints of foreignness in their speech nod to Eastern wisdom literature, similar to Job's location in the land of Uz (Job 1:1). These hints include the Aramaisms of *bar* (vv. 2–3) and *mlkn* (v. 3), the mention of *massa* (v. 1) as possibly referencing a northern Arabian tribe, and the etymology of Lemuel as possibly meaning, "Lim is God," a reference to a foreign deity.[27] Alternatively,

---

25 Massey, *Space, Place and Gender*, 180.
26 Lindemann Nelson, *Damaged Identities, Narrative Repair*, 164.
27 Fox, *Proverbs 10–31*, 884; McKane, *Proverbs*, 408.

some scholars suggest that Lemuel means "belonging to God" or "dedicated to God,"[28] in pattern similar to Samuel or Solomon, both known for their wisdom and their mothers.

Lemuel and his mother share *privilege*. He is a king, expected to rule. She is the mother of a king. Such status entails wealth and power and is confirmed through the mother's warning against Lemuel squandering his *chayil* (v. 3), the semantic range of which includes "wealth," "power," "status," "property," "sexual virility," and more.[29] Further, in articulating her vision for her son, she distinguishes him from those whom he rules in her language choice. Her son is *bar*, a Persian-sanctioned Aramaic term for "son," while peasants are *ben*, which is Hebrew, also for "son." In addition, differing modifiers in the construct chains within which "son" occurs—"son of my *womb*" for her son and "sons of those who are *perishing*" for these others—respectively convey connection and distance. She and her son together belong to the elite upper class.

Yet, Lemuel and his mother are in some quarrel; they do not share *everything* in common. They also differ. It is interesting to consider within the polyphony of these words how each character jockeys for dominance in both relationship and in rhetoric. According to one reading, we could say Lemuel has the upper hand. He is mentioned first in the text, and initially its words are ascribed to him, leaving uncertain the degree to which they borrow from his mother. We do not know how heavily Lemuel filters his mother's words before passing them on to the reader, but as the narrator sets the scene, it is clear that Lemuel, not his mother, is that filter.

Lemuel also benefits through being named, while his mother is not. A proper name promotes individualization. Its etymology can suggest traits about a character (as above, "belonging to God," etc.), as can its associations with other persons bearing that name. A name distinguishes one character from others and unifies disparate traits

---

28 Waltke, *Book of Proverbs*, 502.
29 *HALOT*, 311.

into one figure.[30] Lemuel's mother lacks these advantages. Adele Reinhartz writes, "The centrality of the proper name to the perception and construction of identity implies the converse: that the absence of the proper name contributes to the effacement, absence, veiling, or suppression of identity."[31] Because real people have names, Lemuel's name makes him seem more real and worthier of remembrance. No doubt his having a name is what causes some commentators to assume Lemuel is a historical person.[32]

Lemuel also has a title. He is king. His mother does not have one. She even lacks the descriptive term, *gebirah*, that other biblical texts attach to the mothers or wives of kings (1 Kgs 11:19; 15:13; 2 Kgs 10:13; 2 Chr 15:16; Jer 13:18; 29:2). Often treated by commentators as a title, *gebirah* means "great lady." It is the female-gendered and singular equivalent of King David's *geborim*, "mighty men." The effect of this disparity in naming and titling is clear: Lemuel is the speaker and subject over his mother.

Yet, we need not interpret Lemuel's mother as subsumed beneath him. She also asserts herself. As Proverbs 31:1 develops, ambiguity as to speaker shifts focus from Lemuel to his mother: "She rebuked him, his mother." The very act of speaking implies a certain amount of agency, confidence in her ability to influence (else she would not bother to speak), and value of her judgment (else her words would not have been remembered).

By characterizing Lemuel's mother's words as *yasar* (whether rendered as "rebuked" or "taught"), the text sets her up as an authority. Lemuel thereby appears less capable than she in knowing or doing what is right. In verse 5, his mother introduces two of several legal terms that inform the verses to follow: "forget the decrees" and "change the verdict." These phrases address two

---

30 Adele Reinhartz, *Why Ask My Name? Anonymity and Identity in Biblical Narrative* (New York: Oxford University Press, 1998), 6.

31 Reinhartz, *Why Ask My Name?*, 9.

32 E.g. Roland Murphy, *The Tree of Life: An Exploration of Biblical Wisdom Literature* (Grand Rapids: Eerdmans, 2002), 26; Waltke, *Book of Proverbs*, 503; Perdue, *Proverbs*, 269.

distinct concerns: first, that a drunken judge will forget the laws and render a faulty verdict; second, that a drunken judge will unfairly change a verdict already made.[33] The distinctions show Lemuel's mother to be not only interested in her son's personal welfare but also knowledgeable about legislative and judicial functioning.

With Lemuel and his mother both asserting themselves, identity construction occurs in multiple and varied ways. The depiction of Lemuel through his mother's urging promotes qualities typical of ancient ideals of masculinity. He must be quite virile, as signaled by his mother's warning about women and the sexual connotations of *chayil*. Yet, it is expected that he ought to bond with other men, reserving women only for sexual contact. The advice to resist both women and alcohol (vv. 3–4) fits ancient masculine conventions around self-discipline and self-control.[34] These two traits were expected to channel strength toward dominating others.[35] Such may explain why Lemuel's mother integrates her advice to resist temptations with advice on how to rule (vv. 4–9). Speaking, too, could be an ancient mode of domination.[36] Its promotion occurs in Proverbs 31 not only in Lemuel's being urged to speak on behalf of others (vv. 8–9) but also in the way he filters and transmits his mother's words (v. 1). Lemuel exhibits here "male logo-centricity," a quality Ovidiu Creanga defines as "the circular power and prestige that biblical men acquire through being institutionally privileged over women

---

33 Fox, *Proverbs 10–31*, 887.

34 Hilary Lipka, "Masculinities in Proverbs: An Alternative to the Hegemonic Ideal," in *Biblical Masculinities Foregrounded*, ed. Ovidiu Creagna and Peter-Ben Smit (Sheffield: Sheffield Phoenix, 2014), 90.

35 Stephen Moore, "Final Reflections on Biblical Masculinity," in *Men and Masculinity in the Hebrew Bible and Beyond*, ed. Ovidiu Creanga (Sheffield: Sheffield Phoenix, 2010), 247.

36 Moore, "Final Reflections on Biblical Masculinity," 248. See also David Clines, "David the Man: The Construction of Masculinity in the Hebrew Bible," in *Interested Parties: The Ideology of Writers and Readers of the Hebrew Bible* (Sheffield: Sheffield Academic, 1995), 219.

to speak in public gatherings, usually at critical moments in the life of the Israelite community."[37]

Lemuel's mother, for her part, has but one primary identity marker: mother. That this noun is placed at the very end of verse 1 gives it special emphasis: "The words of Lemuel, a king, the burden with which she rebuked him, his mother." "Mother" is the title or label equivalent to Lemuel's "king." A person becomes a mother only through relation to someone else. So being a mother comes with expectations of being highly relational, connected to others, more so than a title or label related to talent or occupation. Lemuel's mother references her son three times. She also references her womb (v. 2), the space where Lemuel was formed and grew. Given that mothers devote so much to their children (personal health, convenience, emotional energy, resources, time, hopes . . .), a mother can oblige a son, even a king, to act in accordance with her wishes, a partial but never total repayment for all she has provided. A mother is unique among every other person in her experience and knowledge of her son. She alone felt him in her body; she watched him leave the womb, nursed him as he grew, and reared him into manhood. A mother is uniquely qualified to advise her child, and her advice ought to be heeded.

But the impact of Lemuel's mother's identity is better to be described as influence rather than authority. Authority is direct, publicly acknowledged, and based on status and roles; King Xerxes either extends or withholds his scepter to decide between life or death. Lemuel's mother shows the limits of her power in opting to rebuke her son rather than herself banishing suspect women, banning beer from the banquet hall, or solving the problems of the poor. Mothers, as most women in biblical texts, work behind the scenes and indirectly. Like Esther, who had to charm, flatter, and curry her husband's favor to avert genocide, Lemuel's mother frames her message with appeals to family ties, with displays of emotion, and with appeals to personal vanity ("Not for *kings*, Lemuel," v. 4).

---

[37] Ovidiu Creanga, "Introduction," in Creanga and Smit, *Biblical Masculinities Foregrounded*, 6.

PERIPHERAL FIGURES

Lemuel and his mother are not the only characters in verses 1-9. Between and below the poem's ostensible protagonists lie dangerous women (v. 3) and peasants (vv. 5-9). These figures are not developed as individuals but as "readily recognizable character types."[38] They lack names. They lack personalities. But they contribute to the "socially shared understandings" that narratives rely on and develop.[39] Recognizing this text's subtensions and subplots requires us to examine and creatively center these peripheral, partial character types.

Lemuel's mother commands, "Do not give to women your *chayil*, or your *derek* to *makhoth* kings" (v. 3). This verse is difficult to translate because of multiple possible meanings of three key words. *Chayil* can mean "wealth," "power," "status," "property," "sexual virility," and more.[40] *Derek*, usually translated, "ways," can also mean "business" or "enterprise."[41] William McKane recommends an emendation to *derek* that would give it the meaning of "thighs," a sexual allusion, thus paralleling the sexual innuendo in *chayil*.[42] *Makhoth* appears only here in the entire Hebrew Bible. Some scholars have concluded that it is an unresolvable textual corruption. Most translators take it as an infinitive construct of *makhah*, "to ruin, to wipe out,"[43] and propose something like, "destroyers of." This translation is supported by *makhoth*'s feminine ending, its parallelism with "women" in the previous phrase, and its resemblance to Proverbs 30:20, which employs *derek* in proximity to *makhah*: "This is the way [*derek*] of an adulterous woman: she eats and wipes [*makhatah*] her mouth, and says, 'I have not done wrong.'"

---

38 Lindemann Nelson, *Damaged Identities, Narrative Repair*, 6.
39 Lindemann Nelson, *Damaged Identities, Narrative Repair*, 6.
40 *HALOT*, 311.
41 *HALOT*, 232.
42 McKane, *Proverbs*, 409. Also Waltke, *Book of Proverbs*, 507; Fox, *Proverbs 10-31*, 885.
43 *HALOT*, 567-68.

No translation can perfectly replicate its original. Keeping the nuances above in mind when interpreting produces an impression of the women Lemuel's mother warns about as a threat not only to personal virtue or happiness but also to wealth and political stability in ways that could affect those around him. Scholars associate the warning here with the biblical stories of David and Solomon, kings who compromised their reigns through engagements with women.[44] Proverbs 31:3 triggers a "person-cliché," a character type whose inclusion reminds an audience of a set of shared beliefs.[45] In this case, the belief is that women are dangerous and deserve blame when things go badly for men. This "truth" is taught via multiple biblical narratives that echo and reinforce one another. Vashti's defiance of her husband Xerxes, Delilah's betrayal of Samson, and, of course, Eve's screwup in the garden fit this familiar type.

The dangerous woman person-cliché occurs also in biblical wisdom literature, for example:

> The lips of an alien woman drip honey,
> her mouth is smoother than oil,
> but her end is as bitter as gall,
> sharp as a two-edged sword . . .
> keep your way far from her,
> don't go near the entrance to her house,
> so that you don't give your wealth to other people,
> your years to someone cruel. (Prov 5:3–4, 8–10)[46]

Alluring but deceptive, with torturous, ruinous objectives: notice the poem's first characterization of the women in question, *zarah*, which refers to a strange, different, illicit or unauthorized woman.[47] This adjective appears elsewhere as part of the dangerous woman

---

44 Yoder, *Proverbs*, 291.
45 Lindemann Nelson, *Damaged Identities, Narrative Repair*, 84.
46 John Goldingay, *The First Testament: A New Translation* (Downers Grove, IL: InterVarsity, 2018).
47 *HALOT*, 279.

person-cliché. Proverbs 2:16 and 7:5 through parallelism equate a *zarah* with a foreigner who speaks "smooth words." Undefined in these uses, though, is whether only certain women are the threat (those from outside the community) or whether potentially all women are suspect, being in their essence "other" than men (and therefore, to focalizing men, *zarah*). Proverbs 31 does not include the word *zarah*, but similarities of vocabulary and theme with other renderings of this person-cliché extend the stereotype via readers' minds onto the women of Proverbs 31.

The descriptive adjective that verse 3 does contain—*makhoth*—works similarly. Are all women being characterized as the ruination of kings or only some fewer number? According to the conventions of poetic parallelism, either can be understood as communicated here. Such ambiguity bleeds the pejorative of the second phrase onto the first. Regardless of whether all women are intended, all are indicted. So in Proverbs 31:1–9, women are identified as unsavory participants in sexual dalliances. They are dangerous, suspect in gaining possession of men's assets and causing their downfall.

The second set of character types in Proverbs 31:1–9, the peasants, rely less on person-cliché for communicating their nature because more descriptives are provided about them. Whereas the women in verse 3 have just one modifier (*makhoth*), Lemuel's subjects in verses 5–9 receive nine. Seven labels convey some type of suffering or deprivation: *bene-'oni* (literally, "sons of the oppressed," meaning "belonging to the class of people who are oppressed"),[48] *oved* ("perishing"), *mare-nephesh* ("bitter of soul"), *'ilem* ("speechless"), *bene-khaloph* ("perishing"), *'ani* ("poor"), and *'evyon* ("oppressed"). They wallow in *rish* ("misery") and *'amal* ("toil"). Semantic distinctions among these words are difficult to establish. Connotations include lacking property, being orphans, beggars, and immigrants, and teetering on the brink of death. Jean-Jacques Lavoie writes of the key term, *'ani*, that it "refers to the one who bends and flees, the

---

48 Jean-Jacques Lavoie, "Vin et Bière En Proverbes 31,4–7," *SR* 44, no. 1 (March 2015): 42.

one who is unable to resist, the bent, the humiliated, the weak, the oppressed."[49] As earlier with women of verse 3, ambiguity in verses 5–9 prevents distinguishing whether all or only some of Lemuel's subjects experience life in this way.

DAMAGED IDENTITIES

These two groups, women and peasants (who, of course, also include women), experience damage to their identities through their portrayal in Proverbs 31. To invoke the categories of oppression defined by Iris Marion Young,[50] the women are *marginalized* when othered and distanced from men. They are *disempowered* when prevented by others (here a fellow female, no less) from accessing those with power and the resources that those with power possess. They are *stereotyped* as sex objects, tempters and temptations, dangerous, malignant. Even a privileged woman such as Lemuel's mother indicates damaged, disempowered female identity in namelessly lobbying her son to act rather than acting herself.

The peasants also fit several of Young's categories of oppression. Labeled speechless (v. 8), their nonparticipation in the conversations about justice that Lemuel's mother urges for her son (v. 9) illustrates *marginalization*. Marginalization also appears in their being the ones who are judged, not those who judge (v. 5). Lemuel, even if inebriated and unfit, still functions as lawmaker and enforcer. His subjects can only accept his verdicts, no matter how unjust; they are *disempowered*. Twice-noted poverty (vv. 7, 9) also indicates powerlessness, lacking resources to protest or strive for better outcomes. Instead, Lemuel's mother recommends plying the poor with alcohol to "forget" their poverty (v. 7), in other words, rendering them incapable of even knowing how bad off they are. "'Give beer to the perishing, and wine to the bitter of soul'—Let him drink and forget his poverty; let

---

49 Lavoie, "Vin et Bière En Proverbes 31,4–7," 44 (my translation).
50 See Iris Marion Young, *Justice and the Politics of Difference* (Princeton: Princeton University Press, 1990).

him not remember his toil anymore" (vv. 6–7). South African scholar Makhosazana Keith Nzimande writes of this line, "No doubt, the giving of alcohol to the poor is a well known dehumanizing strategy in colonial and postcolonial contexts."[51] These peasants are *stereotyped* when labeled as miserable, oppressed, mute, and unstable.

Finally, reference to toil indicates a fourth of Young's named oppressions: they are *exploited*. No measure of hard labor can free them from their function as suppliers of the resources elites need to maintain themselves. Roland Boer's explanation of class exploitation helps to understand the organization of society taken for granted in Proverbs 31:1–9: "A certain group is disconnected from the production of essential items for survival such as food and clothing. This class then relies on those who do produce these essentials and must extract it from them in some fashion, whether by coercion or persuasion or some mix of the two."[52]

FOCALIZING POWER

The marginalization, powerlessness, stereotyping, and exploitation of Proverbs 31:1–9 have been largely unacknowledged, with commentators almost universally characterizing Lemuel's mother as unproblematically modeling virtue through concern for the poor. Such is the power of focalization to cause readers not to even notice who is being harmed as they sympathetically align with the speaker. Lindemann Nelson labels such focalizing "the arrogant eye," which "takes one's own standpoint as central" while undervaluing or erasing the needs, opinions, and desires of others.[53] Readers conventionally accept a narrator's assertions as authoritative, which, as Frank

---

51 Nzimande, "Postcolonial Interpretation in Post-apartheid South Africa," 194.

52 Roland Boer, "The Sacred Economy of Ancient Israel," *SJOT* 21, no. 1 (2007): 36.

53 Lindemann Nelson, *Damaged Identities, Narrative Repair*, 173.

warns, can cause them to sympathize with and support bad people.[54] Focalization, writes Bal, is "the most important, most penetrating, and most subtle means of manipulation."[55]

This subtlety manifests in Proverbs 31:1–9 through employ of a mother as speaker. Mothers are commonly perceived as vulnerable, in part because they suffer so visibly over their children's pains. Readers, with their own bonds with mothers, feel prompted to alleviate a mother's distress, and the only means available is sympathetic assent to her projections. Mothers also tend to be associated with care. If a mother says something, readers are inclined to assume that her words must come from a good place and that they must be true (especially a mother who, like Lemuel's, emphasizes a maternal bond). Lemuel's mother prioritizes her son's well-being above marginalized women and the poor, even though the latter's circumstances must be immeasurably more severe. Readers mostly do not ask whether what is good for Lemuel is good for those he rules.

Even his mother's advice to inebriate the poor has been justified as showing "deep concern for those who are suffering." After all, reasons John Hartley, the ancients did not have medicinal reliefs such as "aspirin and ibuprofen."[56] Alcohol was it. Waltke says the remark can only be understood as sarcastic, because to take it literally would produce a meaning "completely out of harmony with wisdom."[57] But readers need not join Waltke here in equating Lemuel's mother with Lady Wisdom of Proverbs 1–9. We can group her with the likes of Sarah, who to protect her son's inheritance demanded Abraham send into the wilderness Hagar and her son. In a rare contrasting opinion on Lemuel's mother, Stiebert writes, "The words attributed to the king's mother do not actually express *ubuntu* for the oppressed

---

54 Frank, *Letting Stories Breathe*, 32.
55 Bal, *Narratology*, 176.
56 John E. Hartley, *Proverbs: A Commentary in the Wesleyan Tradition* (Kansas City, MO: Beacon Hill, 2016), 326.
57 Waltke, *Book of Proverbs*, 508.

but quite the opposite: They reinforce the systems that create and maintain social oppression."[58]

ADVANTAGE ELITES

While damaging some, Proverbs 31:1-9 advantages others. Of course males possess and control; Lemuel and his mother project this as natural, a given, beneficial to all. This hierarchy is reinforced through impugning women: they cannot be trusted and do not deserve any more than what they have. But the main advantage they press concerns the peasant class. Although Lemuel's mother initiates her rebuke through repeated mentions of the word "son" (v. 2), as she continues, her subject shifts to target "kings": "Do not give to women your strength [*chayil*], or your ways to devourers [*makhoth*] of kings." Kings, those who rule, should avoid ruin through distancing from women (v. 3). In verse 4, she mentions them twice: "Not for kings, Lemuel, not for kings . . ." The repetition reveals her true interest. She is not advocating purely for Lemuel, her son, the individual object of affection. No: it is her son with respect to his station that concerns her, the position of dominance they both occupy as elites. Differences in identity validate differences in roles, responsibility, agency, and opportunity. So the ruling class must act and speak differently to those they would seek advantage over. As those with damaged identities are not capable, Lemuel and his kind must be the ones to establish laws and enforce them (v. 5). Lemuel must allocate societal resources; the peasant class are helpless, speechless, inconsequential, so they could not and should not try.

Lemuel and his mother express no curiosity as to why so many of their own subjects are so badly off, much less whether they, the ruling class, contribute to this state. There is no room for such in a scene crowded with emotional appeal and ethical posturing. Lemuel's mother cries—vaguely—for righteous judgements (v. 9). Oh, how

---

58 Stiebert, "People's Bible, Imbokodo," 247.

she suffers! Oh, how she cares! If her counsel in verses 2–9 serves as example, such judgments would blame true victims and obscure the nature of and reasons for the harm done to them. Nzimande writes, "Lemuel's Queen Mother is a hauntingly tricky figure who can easily dupe the marginalized into believing that she cares about their plight while she covertly silences their struggles."[59] Lemuel's mother communicates no ideas for including or empowering the underclass, no plans for relieving them of their poverty, their hopeless, miserable toil. These conditions simply remain eternally so, just as Lemuel and his mother will, as things go, retain their wealth, positions, and power. This messaging is no accident but actually a substantial work, or purpose, of the poem.

THE WORLD BEHIND THE TEXT

Why is this text doing this work? Earlier we wondered what crisis might have provoked Lemuel to remember his mother in this way. We asked: What is the question to which this rebuking mother is an answer? What is the agenda, the hoped-for impact of this poem?

Considering features of its likely Persian-era historical and social context provides insight. As the Babylonian Cyrus Cylinder and Second Isaiah illustrate, ideas about the Persian Empire that circulated within its political domain were almost always positive. Cyrus, for example, was portrayed as a liberator. The Persian Empire did not force a certain language or religion on conquered territories, nor did it install foreign leaders at the local level. Instead, it integrated local authorities, laws, and customs into its administration. It developed high-quality roads and an efficient postal system, which fostered trade.[60] Such conditions enabled many conquered peoples to thrive, including Yahweh worshippers, both those living in diaspora and

---

59 Nzimande, "Postcolonial Interpretation in Post-apartheid South Africa," 184.

60 Benjamin R. Foster and Karen Polinger Foster, *Civilizations of Ancient Iraq* (Princeton: Princeton University Press, 2011), 142-143.

those in Yehud. Jews in Babylon, for example, were able to materially support those left behind (Ezra 1). Even in the poverty of Yehud, Nehemiah worked for the emperor amid lavish circumstances (Neh 5:17). Other examples are not hard to find.

Yet Persian-sanctioned propaganda should not be mistaken for actual benevolence. The empire conscripted men to serve throughout its provinces as soldiers in exchange for agricultural land. The result was larger numbers of troops that were readily available to quash rebellions.[61] The empire also imposed tributes, income taxes, and wealth taxes. These requirements made no exceptions for economic disruptions caused by natural disasters. Payments, moreover, needed to be made in silver rather than in goods, thus requiring extra effort and costs that were shouldered by those on whom these transfers were levied.[62]

Such conditions motivated Yahweh worshippers across the empire to strategize to preserve or even enhance their wealth and stability. Some elites entered marital alliances with Persian officials (Neh 13:28). Some made deals with Persian landlords that enabled them to speculate on the harvest of local peasants. But peasants were left out of such arrangements, resulting in increased debt and economic servitude of the imperial underclass.[63] A substantial number of people without land to call their own moved from farm to farm to work as day laborers, while their families broke apart through distance.[64] As Mario Liverani describes, "Social unrest was generated by the process of indebtedness, endemic in peasant societies in the ancient Near East, including Palestine; this was met by paying interest and mortgaging property (homes and land) and personal service ('debt slavery'). These processes were highly corrosive for the socioeconomic system, destroying the theoretical model of a fabric of families that were all free (with their own productive means)

---

[61] Foster and Foster, *Civilizations of Ancient Iraq*, 144.
[62] Rainer Kessler, *The Social History of Ancient Israel*, trans. Linda M. Maloney (Minneapolis: Fortress, 2008), 140.
[63] Foster and Foster, *Civilizations of Ancient Iraq*, 144.
[64] Kessler, *Social History of Ancient Israel*, 135.

THE DRAMA OF MOTHERS AND KINGS

and of equal status; and also because they increased the number of servants in the latifundia, basically without limit."[65] Nehemiah 5 records complaints of this nature by the suffering underclass, not against Persian overlords but against fellow Jews who exploited their impoverished countrymen.

In Yehud, those newly arrived from Babylon following Cyrus's recommendation to return clashed with locals over land ownership. A new upper class had formed in Judea (Yehud) during the time the Israelite aristocracy was in exile in Babylon.[66] Not necessarily related by blood to the former Israelite people, these new elites now occupied the land. The so-called (self-identified) returnees from Babylon, also not exclusively related to the former Israelite kingdom, pressed their advantage, developing genealogically based claims to land, working Persian connections to extract edicts in their favor, maneuvering for political and religious positions of leadership. As the privileged few who could read and write (or employ scribes to do so), the returnees developed master narratives to strengthen their claims, such as telling the story of the fall of Jerusalem as a "total exile" that left an "empty land."[67] According to this narrative, those returning to Yehud were the ones who truly belonged, an ideological perspective that is reflected in the biblical narrative itself.

Earlier, the Babylonians had settled the Judean exiles into their own communities in Babylon; they did not disburse them into oblivion as had happened during the Assyrian exile of the northern tribes a few centuries earlier. Yet during Babylonian and Persian rule, Jewish exiles experienced considerable interaction with non-Jews. This experience sparked debate about how much integration is beneficial and at what point intermingling dismantles communal identity and

---

65 Mario Liverani, *Israel's History and the History of Israel*, trans. Chiara Peri and Philip R. Davies (London: Equinox, 2003), 348.

66 Kessler, *Social History of Ancient Israel*, 136.

67 As detailed by Ehud Ben Zvi, "Total Exile, Empty Land and the General Intellectual Discourse in Yehud," in *The Concept of Exile in Ancient Israel and Its Historical Contexts*, ed. Ehud Ben Zvi and Christoph Levin (Berlin: de Gruyter, 2010), 155–68.

strength. Much of this discussion focused on women and marriage. Would Jewish men marrying non-Jewish women dilute Jewish distinctives through passing on to their children non-Jewish beliefs and practices? Rules against exogamy (Ezra 10) knocked against inspiring tales of heroic outsiders (Ruth, Rahab). Questions about women also factored into issues of land. If women inherited land, would marrying outside their tribe deplete communal resources?

As we can see from even a broad, cursory overview of the text's social and political context, concerns over social organization, class conflict, distribution of resources, and cooperation with empire were circulating widely among Yahweh worshippers across Persia's domain. Those concerns are reflected in narratives, histories, and even wisdom literature produced or edited in this period. In the case of Proverbs 31, a grasp of exilic and postexilic politics helps us modern readers to find the voices of the oppressed even in texts that largely reflect the politics of their oppressors. Upper-class Yahweh worshippers in Yehud and in diaspora communicated freely with one another through Persia's postal and travel systems.[68] It would be fitting for members of these communities to have produced, circulated, and/or discussed a text like Proverbs 31:1–9, in which an elite mother cannot abide her son risking the family wealth on inappropriate dalliances and cannot stomach profligacy when he should be soberly assessing their situation and looking for ways to enhance their influence and stability.

The king and his mother have postexilic social and political dilemmas quite distinct from those they rule. The text accordingly focuses on the strategies they can deploy to advance their interests. Lemuel-types must keep their wits about them. They must display deference to the Persian authorities and demonstrate that they are qualified to direct and administrate those beneath them, judging accurately and enforcing consistently (vv. 4–5). But they must also

---

68 Mary Joan Winn Leith, "New Perspectives on the Return from Exile and Persian-Period Yehud," in *The Oxford Handbook of the Historical Books of the Hebrew Bible*, online ed., ed. Brad Kelle and Brent Strawn (Oxford Academic, November 10, 2020), https://academic.oup.com/edited-volume/34226, 148.

understand the underclass well enough to address their privations and maintain social cohesion: "Open your mouth for the speechless." They must dole out just enough sustenance to secure compliance and keep peasants from rebelling: "Give beer to the perishing.... Let him drink and forget his poverty." In Genesis, Joseph's arc forms a parallel. He rose to power serving a foreign ruler but also took care of his own—in both senses of that phrase: he provided for and controlled his family, establishing them in Goshen, protected from but also utterly reliant on Egyptian rulers and eventually enslaved by them. Perhaps sincerely, perhaps cynically, Proverbs 31:1-9 depicts the complex social negotiation of postexilic elites in their struggle to survive and thrive.

BEYOND THE DOMINANT IDEOLOGY

We see more clearly now the ideological agenda of Proverbs 31:1-9, the how and the why some community members seek to maintain their positions by moving others to the margins. But this text can be pressed beyond the dominant ideology. Other combinations of its meanings can release the marginalized from their assigned margins. No utterance occurs in isolation. Rather, each utterance "is accompanied by a continual sideways glance at another person."[69] Listeners are not passive containers for speech. They form a simultaneous response to a speaker's utterance. The experience or anticipation of such responses in turn influences how a speaker speaks. This inherent dialogical dynamic of written language enables us to infer the perspectives, interests, and even ideologies not only of the speaker but also of the listeners. "The listener," Bakhtin writes, "becomes the speaker."[70] He asks us to "imagine a dialogue of two persons in which the statements of the second speaker are omitted, but in such a way that the general sense is not at all violated." In such a dialogue,

---

69 Bakhtin, *Problems of Dostoevsky's Poetics*, 32.
70 Bakhtin, "Problem of Speech Genres," 68.

"The second speaker is present invisibly, his words are not there, but deep traces left by these words have a determining influence on all the present and visible words of the first speaker." We cannot but name the meeting of these two modes of presence as conversation. Indeed, "It is a conversation of the most intense kind, for each present, uttered word responds and reacts with its every fiber to the invisible speaker," and each "points to something outside itself, beyond its own limits, to the unspoken words of another person."[71]

In Proverbs 31:1-9 the "absent interlocutor"[72] is made present through the text's questions: "What . . . ? And what . . . ? And what . . . ?" (v. 2) Questions imply the presence of an addressee and invite their reply. Lemuel may at first appear to be the one his mother addresses, with the lack of recorded dialogue signaling silence itself as his response. Cynthia Miller argues that in some cases, "the absence of speech results in communication just as surely as its spoken counterpart."[73] Silence can signal assent or dissent. Riad Aziz Kassis groups several types of silence that occur in Proverbs, including expressions of respect, ignorance, response to fools, concealment of information, compassion for the poor, and strategic advantage.[74] Lemuel's silence could convey *respect*, reflecting the appropriate posture of offspring toward a parent. Or perhaps a type of *ignorance*, implying that Lemuel is incapable of marshaling a reply. If we take Lemuel to be an adolescent (we do not know his age, after all), silence here could be a *response to fools*, the withdrawal of one who has concluded his mother will not listen and does not care about his point of view. Silence then can mean resistance.

Though the punctuation added by translators encourages readers to imagine Lemuel as this mother's addressee, such an interpretation

---

71 Bakhtin, *Problems of Dostoevsky's Poetics*, 197.
72 Bakhtin, *Problems of Dostoevsky's Poetics*, 120.
73 Cynthia L. Miller, "Silence as a Response in Biblical Hebrew Narrative: Strategies of Speakers and Narrators," *JNSL* 32, no. 1 (2006): 23. See also Mark Sneed: silence "is an active virtue which stops quarrel and combat." Sneed, *The Social World of the Sages* (Minneapolis: Fortress, 2015), 274.
74 Riad Aziz Kassis, *The Book of Proverbs and Arabic Proverbial Works* (Leiden: Brill, 1999), 148.

of the facts is not required. *Mah beri*—"What my son"—could identify the topic that another is invited to weigh in on ("What: my son!") and not necessarily constitute a direct address ("What, my son?"). Readers may take the mother's opening as extended not to Lemuel (or not *only* to him) but to any number of others, including Proverbs 31's ruinous women and/or the poor. What would *they* say, having been invited here to speak? Would they note the contradictions in her speech? A woman warns against women. Why should she, then, herself a potential ruiner of kings, be trusted? Queen mothers are not always respected: Is this one a role model, or is she more akin to the reprehensible Maacah (1 Kgs 15:9–14) or Athaliah (2 Chr 22:2–4)? The words of Proverbs 31:2–9 are Lemuel's, and yet they are his mother's. Who is the true authority, the true competent? If we take Lemuel to be the speaker, he is telling the reader that his own mother believes his rule is failing. So is this unreliable king the one in whom the "mute" are supposed to place their hope?

Additional "others" in this scene can be detected when we pay attention to the change of address that occurs between verses 5 and 6. In the first half of the poem, Lemuel's mother inflects her imperative in the singular: "Do not give to women." But then in verse 6, her command to "Give beer" inflects as a plural, which seems to suggest, as Jean-Jacques Lavoie notes, that "the queen is no longer exclusively addressing her son."[75] Some scholars consider verse 6 to be an insertion of a traditional communal proverb into the queen mother's lecture.[76] Indicators of proverbs performance include the presence of conflict and an "out-of-context intrusion of figurative language."[77] Such proverb citation is a strategy of persuasion that invokes a traditional saying to offer a clarifying appraisal in an ambiguous situation.[78] It is a way of noting within an argument, "It's not just I who thinks so!"

---

75 Lavoie, "Vin et Bière En Proverbes 31,4–7," 46 (translation mine: "il semble bien que la reine ne s'adresse plus exclusivement à son fils,...").

76 Fox, *Proverbs 10–31*, 887.

77 Carole R. Fontaine, "The Proof of the Pudding: Proverbs and Gender in the Performance Arena," *JSOT* 29, no. 2 (December 2004): 185.

78 Fontaine, "Proof of the Pudding," 182–183.

With verse 6's injunction to provide libations to the suffering, Lemuel's mother, through use of a traditional communal proverb, brings into the discussion a chorus of communal stakeholders. She likely intends for them to back up her assertion that it would be better for the poor to get drunk rather than the king. But she cannot control the reception of these words once unfurled. Waltke notes that *oved* ("perishing," v. 6) is most frequently used in the Hebrew Bible to describe the "devastating, destructive" end that God inflicts on the wicked. Elsewhere in Proverbs, it is always used pejoratively with regard to the poor.[79] So alongside this mother's purported moral sensibilities, bolstered through a proverbial citation, exists a longstanding communal prejudice against the poor.

We are attempting to hear the fainter voices of Proverbs 31:1-9. But dialogism exists not only between characters expressing differing interests and points of view. It also exists within characters themselves, as evidenced by internal debate, argument, and struggle.[80] The literary remains of this "plurality of consciousnesses"[81] are revealed through instances of repetition. In addition to the repeated "what" (v. 2) and "not for kings" (v. 4), already discussed, alcohol (v. 6) and the instruction to "open your mouth" (vv. 8-9) are mentioned twice. Extensive repetition of legal terminology and references to the underclass also recur throughout the poem. Lemuel's mother mentions "decree," "verdict" (v. 5), "open your mouth," "judge rightly," and "plead the case" (v. 9), all recalling judicial actions where argumentation either condemns or upholds the accused.

Why the repetition? Why say something twice, four times, or nine; does once not suffice? Conventions of parallelism in Hebrew poetry invite the phenomenon, but why choose *these* particular conventions? What is their contribution to the text's meaning? Perhaps the goal is mere emphasis. Perhaps the characters' intentions are confused. Perhaps the whole scene is marked by uncertainty. Perhaps the solution is more elusive than the problem. Mother (as speaker) and son

---

79 Waltke, *Book of Proverbs*, 505.
80 Bakhtin, *Problems of Dostoyevsky's Poetics*, 32.
81 Bakhtin, *Problems of Dostoevsky's Poetics*, 9.

(as rememberer of her speech) in their repeated graspings show their frailty and the limitations of their understanding. This mother is anxious; her son is vulnerable. In the midst of such fallibilities, an opening exists for marginalized others to step onto the stage to disturb the arrangements these elites work so hard to project to the world as good, natural, and permanent. The suffering underclass need not submit to the emotionalism and maternal manipulation Lemuel's mother deploys. She is not their mother. She is not looking out for them. Neither she nor Lemuel has nourishing words to feed them.

NARRATIVE REPAIR

Recognizing damaged identities and resisting the master narratives offer some benefit to those whose opportunities and basic welfare are threatened by the status quo. These tactics call into question the veracity of unfavorable beliefs as well as the credibility of those who perpetuate them. But recognition and resistance do not in and of themselves *repair*. Repairing damaged identities requires developing and circulating a counterstory that shifts social understanding. Stories emphasizing a group's perceived negative qualities must be rewritten and retold so that group can be redefined by positive attributes and abilities.[82] An effective counterstory replaces an "arrogant eye" with a "loving eye."[83] It contests damaging master narratives through depicting the group in question as morally worthy, not defective.

A dialogical reading of Proverbs 31:1–9 allows marginalized characters to be recognized and elite prejudices to be resisted, but can it also produce a counterstory within the text itself? The raw materials for such a project seem sparse. We might note that, in contrast to Lemuel's mother's effort to portray other women as "ruiners of kings," she herself is portrayed positively as a qualified, helpful, contributing

---

82 Lindeman Nelson, *Damaged Identities, Narrative Repair*, 69.
83 Lindeman Nelson, *Damaged Identities, Narrative Repair*, 174.

member of society and its rulers. She, modeled through vocabulary choices and subject matter as a prophet, is an adviser of kings. She thus embodies a counterstory to the narrative about women she is herself telling. We could also note that even the capacity to be a ruiner of kings (ascribed to women in v. 3) involves possessing some measure of power. Though Lemuel's mother lobbies him to prevent women from gaining *chayil* ("strength"), they must in some sense already possess it. But are these materials enough to tell a new story?

CONCLUSION

Lindemann Nelson argues that for a story to effectively counter a damaging master narrative and contribute positively to a person's identity, it must have "heft."[84] Heft refers to the connection between those elements of identity inherent to a counterstory and the values shared within a community. The community must care about whatever characteristic is being promoted. Otherwise it will not notice the narrative shift at all. The ancient postexilic community did value both prophetic wisdom and strength, as attested in other biblical literature. So, we can identify some viable components toward repairing damage to women's identity present in this text. But this poem in and of itself lacks broader concern for the suffering underclasses. More is required to cultivate a different story about the elites and the poor, and especially the intersections of wealth and gender. This fuller counterstory begins to emerge when we apply the lessons of dialogical reading to other narrative elements of Proverbs 31.

---

84 Lindeman Nelson, *Damaged Identities, Narrative Repair*, 96.

Proverbs 31:10–23

10 *Eshet chayil*, who can find?
   Her value is far beyond jewels.
11 Her husband takes shelter in her
   and never lacks for plunder.
12 She supplies for him good things,
   not bad, all the days of her life.
13 She pursues wool and flax
   and applies her hands with pleasure.
14 She is like trading ships;
   from far away she brings her food.
15 And she rises while it is still night and provides prey to
   her household and assigned tasks [/portions] to her girls.
16 She schemes to get a field and seizes it;
   from the fruit of her hand she plants a vineyard.
17 She binds with strength her loins
   and she braces her arms.
18 She knows that her trading is good,
   and her lamp does not go out at night.
19 Her hands thrust toward the distaff;
   her palms grasp the spindle-whorl.
20 Her palm she stretches toward the poor;
   her hands thrust toward the oppressed.

21 She does not fear snow for her household,
   for all her household are clothed in double layers.
22 She makes bed coverings for herself;
   linen and purple are her clothes.

CHAPTER THREE

Of Wifely Exertions
Proverbs 31:10–22

Proverbs 31's second poem, like its first, commences with a question, implying an audience and inviting reply. This dialogic element joins others—gaps, ambiguities, contradictions, and multiplicities of meaning—to form worlds of subtensions and subplots that add layers of meaning waiting to be recognized.

Eshet chayil, mi yimtsa? Woman (or is it "wife"?) of—what? worth? virtue? competence? strength? A monologic reading must select one word for translation and thereby reject all others to know and to enforce *the* meaning of the poem. But dialogism acknowledges multiple, concurrent meanings as significant. A monologic reading fixates on this first focalized figure and reads the poem as her portrait, but we will consider this woman as a member of a community in which several factions speak: both men and women, affluent and poor. We will ask always and again: What is the communal question to which *this* mother is an answer?

A question, by its very nature, expresses lack and desire: something is not known, but someone wants to know it. This poem's opening question invites its audience into a drama, a journey to find the thing that is sought. Verse 10's polyphony allows for multiple answers to the question. Is it an ideal woman, about to be described?

"*Eshet chayil*, who can find?" Perhaps emphasis falls on the *who*, with the speaker seeking to know the person who could find this woman, what type of "ideal" man would be qualified to discover or obtain her. Or should we focus on the final word: "Who can *find*?" Perhaps this question is really about locations, real or imagined, dissatisfaction with current circumstances, seeking something better, somewhere. Will this poem, then, probe the *conditions* that produce an idealized wife and therefore an idealized life?

Readers familiar with the preceding poem of verses 1–9 are primed for such questions, given verse 3's words of wisdom to a son, a king, commenced as a warning about women, to guard against giving them *chayil*, a word whose meanings encompass power, wealth, and sexual virility. Now here, a second poem envisions a woman, one already possessing *chayil*, and this one is desired. Is she an exception to the previous principle, a contradiction, or somehow transcendent of it?

Both poems share '*ani* and '*avyon*, which reference the peasant underclass as suffering and oppressed. Both promote elites as "opening mouths" (*petach peh*; vv. 8–9, 26) seemingly to speak or to judge for communal good. Yet our dialogical reading of verses 1–9 unearthed, with regard to the underclass, Lemuel and his mother's conflicted motives, oppressive behavior, and damaging identity constructions. What about here in the second poem? An *eshet chayil* is prosperous and powerful. How does this one treat the poor? Does she come through for them with interventions of genuine justice? Or is she just another of the ruling class who, in the words of Nzimande, "dupe the marginalized into believing that she cares about their plight while she covertly silences their struggles"?[1]

In verses 1–9, a quarrel between *mother and son* surfaces Persian-era anxieties and strategies related to class conflict, distribution of resources, and cooperation with empire. A substantial work of that poem is defending the elites' position of dominance in order to protect resources and access to power. The poem in verses 10–31 uses

---

1 Nzimande, "Postcolonial Interpretation in Post-apartheid South Africa," 184.

another fundamental familial relationship, that of *husband and wife*, to process these same issues, like a musical composition exploring variations on a theme. In this chapter, I will analyze verses 10–22, the second poem's first half, attending to its narrative features of setting, characterization, and plot. We read dialogically to hear the multiplicity of voices present in the text, especially those offering testimony as to who is helped and who harmed via the text's vigorous identity construction. In such manner we continue probing the intersections of wealth, class, and gender in Proverbs 31 and in the world producing it, the civilizational precarity that these dynamics reveal.

SETTINGS

The importance of location in this poem is first suggested in the poem's opening verse: the quest to "find" a desired woman and mention of her price (*mekhir*) as "far beyond" (a spatial term) jewels (*rakhoq*). Seeking implies locations where whatever is sought could be found. The distancing of this woman's price (or perhaps, value, or quality) from jewels in verse 10 discourages envisioning the *eshet chayil* in a palace throne room, banquet hall, or any other place where refined aristocratic ladies might wear their jewels. The poem moves readers through several other spaces where the *eshet chayil* might be found due to her notable impact. She brings food *from far away* (v. 14), gives prey to her *house* (v. 15), schemes to acquire a *field*, and plants a *vineyard* (v. 16). Within the poem's climactic ending in verse 31, she becomes associated with *city gates*. These locations and distances form a nexus of potential settings where this sought-for woman might be found.

Scholars debate the extent to which such descriptions indicate the *eshet chayil*'s occupation of spheres outside the home. Bernard Lang compares her to the wife described in the contemporaneous text *Oeconomicus* and concludes that Proverbs 31 conforms to a common practice in ancient Mediterranean cultures of women staying at home while men go out in public, commensurate with the separate spheres of their responsibilities and roles.[2] Other scholars assume that the *eshet chayil* must move freely in public spaces.[3] Yoder has amassed an extensive list of occupations in which Persian-era women participated, including as stockyard workers, treasury workers, goldsmiths, keepers of fruit, irrigation workers, winemakers, tax handlers, extenders of loans, renters and managers of fields.[4] A network of roads throughout the Persian empire enabled Yehudites to interact with and be influenced by surrounding culture, as is even implied in Proverbs 31 through its mention of *Kena'ani*, "Canaanites," (v. 24), which likely refers to Phoenician maritime traders, and also its mention of flax (v. 13) and dyed linen (v. 22), exports from Egypt.[5] It seems reasonable to expect that the *eshet chayil* would occupy these spaces she is associated with in the poem.

But it is notable that this celebration of an *eshet chayil*, introduced as a quest to find her, does not explicitly locate her in any of these spaces, certainly not to the degree of specificity that her husband enjoys, seated as he is on the elders' bench (v. 23). Readers locate the woman through inference or assumption amid ambiguities that produce uncertainties. For example, "From afar she brings her food" (v. 14) could mean she travels to foreign lands, or it could mean that she stays put and purchases locally goods imported from afar. The woman makes plans concerning a field (v. 16), but the text does not say, like a Boaz-type from Ruth, that she visits her fields for inspection. Readers must insert her there, and only if they wish to do so. The text does not say she plants a vineyard but actually, "*from the fruit of her hands* she plants a vineyard." What does that mean? Is she the one actually planting or not? Even the thrice-repeated mention of

---

2 Lang, "Hebrew Wife and the Ottoman Wife"; also Bernard Lang, "Women's Work, Household and Property in Two Mediterranean Societies: A Comparative Essay on Proverbs xxxi 10–31," *VT* 54, no. 2 (2004): 188–207.

3 E.g., Longman, *Proverbs*, 543; Claassens, "Woman of Substance," 11; Masenya, *How Worthy*, 103.

4 Yoder, *Wisdom as a Woman*, 60.

5 Yoder, "Woman of Substance," 441–42.

"her house" (*betah*; vv. 15, 21, 27) does not locate her there but rather identifies the people of her household, not the physical space itself.

NEBULOUS POSITIONING

These instances make nebulous the *eshet chayil*'s positioning. While the several mentions of diverse spaces in the poem's first half allow a sense that her impact is everywhere felt, her own lack of explicit location emphasizes her labor and what she produces rather than herself. It is surprising that such an elite woman would be so characterized, since in biblical texts members of the upper class generally prefer depictions of leisure to signal their status,[6] as in the case of Job (Job 29) or the *eshet chayil*'s husband in Proverbs 31:23. Sirach 38:24 states, "Scribal wisdom is dependent on the opportunity of leisure, and whoever is free from toil can become wise."[7] According to Ehud Ben Zvi, a postexilic female figure could be better suited than a male to promote labor and productivity because the elite sector of society developing and contemplating such a poem looked down on trade, with several ancient texts referencing it disparagingly. The leisure class did not want association with the working class, so any commercial or manual activity was vulgar.[8] Therefore, depicting the wife and not the husband engaging in trade could spare a male audience's concern for honor, playing up the benefit to the community while deflecting attention from actual male participation. Women in relation to men are the "other" and often lack agency and voice, so a female figure could more effectively personify the *golah* community,

---

[6] Tamara Cohn Eskenazi, "The Lives of Women in Postexilic Era," in *The Writings and Later Wisdom Books*, ed. Christl M. Maier and Nuria Calduch-Benages (Atlanta: SBL Press, 2014), 13.

[7] As cited by Christopher A. Rollston, "Scribal Curriculum in the First Temple Period: Epigraphic Hebrew and Biblical Evidence," in *Contextualizing Israel's Sacred Writing: Ancient Literacy, Orality, and Literary Production*, ed. Brian Schmidt (Atlanta: SBL Press, 2015), 71.

[8] Ben Zvi, "'Successful, Wise, Worthy Wife,'" 34.

whose leaders, even though considerably better off than peasants, saw themselves as the marginalized other of the Persian Empire.[9]

In light of such considerations, scholars seeking to defend the *eshet chayil*'s husband against accusations of laziness miss the point. The husband also works, Fox assures, otherwise he would not be worthy of an *eshet chayil*.[10] The text "lopsidedly" depicts only the female as breadwinner, writes Waltke, neglecting males, but surely in reality "the husband has founded the home on a sound economic foundation" that enables his wife to "settle down and function to her maximum capacity."[11] Biwul detects markers of male contribution in the text, overlooked amid (in his view) excessive praise for the wife.[12] He writes, "The salient roles [the husband] performs both at the familial and societal levels embedded in this poem (Prov 31:11, 23, 28b–29) singles him out as a celebrity and role model *par excellence* who should elicit an equal amount of public praise, and perhaps, even higher praise than the female figure."[13] But labor, productivity, profit, and the comforts these bring are what is really celebrated here. The *eshet chayil* is a postexilic fantasy insulating against anxiety concerning lack of security and essential resources. These are alluded to when the poem mentions having shelter, never lacking (v. 11), receiving "good things, not bad" (v. 12), and not fearing snow (v. 21).

Scholars fretting over the *eshet chayil*'s husband receiving the credit he is due are correct, however, in sensing that what a person does within a given setting affects their identity. Cresswell points out that expressions "know your place" and "put him in his place" imply that spaces are not just physical locations; they are mental conceptions bound up with "a sense of the proper,"[14] including who

---

9 Eskenazi, "Lives of Women," 26, referencing Orit Avnery, "The Threefold Cord: Interrelations between the Books of Samuel, Ruth and Esther" [Hebrew] (PhD diss., Bar Ilan University, 2011), 105.
10 Fox, *Proverbs 10–31*, 893.
11 Waltke, *Book of Proverbs*, 520–21.
12 Biwul, "What Is He Doing," 35.
13 Biwul, "What Is He Doing," 47.
14 Cresswell, *In Place/Out of Place*, 3.

belongs where and who should behave how in any given place. In Proverbs 31, these places of labor—trading routes, home, fields and vineyards—and their mention in relation to the *eshet chayil* encourage associating the wife with labor and thereby attaching labor connotations to her identity. At the same time, the *eshet chayil*'s frenetic activity ("she rises while it is still night. . . . Her lamp does not go out at night") combined with her nebulous location in so many communal spaces advances the sense of unsettledness and seeking embedded in the poem's opening question: "*Eshet chayil*, who can find?" Who is the *eshet chayil*, and by extension, who are the ones envisioning and seeking her?

CHARACTERIZATION

The *Eshet Chayil*

The characterization of this much-exalted woman begins with her first modifier: *chayil*. As a noun, *chayil* throughout the Bible means primarily "army," or secondarily "wealth." It occurs more than two hundred times, most often as an adjective, almost always modifying a male subject: a man, a ruler, or God. While occasionally context suggests a meaning of "capable," most often *chayil* used adjectivally concerns fighting and so results in translations of "warrior," "men of valor," "brave" or "fierce" fighters. But Proverbs 31:10 uses *chayil* in relation to a woman. Is she, too, a warrior? A brave or fierce fighter? English translations do not render her as such. The woman (or wife) in Proverbs 31:10 is a "worthy woman" (ASV), an "excellent wife" (ESV), a "virtuous wife" (NKJV), a "good woman" (MSG), a "wife of noble character" (NIV), a "capable wife" (NRSV). Presumably the context of a female subject has for translators necessitated an uncommon rendering for *chayil* in verse 10: neither its primary nor secondary meanings. This makes quite a difference in understanding what this woman is like and why she is sought after and praised. But is this choice really warranted?

In the Bible, *chayil* only rarely attaches to females: the queen of Sheba (1 Kgs 10:2; 2 Chr 9:1), the Moabite widow, Ruth (Ruth 3:11), and in Proverbs (Prov 12:4; 31:3, 10, 29). In 1 Kings 10:2/2 Chronicles 9:1, *chayil* is a noun and is translated "entourage" or "retinue," a summation of the great wealth the queen of Sheba brings with her to visit Solomon. This translation, consistent with *chayil*'s secondary meaning, derives from context, with mention later in the verse of her servants, camels, spices, and jewels. But translation and meaning get trickier when *chayil* appears as an adjective directly modifying a female subject. Boaz deems Ruth an *eshet chayil*, but why? Ruth at the threshing floor, washed and anointed, alone at night, lying at his feet, has taken great risk to secure her own and her family-in-law's interests. Proverbs 12:4 reads, "*Eshet chayil* is the crown of her husband, but she who brings shame is like rottenness in his bones." Here, antithetical parallelism suggests that *chayil* must have some meaning opposite to bringing shame. Honor is the opposite of shame, to have a good reputation, positive standing within one's community. This adjectival meaning of *chayil* gains support through Boaz's use: "All the gate of my people know that you are an *eshet chayil*" (Ruth 3:11). It's the community's high opinion of Ruth that earns her status as an *eshet chayil*.

An appropriate translation of *chayil* in Proverbs 12:4 would be "an honor-bringing wife" or "a *creditable* woman." "Creditable" conveys a nuance of value, which correlates to *chayil*'s secondary meaning, "wealth." When someone is a credit to their family, they bring value to it. The closest common translation of Proverbs 12:4 communicating this nuance of meaning is "a worthy woman" (ASV), but most translations choose a modifier that conveys a different moral quality: an "excellent wife" (ESV), a "virtuous woman" (KJV), a "noble wife" (NIV), or a "good wife" (NRSV). Such translations no doubt reflect the same reasoning as that surmised above concerning Proverbs 31:10. But the favor that popular translations have done to imagine on readers' behalf what quality is so desired in a wife distorts the meaning actually conveyed by the phrase *eshet chayil*. We must retain all three shades of meaning for *chayil*, warfare, wealth, and honor, because multiple phrases throughout the poem expand on them to honor the *eshet chayil* as a warrior for wealth.

WARRIOR FOR WEALTH

Let us explore these several places where the *eshet chayil* is honored as a warrior for wealth. The second warrior image (following her initial descriptor, *eshet chayil*) occurs in Proverbs 31:11 with "Her husband takes shelter in her." The verb here rendered "takes shelter" (commonly translated as "trust") is *batach*. It occurs over one hundred times in the Bible and often involves seeking protection from threat via some more powerful person or object such as Yahweh, military leaders, foreign powers, chariots, city walls, and so on. Deuteronomy 28:52 mentions the "high and fortified walls, in which you [*batach*] trusted." Second Kings many times depicts the Israelites "trusting in" (*batach*) the Lord or Egypt (18:5, 19–22, 24, 30; 19:10). Here in Proverbs 31 the husband focalizes his wife as an object effective for hiding behind. Ben Zvi explains the husband's "trusting in" his wife as "she is their fortress and army, upon whom they can reliably lean."[15]

Another warrior reference occurs at the end of verse 11: "he never lacks for plunder." Plunder (*shalal*), like *chayil*, has both martial and economic associations. But how does this image of the husband enjoying plunder serve to characterize the wife? Where does she fit? Women are commonly listed or presumed among the valuables seized by conquerors (Deut 21:11; Judg 5:30; 1 Sam 30:2). So we could presume that the *eshet chayil* is the plunder of verse 11, an asset seized to enrich him, serve him, pleasure him. Yet we can also understand the *eshet chayil* not as plunder herself but as the plunderer. The next phrase references the wife as "supplying good things" (v. 12). She is perhaps being likened to a proxy soldier, one of her husband's troops, like David's "mighty men" (2 Sam 23:8) or Joshua's "mighty men of

---

15 Ben Zvi, "'Successful, Wise, Worthy Wife,'" 37.

fighting strength" (*gibbore hachayil*; Josh 8:3; 10:7). She is a battlefield power to strategically deploy for surefire gains, an idea blending, like the term *eshet chayil* itself, warrior imagery and wealth acquisition.

Yoder argues that "plunder" (she translates "loot") references the hefty dowry this woman must have brought to the marriage.[16] But the wealth she brings as bride is only the first haul. Subsequent descriptions of her activities as wife attest to her continual success expanding household coffers. Her bringing of food from afar (v. 14) indicates that her household produces more than is needed for immediate consumption, thus enabling trade for choicer goods. The *eshet chayil* has multiple servants (v. 15) in a culture where to have even one would have been a mark of privilege.[17] Reference to her lamp not going out at night (v. 18) signals prosperity in having oil to burn rather than conserving and waiting for daylight.[18] She and her household are abundantly clothed (vv. 21–22). Wearing dyed linen conveys not only affluence but membership in the ruling class.[19]

Three primary sources drive the *eshet chayil*'s income: farming, textile production, and trade. Participation in all three maximizes profits by managing the entire supply chain of her finished goods. Owning land (v. 16) enables her to grow flax and cultivate sheep for wool (v. 13), from which she produces clothing and other linens (vv. 19–21), with which she trades with foreign merchants (vv. 18, 24). The profits from these transactions she reinvests to diversify her crops ("From the fruit of her hands she plants a vineyard," v. 16). Throughout the poem, all this economic activity is couched within warrior allusions. The *eshet chayil* hunts for and brings back "prey" (v. 15). She girds her loins and strengthens her arms (v. 17). She schemes for land and seizes it (v. 16) just as a military leader would do—or a savvy landowner. Through such imagery the text promotes, for Yoder, the business dimensions of marriage, or, in Ben Zvi's view,

---

16 Yoder, "Woman of Substance," 435.
17 Yoder, *Proverbs*, 293.
18 Yoder, *Proverbs*, 295. Also Richard J. Clifford, *Proverbs: A Commentary* (Louisville: Westminster John Knox, 1999), 275.
19 Perdue, *Proverbs*, 278.

"ideal economic behavior at the level of a single household."[20] Warrior imagery drives home the message that the affluence enjoyed by this elite couple is not passive income. It must be fought for.

CHARACTERIZING HER LORD

Within this expansive description of the *eshet chayil* exist clues characterizing also her husband, a second key character in Proverbs 31:10–31. What can we know about him? He is the lord of the household. To reference him, the poem three times uses the term, *ba'al*, meaning "owner, lord, husband" (sometimes, "landowner") (vv. 11, 23, 28).[21] Camp labels the use of *ba'al* in Proverbs 31 as "almost ironic" in light of the wife's evident command of her household.[22] Yet *ba'al* fits if we remember the *eshet chayil* as a soldier fighting on his behalf.

As lord of the household, the husband is the beneficiary of all her endeavors: "She supplies for him good things, not bad, all the days of her life" (v. 12). He is a man of privilege, a privilege that extends not just to enjoying the spoils of her economic battles but also to being the arbiter of what even constitutes valued spoils and who should enjoy them. This privilege is communicated overtly in verse 23, where the husband is classified as an elder sitting in the gates, the place to settle communal issues and establish local law. It is also conveyed more subtly through the narrator's "arrogant eye," which centralizes one particular point of view and experience[23]—in this case, the husband's—as the lens through which the subject (the wife) will be observed, described, and evaluated.

Proverbs 31 several times mentions the *eshet chayil*'s body: her hands (seven times: vv. 13, 16, 19–20, 31), and also her arms, loins

---

20 Yoder, *Wisdom as a Woman*, 78; Ben Zvi, "'Successful, Wise, Worthy Wife,'" 30–31.
21 *HALOT*, 142.
22 Camp, *Wisdom and the Feminine*, 91.
23 Lindemann Nelson, *Damaged Identities, Narrative Repair*, 16.

(v. 17), and tongue (v. 26). The husband's body is not mentioned. In such manner the narrator positions his audience to look through the husband's eyes at the wife, seeing her and valuing her as he does. The opening line asks who can find a *wife*—a male interest and concern. What is sought is not just any wife but a *chayil*, "creditable," wife. Creditable to whom? Her husband! A creditable wife is actually "incredibly" (that is, above and beyond crediting) valuable (v. 10b, "far beyond corals"). For whom is this true? The husband! Why? Because he will always be safe with her around, will always enjoy ample pleasures (v. 12), and will live a life of both ease and authority—all because of her (v. 23).

SOCIAL IDENTITIES

This focalization contributes not only to characterization of the husband as lord but also to the *eshet chayil*'s identity. As explained in chapter 2 with regard to the characters of verses 1–9, identities form through the combined impact of an individual's interests and capabilities with the interests and assessment of those with whom that individual interacts, their community. What do they notice, value, and cultivate? What do they ignore, discourage, or obstruct? These communal activities largely determine individual opportunities, shaping identity in either empowering or damaging ways.

In Proverbs 31, the husband characterizes the *eshet chayil* as both extraordinary and *rare*. Such rarity is indicated in two ways: (1) by employing a rhetorical question, "Who can find," a phrase employed elsewhere in biblical texts to suggest that the answer is "not many" or "no one"; and (2) through comparing this woman's value to rare stones.[24] According to Richard Clifford, the implication of verse 10

---

24 Bruce V. Waltke, "The Role of the 'Valiant Wife' in the Marketplace," *Crux* 35, no. 3 (1999): 31; also Fox, *Proverbs 10–31*, 891; Yoder, *Wisdom as a Woman*, 77. A similar example would be Mic 7:18. Yoder cites Prov 20:6 and Qoh 7:24. See also Thomas P. McCreesh, "Wisdom as Wife: Proverbs 31:10–31," *RB* 92, no. 1 (1985): 36–37.

is that finding such a wife requires a miracle.[25] Any woman around, if she is *easily* seen, would therefore likely *not* be an *eshet chayil*. Emmanuel Nwaoru's commentary on Proverbs 31 reveals the impact of this focalized gender construction. In describing the *eshet chayil* as a real woman, a successful career person, and devoted household manager, not domineering but meek and quiet, he writes, "Unfortunately, indeed, such women are rare to find."[26] The very first verse of this acrostic, then, conditions readers to accept as normal and appropriate women's evaluation by men, an evaluation predisposed to be negative. As Yoder notes, "What is a tribute to the lives and work of real women is, at the same time, an objectification of the same."[27]

In addition, the speaker channeling the husband to celebrate what benefits him ignores or erases critical features about this woman, and in so doing affects her characterization and identity. Basic needs for self-care constitute one example of such critical features. The *eshet chayil* rises early (v. 15) and stays up late (v. 18), obtaining sustenance for others in her household (v. 15). But the poem makes no mention of her own need to eat or rest or receive support from others. She exhibits no pesky negative emotions: does not fear snow (v. 21) or any material lack. She is not angry, worried, or sad but works constantly "with pleasure" (v. 13). "This woman is unbelievable and unbalanced," writes Kirk-Duggan.[28] Although she does have children (v. 29), activities of childbearing and rearing that take up tremendous time and energy are not mentioned.[29]

Perhaps most appealingly of all for this male fantasy, the *eshet chayil* does not speak, a constraint that permits assuming her views and experience contentedly align with those of the speaker, her husband, any community member, really, concerning this life of ceaseless toil and service. These details fit Fontaine's characterization of biblical texts as containing "overdrawn caricatures by men whose

---

25 Clifford, *Proverbs*, 274.
26 Nwaoru, "Image of the Woman," 62.
27 Yoder, "Woman of Substance," 446.
28 Kirk-Duggan, "Rethinking the 'Virtuous' Woman," 107.
29 Eskenazi, "Lives of Women," 29.

obsession with their own honor and wisdom made them less than accurate observers of Woman and women, Wisdom and wisdom."[30] Characterizing the *eshet chayil* in such manner denies her the material and communal support that she would actually need to achieve even a fraction of the domestic, agricultural, and entrepreneurial success ascribed to her. Her identity—and that of all who identify with her or are likened to her—is damaged.

THE UNDERCLASS

Finally, let us mark how the underclass are characterized within this poem. They are first alluded to in verse 15, with mention of the servant girls who work in the *eshet chayil*'s household, undeveloped except as being ones who receive something from the *eshet chayil* (just what they receive is unclear.) The underclass can also be inferred in scenes where they are not overtly mentioned, for example, in verse 16, commonly translated "She considers a field and buys it" (NIV, ESV, NASP, NKJV). From whom is the *eshet chayil* obtaining this land? Under what circumstances? The sellers are unrecognized and unknown. For an ancient, agrarian society, giving up land is deeply destabilizing not only to oneself and family but also potentially to one's tribe. The translation cited above obscures this reality in choosing "to buy" to translate, *laqach*, the second verb of the verse. "To buy" connotes a fair, free, legally moderated economic exchange. But *laqach* means "to take, grab, seize."[31] It is used frequently in the Bible to describe taking, not buying, any number of objects, including women as wives (whether through warfare or some other means).

---

30 Fontaine, "Proof of the Pudding," 197.

31 *HALOT*, 534. Margaret Crook and, more recently, Philippe Guillaume have contested the translation of "to buy" in v. 16. See Crook, "The Marriageable Maiden of Proverbs 31:10–31," *JNES* 13, no. 3 (1954): 137–40; Guillaume, "Wonder Woman's Field in Proverbs 31: Taken, Not Bought! Economic Considerations on Proverbs 31:16," in *Ugarit-Forschungen: Internationales Jahrbuch für die Altertumskunde Syrien-Palästinas*, ed. Manfried Dietrich and Ingo Kottsieper (Munster: Ugarit-Verlag, 2016), 85–102.

Where land is purchased, as in Genesis 23:13, the verb *nathan* is used, as in "to give silver." So in Proverbs 31 there is actually no indication that the *eshet chayil* purchases land from anyone. She just takes it, as if it were her right to do so, and as if any prior occupants or owners did not count at all.

Such impression is reinforced through the first verb used in verse 16 as well: *zamam*. Scholars render it in English as "consider," "survey," "ponder," and so on. However, it should be noted that, without exception, this word's use in the Hebrew Bible (13 times) always involves sinister intent. It pertains to evil people scheming evil deeds, such as the builders of the tower of Babel (Gen 11:6) and false witnesses (Deut 19:19). Or it refers to Yahweh intending some violent destruction as punishment for a people's sin (Jer 4:28; 51:12; Lam 2:17; Zech 1:6, 8:14).[32] These uses elsewhere warrant suspecting some nefariousness in *zamam*, even in Proverbs 31:16, even with regard to the *eshet chayil*: "She schemes to get a field and seizes it." While praising the *eshet chayil* as a conquering warrior for wealth, the line is also characterizing those from whom she takes this land as victims. They are displaced, not justly compensated, and possess no strength to resist.

The second line of verse 16 repeats erasure of the underclass: "From the fruit of her hand she plants a vineyard." This line is ostensibly about the *eshet chayil*, but is it likely that she really would plant a vineyard? Some commentators take literally that the *eshet chayil* herself is completing this arduous labor, concluding, along with Jana Riess, that "she was probably a prosperous farmer's wife."[33] But it seems more likely a vineyard would be planted with the hands, rough and dirty, of a common laborer. Note that the planting referenced here is accomplished not just by "hands" but "with *the fruit* of her hands." A metaphor here appears, one that depicts the profits of

---

32 An exception is Zech 8:15.

33 Yoder, *Proverbs*, 298; Katherine Low, "Implications Surrounding Girding the Loins in Light of Gender, Body, and Power," *JSOT* 36, no. 1 (2011): 28; Jana Riess, "The Woman of Worth: Impressions of Proverbs 31:10–31," *Dialogue* 30, no. 1 (1997): 149.

this woman's industry, used for such activities as purchasing seed, tools, and perhaps laborers. "She plants" also constitutes a metaphor, imaginatively communicating how the woman and her profits enable still more productivity and profit through imaging these as peasant laborers planting a vineyard. As Waltke interprets, this "wealthy woman" has "the capacity to do the required, sustained manual labor ... though undoubtedly she employed male slaves to do much of the work."[34] The text here borrows from the real lived experience of the underclass to praise a member of the upper class. This elite presumption communicates that it is acceptable to appropriate images of the poor for one's own enhancement instead of crediting them their actual contribution. It is a form of exploitation, an identity-shaping plundering of laborers in which the elites—Proverbs 31's narrator, husband, and wife—all collaborate. The specific association of the *eshet chayil* with a *vineyard* may very well allude to the luxury crops required of the empire, thus blatantly locating her as a participant in transnational system of extraction and exploitation. The hands doing the planting are the very ones from whom the resulting fruits are deprived.

HANDLING THE POOR

Most interesting of all is the *eshet chayil*'s treatment of the poor as described in the chiasm that occurs in verses 19–20:

> Her hands thrust toward the distaff;
>   her palms grasp the spindle-whorl.
> Her palm she stretches toward the poor;
>   her hands thrust toward the oppressed.

This chiasm forms through mention of *yadeha shelkhah* ("her hands thrust") and *kapheha* ("her palms") in verse 19 coupled with these

---

34 Waltke, *Book of Proverbs*, 525.

same two elements mentioned again in verse 20 but in reverse order: first *kaphah* ("her palm") and then *yadeha shelkhah* ("her hands thrust"). Through this pattern the poem connects the *eshet chayil*, textile production, and the underclass. Why? These verses have not received full recognition for their complexity: polysemic nouns, metonymy, multiple word pairs interlaced within an extended "double chiastic structure," as well as a hendiadys in "poor" (*'ani*) and "oppressed" (*'avyon*) that repeats two keywords of the chapter's previous poem, thereby thematically linking the two.[35]

David Noel Freedman observes, "As with much of literature, especially poetry, ambiguity and obscurity are inherent in the form and content: chiasm only adds to the uncertainty and mystery."[36] Scholars attending to the chiasm of Proverbs 31:19-20 generally resolve the mystery of its meaning via some correlation between industriousness in textile production and the virtue of charity. Fox claims the chiasm depicts these as "two aspects of the woman's handiwork."[37] Van Leeuwen summarizes verses 19-20 as "hands that grasp to produce open wide to provide."[38] Representative of the views of most interpreters, Waltke writes, "Pride of place is given to her ministry to the afflicted and destitute in the community."[39] Such interpretations no doubt spring from commentators' assumptions that if an admirable, wealthy woman and the destitute are to be paired, charity must surely link them. Perhaps, as Waltke speculates, the *eshet chayil* aims to "invite home or to give material aid."[40]

But the ambiguity and gaps within this text do not require us to assume charity here. The *eshet chayil* is not someone who heretofore has been promoted as charitable, gracious, or kind. She is the wealth warrior, the aggressive, intimidating, scheming fighter, arms braced

---

35 See Gary A. Rendsburg, "Bilingual Wordplay in the Bible," *VT* 38, no. 3 (1988): 272; Waltke, *Book of Proverbs*, 527.

36 David Noel Freedman, "Preface," in *Chiasmus in Antiquity: Structures, Analyses, Exegesis*, ed. John W. Welch (Hildesheim: Gerstenberg, 1981), 7.

37 Fox, *Proverbs 10-31*, 895.

38 Raymond Van Leeuwen, "The Book of Proverbs," *NIB* 5:262.

39 Waltke, *Book of Proverbs*, 529.

40 Waltke, *Book of Proverbs*, 529.

for battle and loins bound with strength (v. 17). She is a towering figure (vv. 11, 27), now here grasping and thrusting toward the poor. Her earlier depiction justifies examining more carefully what verses 19 and 20 are actually communicating about the *eshet chayil* and her relationship to the underclass.

Let us first note the words that begin each of these verses: *yad* and *kaph*. These contribute to the poem's acrostic form, which begins each line with a succeeding letter of the alphabet. Verses 19 and 20 contribute letters *yod* and *kaph* to the acrostic via the words *yadeha* ("her hands") and *kaphah* ("her palms"). This feature is structurally clever in not just including the acrostic letter at its appropriate point but also incorporating the actual name of the letter into the message of the poem: *yod* and *kaph*, hands and palm. In addition, *yad* in biblical texts commonly means power exercised over or against another.[41] For example, Genesis 9:2: "Into your hand they are delivered"; Genesis 16:6: "Behold, your servant is in your hand, do to her as you please"; Genesis 16:12: "He shall be a wild donkey of a man, his hand against everyone." *Kaph* is its synonym. Including these two terms with respect to the *eshet chayil* constitutes yet another depiction of her as a powerful woman, extending that power now in her relations with, and functionally over, the underclass.

Second, we should note in verses 19–20 the objects toward which the *eshet chayil*'s hands are directed. These are set at the end of each line in parallel fashion. The first two lines end with the objects *kishor* and *pelek*, and the second two lines, with *'ani* and *'avyon*. *'Ani* and *'avyon*, as mentioned above, form a known hendiadys, the distinction between these two words difficult to discern, encompassing some type of suffering and deprivation.[42] The first pair of nouns is more difficult to translate. *Kishor* does not occur elsewhere in biblical texts; it is a *hapax legomenon*. Most scholars presume synonymous

---

41 Michaela Geiger, "Creating Space through Imagination and Action: Space and the Body in Deuteronomy 6:4–9," in *Constructions of Space IV: Further Developments in Examining Ancient Israel's Social Space*, ed. Mark K. George (London: Bloomsbury T&T Clark, 2013), 54.

42 Longman, *Proverbs*, 535.

parallelism between lines a and b of verse 19 and thus render *kishor* as a synonym of *pelek* ("spindle whorl"), hence "distaff" or some such part of a spindle. Based on these assumptions, *kishor*, with *pelek*, focuses the *eshet chayil*'s area of expertise: textile production, a highly valued and wealth-producing skill. Murray Lichtenstein understands *kishor* to mean "with dexterity."[43] Based on the context in Psalm 68:7 of a cognate (*koshrah*), he identifies the semantic range of *kishor* as including both technical skill and physical ability, power, and heroic prowess.[44] As adverbial phrase, then, *kishor* qualifies the manner in which the *eshet chayil* accomplishes her labor—once again, as a strong and clever warrior.

Third, we must note the verbs employed to bind these nouns of *yad* and *kaph*, *kishor* and *pelek*, *'ani* and *'avyon*. The first verb, *shilkhah*, forms the outer element of the chiasm and is commonly rendered neutrally by commentators and translators, for example, as "she holds out her hands" or "her hands she stretches."[45] But elsewhere in biblical texts the idiom combining *shilkhah* with "hands" always has a negative, even aggressive connotation.[46] In Genesis 3:22, God worries that Adam, having once disobeyed, may now inappropriately *yishlakh yado* ("stretch out his hand") "and take also of the tree of life and eat and live forever." In feminine inflection, the phrase occurs in the Song of Deborah to describe Jael's act of driving a tent peg through Sisera's skull: "Her hand she put to the tent peg, her right hand she shot out [*yadah tishlakhanah*] to the driving hammer" (Judg 5:26). The vocabulary and rhythm of Proverbs 31:19/31:20 and Judges 5:26 are markedly alike. Both texts are set within poems classified as warrior hymns that celebrate women as fighters. In Judges, Jael is not a soldier, not even an Israelite, but she uses what assets she has to fight

---

43 Murray H. Lichtenstein, "Chiasm and Symmetry in Proverbs 31," *CBQ* 44 (1982): 206.

44 Murray H. Lichtenstein, "Psalm 68:7 Revisited," *JANES* 4 (1972): 108–9.

45 Waltke, *Book of Proverbs*, 529; Fox, *Proverbs 10–31*, 889; Yoder, *Proverbs*, 295.

46 Wolters, "Proverbs 31:10–31 as Heroic Hymn," 453.

for Israel, and she wins. In Proverbs 31:19 and 31:20, it is the *eshet chayil* whose hand shoots out—with what weapon? Against whom?

It is not hard to imagine why, in verse 19, textile production (signaled via "distaff" and "spindle whorl") could be depicted using the violent imagery of *yadeha shilkhah*. Militaristic language has already been deployed to describe this woman's wide-ranging economic accomplishments. According to Ben Zvi, characterizing these activities in such manner communicated to the postexilic community, now lacking a king and army, that the new, more effective way to fight was through increasing wealth.[47] Longman adds substance to this interpretation in suggesting that verse 19 may intend to conjure Anat, the warrior goddess of Ugarit, who used distaff and whorl as weapons.[48]

But in the chiasm's second half, verse 20, the *eshet chayil* is no longer engaging her *work* in an aggressive manner (as in v. 19a). Rather, it's the *'avyon*, the "needy" or "oppressed" (v. 20b), who receive the very same gesture: "Her hands thrust toward the oppressed." What is this about? Is this gesture, so blatantly aggressive just one verse earlier, in the first half of the chiasm, somehow charitable here? How would that work? To aid in interpretation, we should recall that this line exists in parallel with line 20a: "Her palm she stretches toward the poor." In verse 19, line b informs concerning the *hapax legomenon* of line a. Could similar parallelism be helpful in verse 20? Does line 20a offer insight as to the meaning of line 20b?

STRETCHING HER PALM

Line 20a translates, "Her palm she stretches [*parsah*] toward the poor." Yoder imagines here the *eshet chayil* lending money, perhaps even at a profit.[49] Fox disagrees, arguing such practice would violate common decency and the ethics of Israel's law codes. Rather, "she

---

47 Ben Zvi, "'Successful, Wise, Worthy Wife,'" 37.
48 Longman, *Proverbs*, 545.
49 Yoder, *Wisdom as a Woman*, 89.

gives charitable aid to the poor."[50] Both views rely on a presumed intertext with Deuteronomy 15:7-9, which urges Israelites to "open" (*pathach*) their hands (*yad*) to the poor (*'ani*) and oppressed (*'avyon*), along with subsequent elaboration of lending generously to them.

Although Proverbs 31:20 and Deuteronomy 15:7-9 do share in common the word "hands" and the hendiadys of "poor and oppressed," we should note against aligning them that Proverbs 31:20 employs different verbs from either the "open" or "lend" that occur in Deuteronomy 15. The verb in Proverbs 31:20a is *paras*. It does occur once in a context having to do with charity: "The children beg for food, but no one *paras* [extends] anything to them" (Lam 4:4). Yet mention of hands does not occur here. Several biblical texts do use *paras* in conjunction with hands (Exod 9:29, 33; 1 Kgs 8:22, 38, 54; 2 Chr 6:12, 13, 29; Ezra 9:5; Job 11:13; Pss 44:20; 143:6; Isa 25:11; Jer 4:31; Lam 1:17). In such cases, the phrase signifies most often a *gesture of appeal*, usually to Yahweh but at other times to the temple or to other gods. In Isaiah 65:2, Yahweh is the one stretching out hands, to Israel, begging them to turn from their rebellion. So in Proverbs 31:20a, when the *eshet chayil* stretches out hands to the poor—could she be appealing to them? But for what? Would an appeal by a wealthy, powerful woman to the destitute, in this context, likely be an act of charity—or something else?

An interesting use of the phrase "stretching out hands" (*yado paras*) occurs in Lamentations 1:10: "Enemies have stretched out their hands over all her precious things." This use has nothing to do with charity, with providing or protecting. It communicates illegitimate seizure of someone else's things. The second-most common use of *paras* in biblical texts accompanies the noun "net," as in stretching out a net to capture quarry (Isa 19:8; Lam 1:13; Ezek 12:13; 17:20; 19:8; 32:3; Hos 5:1; 7:12). In Proverbs 31, then, *paras* harks back to the image of verse 15, wherein the *eshet chayil* provides "prey" to her household.

---

50 Fox, *Proverbs 10-31*, 895.

THE PROVERBIAL WOMAN

There is no reason to interpret *yadeha shilkhah* in line 20b with respect to the *'avyon* any differently from *yadeha shilkhah*'s first appearance in 19a—as aggressive and hostile—since its parallel in line 20a, *kaphah parsah*, is also and similarly aggressive and violating of its object, the *'ani*. Stretching a palm (v. 20a) signifies trapping, poaching. Thrusting hands (v. 20b) means to strike. The *Hebrew and Aramaic Lexicon of the Old Testament* includes within its definition of *shalakh*: "to reach out and touch something with good or malicious intentions . . . alternatively, to help oneself to someone else's property."[51] The lines do not imply charity. The *eshet chayil* here, as elsewhere, is aggressive, violent, and predatory. The *'ani* and *'avyon*—the poor and oppressed—are her victims.

CONTEXTS

This crucial admission concerning the *eshet chayil*'s treatment of the underclass occurs in the central portion of the poem, a location generally considered significant for revealing a poem's central concerns. Such findings may very well shock readers, accustomed as we are to admiring the *eshet chayil*, perceiving her as someone to emulate. They do, however, align with our analysis in chapter 2 of Proverbs 31:5–9, wherein contrasting voices struggle to articulate the conditions and just treatment of the *'ani* and *'avyon* due to the self-interested assertions of the ruling class. They also cohere with elite attitudes toward the poor represented elsewhere in Proverbs. Despite the occasional saying to the contrary (e.g., Prov 19:17), *charity* does not predominantly characterize elite attitudes or behavior. Boer notes Proverbs's multiple contrasts of wise and foolish, industrious and lazy, rich and poor—all channel toward a class consciousness in which being rich evidences possession of wisdom, righteousness, and the blessing of God. Conversely, the poor in Proverbs are depicted as being so because they are "wicked, simple, lazy, rotten." He writes, "It

---

51 *HALOT*, 1512.

requires little imagination to see here the ethics and class consciousness of landlords and of the perpetual dinner guests at the monarch's table. Of course, the despised are precisely those who work the estates or the village communities."[52] Such texts reflect on and respond to postexilic social and economic tensions in Yehud, though not necessarily directly. Boer writes, "Neither windows onto reality, nor expressions of the ideologies of the various groups that purportedly produced them, texts have indirect and contradictory connections with the socio-economic context to which they respond."[53]

The socioeconomic context relevant to Proverbs 31 includes Persian-era shifts in land possession, coerced labor, and burdensome taxes and tributes. A majority of the population engaged in agricultural pursuits, yet settlement of the *golah* into the territory of Yehud destabilized access to land.[54] The Persian government favored the *golah* and extended special terms for them to acquire land in exchange for their assistance with establishing order and extracting tribute in the region of Yehud.[55] Marriage also played a role in shifting land ownership, as some returning elites gained access to land through marrying landowning families.[56] For peasants, land seizures became commonplace. Samuel Adams writes, "Foreign rulers and local elite became proficient in usurping land for themselves, such that long-standing agrarian households often lost the territory and stability that went with one location over many generations."[57] Some peasants subsequently entered into tenant-farmer arrangements.[58]

---

52 Roland Boer, "The Economic Politics of Biblical Narrative," in Fewell, *Oxford Handbook of Biblical Narrative*, 536.

53 Boer, "Economic Politics," 536.

54 Samuel Adams, *Social and Economic Life in Samuel Second Temple Judea* (Louisville: Westminster John Knox, 2014), 82, 46.

55 Herbert Marbury, "The Strange Woman in Persian Yehud: A Reading of Proverbs 7," in *Approaching Yehud: New Approaches to the Study of the Persian Period*, ed. Jon Berquist (Leiden: Brill, 2008), 173.

56 Low, "Implications Surrounding Girding," 29.

57 Adams, *Social and Economic Life*, 13.

58 Jack Pastor, *Land and Economy in Ancient Palestine* (London: Routledge, 1997), 14.

Palatine estates producing luxury goods desired by imperial elites siphoned off other workers from village communes to perform the labor needed for production, further impoverishing already poor rural areas.[59] Burdensome tax measures and the requirement to grow luxury crops such as grapes for the wine preferred as tribute by the empire strained peasants' ability to feed their own families.[60]

Within such context, we may conceive Proverbs 31's *eshet chayil* as navigating multiple challenging routes of a colonized society. Our loyalty to any former conception of the *eshet chayil* should not cause us to ignore what close examination of the language, form, and context of these verses reveals. We should instead press further in our analysis to understand the unique contribution of meaning that the chiasm forms of these two sets of parallel lines. Verse 19 depicts the *eshet chayil* acting aggressively with respect to her textile production. Verse 20 depicts the same aggressive behavior with respect to the poor and oppressed. We know from other verses how successful the *eshet chayil* is in her textile production, with mention of wool and flax (v. 13), good trading (v. 18), double layers for her household (v. 21), bed coverings, and linen and purple garments for herself (v. 22). What the binding of these two lines via chiasm accomplishes is to clarify that such victories *require* the use and abuse of the underclass.

I explained earlier the *eshet chayil*'s economic achievement being credited to her involvement across multiple phases of economic activity: farming, textile production, and trade. But there is a fourth ingredient to her success, implied in verse 16, where the language of strategizing and seizing invites conceiving this hunter (v. 15) as homing in on the vulnerable and wresting away from them their land. In the chiasm, such implications recur. Who will work this elite woman's fields, now that she possesses them? Not the *eshet chayil* herself; we have clarified already that "from the fruit of her hands she plants a vineyard" erases the true laborers to boast about her profits and investments. Who must work the fields? Is it not the

---

59 Boer, "Economic Politics," 530.
60 Sneed, *Social World of the Sages*, 49.

underclass? She needs them to grow and harvest the wool and flax (v. 12) that she will transform into tradable goods. *Parsah* (v. 20a) communicates this need through envisioning hands as reaching out in appeal to those on whom she relies. But *pares* can also mean "to ensnare," so additionally imaging the *eshet chayil* as laying traps for the poor, communicating how limited are the options for the *'ani* and *'avyon* in resisting her designs. She needs them, so she grabs them. *Yadeha shilkhah*, the phrase that forms the outer boundary of the chiasm binding textile production and the underclass: this forceful sending of hands communicates desire, or intention, or ability to exert all her power, superior resources, and connections to push and pull the underclass into those places where she needs them to be. The *eshet chayil* works them as she works a distaff and spindle-whorl. The chiasm communicates that the poor and oppressed are her tools, no different from a spindle. They are raw materials to her, like the wool and flax, to be consumed and transformed into wealth and security for herself and family. They are her plunder and her prey.

PLOT AND SUSPENSE

This lengthy exploration of characterization enables us now to recognize emplotment and suspense within the acrostic of verses 10-31. Emplotment is usually viewed as the series of causally linked events within a narrative. These events can be explicitly identified, implied, or even just inferred as causally linked.[61] In Proverbs 31, each image as it forms within the imagination of a reader becomes a "thing that happens," that is, an event.[62] A lonely bachelor dreams of his ideal wife. A warrior woman battles for her family. A hunter deposits prey on the doorstep; peasants trudge from their ancestral lands, grow crops they cannot themselves consume, are smacked around by landowning lords and ladies. A series of discrete events is not actually

---

61 Shlomith Rimmon-Kenan, *Narrative Fiction: Contemporary Poetics* (London: Methuen, 1983), 18.
62 Rimmon-Kenan, *Narrative Fiction*, 16–17.

even a necessity for readers to form in their minds a narrative of a text. Mere identification with human characters who "live, act, think and feel" is sufficient for readers to invest themselves in imagining what has preceded the moment of their depiction and in wondering what will happen next, how they might resolve their dilemma. This circumstance establishes "a minimal level of narrativity."[63]

Readers may identify with the implied male speaker and want to join his quest for the rare wonderful wife who will defend against harm and harvest every imaginable good. The historical context suggested by his fantasy can enhance emphatic immersion in his plight. As Ben Zvi writes of Proverbs 31:10–31, "It was a utopian world, and such worlds often provided societies ways to address present lacks and express their longings."[64] In verse 11, mention of "never lacks" betrays awareness of need, vulnerability, even danger. A first-century Aramaic Targum of this verse reads the line as saying that her husband "will not *be* plundered or lack,"[65] an even more overt acknowledgment of vulnerability. Some scholars have projected the men of the *golah* community in Yehud to have vastly outnumbered women, perhaps thirty thousand compared to ten thousand women.[66] Thus, presenting the *eshet chayil* as hard to find could express a literal reality.

Compared with other parts of the empire, Yehud was a poor province, its occupation no more than 30 percent its former size.[67] For most households, activities centered on simple survival, for example, the time-consuming task of preparing food.[68] According to Ben Zvi, even the elite among the community were relatively poor and could have conceived themselves as vulnerable to a poor harvest,

---

63 Fludernik, *Introduction to Narratology*, 6.
64 Ben Zvi, "'Successful, Wise, Worthy Wife,'" 40–41.
65 See John F. Healey, trans., *The Targum of Proverbs, Translated, with a Critical Introduction, Apparatus, and Notes* (Collegeville, MN: Liturgical Press, 1991), 62.
66 Eskenazi, "Lives of Women," 13.
67 Ben Zvi, "'Successful, Wise, Worthy Wife,'" 38; Eskenazi, "Lives of Women," 13.
68 Adams, *Social and Economic Life*, 100, 43.

burdensome taxes, or political instability interrupting transportation of goods.[69] The poem praises the *eshet chayil* because she protects her husband and family from starvation, cold, nakedness, homelessness, landlessness. All these things that she obtains for her family are likely deprivations that the community could suffer. Whereas, in Persian-era practice, beds were uncommon and most slept on straw,[70] this utopia depicts the *eshet chayil* making luxurious bed coverings for herself (v. 22). The three-time mention of "house" (*bayit*) represents a settled, secure life, as opposed to one of wandering. Observes Norman Whybray, "The security depicted is the security from the fear of poverty."[71]

Readers also may identify with the ceaselessly toiling wife of Proverbs 31, burdened with impossible expectations, prevented from speaking about her own reality and desires. The poem praises her by depicting her as masculine. A comparable example occurs in a contemporaneous text, Xenophon's *Oeconomicus*, where Socrates compliments a landowner's skill in training his wife by saying, "You show that your wife has a masculine intelligence."[72] The phrase "a manly woman" is even how the Septuagint renders *eshet chayil* into Greek: γυνή ανδρεία. But such "compliments" erase female distinctives and contributions; they damage women's identity by portraying femininity as less worthy of praise than masculinity. Clearly, this *eshet chayil* pleases her husband, but the lack of reciprocal expectations for this husband to please his wife introduces a gendered power differential. Choosing *ba'al* (v. 11), and not the more neutral word for husband, *'ish* (meaning "man"), reinforces the husband's dominance. Madipoane Masenya writes that *ba'al* "denies a woman her full personhood, as she is viewed as someone who can be owned by

---

69 Ben Zvi, "'Successful, Wise, Worthy Wife,'" 38, 41; Adams, *Social and Economic Life*, 45, 2, 7.

70 Gerhard Lensky, *Power and Privilege: A Theory of Social Stratification* (New York: McGraw-Hill, 1966), 271.

71 Whybray, *Good Life*, 161, 163.

72 As cited in Stephen D. Moore and Janice Capel Anderson, "Taking It Like a Man: Masculinity in 4 Maccabees," *JBL* 117, no. 2 (Summer 1998): 267.

her master, the man."[73] Readers may reasonably infer conflict between these two characters, the woman a supposed nucleus of power and her inattentive, uncomprehending "lord."

Adding to the distresses of this husband and wife are those suffered by the underclass. A utopia celebrated by some is dystopian to others. Johannes Ro writes, "The post-exilic society in Palestine created a new upperclass whose ideal was subservient devotion to the foreign superpower without any consideration for whether their own brothers and sisters were exploited in the colonial economic system."[74] The Proverbs 31 acrostic, however, betrays some consideration of the deleterious effects of their actions on others taking place. Elites produced this text; they were the class with the skills and resources to develop, record, preserve, and learn it. The language used to characterize the *eshet chayil*'s behavior—the fighting, the hunting—betrays these elites as the knowing antagonists of those with whom they engage. And they are not, in this poem, engaging those who rule *them*, like a Joseph before Pharaoh or Esther facing Xerxes. No, the poem depicts the *eshet chayil*'s engagement with those over whom she has power. In her handling of those she rules, Proverbs 31 subtly, poetically, presents the same tension as that described in Nehemiah 5:1–5: "Now there was a great outcry of the people and of their wives against their Jewish kin. . . . There were those who said, 'We are having to borrow money on our fields and vineyards to pay the king's tax. Now our flesh is the same as that of our kindred; our children are the same as their children; and yet we are forcing our sons and daughters to be slaves, and some of our daughters have been ravished; we are powerless, and our fields and vineyards now belong to others'" (NRSV).

Ambiguity in verses 20–21 permits continuing unwavering admiration of the *eshet chayil* for any who are so inclined. But ambiguity also invites considering how the poor and oppressed receive her gestures. Do they welcome them? Are they better off because of them?

---

73 Masenya, *How Worthy*, 154.

74 Johannes Un-Sok Ro, "Socio-economic Context of Post-exilic Community and Literacy," *ZAW* 120, no. 4 (2008): 605.

How readers choose to understand the *eshet chayil* here will affect perceived characterization of the underclass. They are victims, no doubt: powerless, exploited, denied freedom, opportunity, and access to subsistence-level resources. But are they victims of the empire, of climate and geography, or of their own kin?

CONCLUSION

In narratives, suspense develops through techniques such as withholding key details, interjecting complications in accomplishing a goal, foreshadowing, and "empathetic immersion in the situation of the various characters."[75] As we consider these characters, relate to them, and care about them, we read on to discover what will happen next. Will we hear the *eshet chayil* herself speak? Have the poor any recourse for justice? In our study of Proverbs 31, we have only reached the center of this acrostic poem. Readers have plenty of verses yet to find out whether these characters will change their circumstances—or change themselves—in ways that resolve the tensions they endure. Danna Nolan Fewell writes, "Plots commonly revolve around boundary-related issues: boundary establishment, boundary maintenance, boundary crossing, and the circumstances under which boundaries should be established, maintained, or crossed."[76] Reading Proverbs 31 with such awareness in mind, we may look to future verses to discover whether the geographical, ethical, and social boundaries promoted in earlier verses are reinforced or challenged. Can the *eshet chayil* and the *'ani* and *'avyon* resist their respective masters? Will they supply positive or negative examples to readers navigating their own power dynamics within community?

---

75 Fludernik, *Introduction to Narratology*, 47.
76 Fewell, "Work of Biblical Narrative," 10.

Proverbs 31:23–30

23 Known at the gates is her husband,
   in his sitting with the elders of the city.
24 Fine linen wraps she makes and sells;
   woven belts she delivers to traders.
25 Strength and honor are her garments,
   and she laughs about the days to come.
26 She opens her mouth with wisdom,
   and the teaching of loyalty is on her tongue.
27 Watching over the actions of her household,
   for laziness does not eat bread.
28 Her sons arise and bless her,
   her husband, and he praises her.
29 "Many daughters do *chayil*,
   but you, you ascend above them all!"
30 'Charm is false and beauty a vapor':
   a woman—fear of Yahweh—she! *She* will be praised.

CHAPTER FOUR

Designing Woman

Proverbs 31:23–30

Aleph (v. 10), *bet* (v. 11), *gimel* (v. 12), *dalet* (v. 13) . . . *lamed* (v. 21), *mem* (v. 22), *nun* (v. 23) . . . Proverbs 31:10-31 is an acrostic; each verse begins with a successive letter of the alphabet, communicating order, completeness, and perfection as concerns the world created in this poem. For the purpose of this study, I have divided Proverbs 31:10–31 into three sections (vv. 10–22, 23–30, 31), but it is important to acknowledge the seamlessness of the poem's acrostic form. Verses 23–30, our focus for this chapter, continue praise of the *eshet chayil* that occurs in previous verses. At the same time, a few particulars in verse 23 invite dividing the poem at this spot. In verse 23, focus shifts from the wife to the husband. Earlier verses describe the *eshet chayil*—her body: strong arms, loins wrapped, her clothes, her vigorous movements affecting others. Now readers view the *ba'al* ("husband" or "lord") sitting among town elders in the city gates. The mention of *ba'al* that occurs in verse 23 also occurs in verse 11 and verse 29. This repetition forms an *inclusio* of the outer verses, with verse 23 a topical center.[1] Verse 23 also introduces a

---

1 Waltke, "Role of the 'Valiant Wife,'" 29. See Murray Lichtenstein for identification of vv. 19–20 as the center of the chiasm ("Chiasm and Symmetry in Proverbs 31," 207).

new setting, the city gates. These are mentioned again in verse 31, the poem's climactic conclusion. Double mention of city gates thus also contributes to verse 23 being a significant verse and appropriate for beginning a new portion for analysis.

One work of Proverbs 31's earlier oracle (vv. 1–9) lay in defending elites' position of dominance in order to protect resources and access to power. Damage to women's identity and to the underclass occurred in this process. The acrostic that follows, commencing in verse 10, swaps a husband and wife for the earlier mother-son pairing to supply another depiction of tensions between elites and underclass. The *eshet chayil* is presented very differently from the women referenced in verse 3, who are a threat. The *eshet chayil* is a protector (v. 11). She is a prosperous landowner, textile producer, merchant. She does not take from her lord; she gives. The *eshet chayil* represents the *golah* in Yehud to promote within that community the values of labor, productivity, and wealth enhancement. She is imaged repeatedly as a warrior to drive home the lesson that all these must be fought for. Portraying her as coercing poor, powerless, oppressed people to aid in her efforts enables the community reciting and pondering this text to acknowledge and wrestle with treatment of their weaker neighbors. In symbolizing the *golah*, the *eshet chayil* is used by the community as a tool to benefit them even as she is depicted using others as tools to benefit her. She is janus-faced. Her identity is damaged along with that of the *'ani* and *'avyon*.

As mentioned at the end of chapter 3, readers can identify with any number of Proverbs 31's characters: the husband, the wife, the underclass, who each experience their own type of lack. We read on to discover their fates, and, through identification with them, to imagine our own. We read to learn whether the one our speaker yearns for can be found, whether the *eshet chayil* can speak her own life experience, whether the plight of the underclass will remain or change. Can an ideal life exist for all members of society, or must some be sacrificed for others?

In this chapter we will analyze the setting, characterization, and plot of verses 23–30 to know how these influence our understanding of the Proverbs 31 acrostic, especially the gender- and class-based tensions introduced in the poem's first half. Attending to these narrative elements as well as gaps, ambiguities, contradictions, and multiplicities of meaning reveals heightening tensions between the *eshet chayil* and her *baʻal*, crowding out, for a time, concerns for the underclass, foregrounding intra-class pressures and expectations concerning survival in Persian-era Yehud.

SETTING

Proverbs 31:23–30 mentions two locations: the "city gates" and "her house." These locations form settings for the drama that readers infer. They also attach to the *eshet chayil* and her *baʻal* and, combined with their positioning, shape character construction and plot development in this portion of the poem.

Gates

"Known at the gates is her husband, in his sitting with the elders of the city" (v. 23). Contemporary readers, with images of gates based on our familiarity with picket or chain-link fences, may not fully appreciate the city gates of the ancient world. Their wooden doors alone could rise as tall as six meters, with a stone or mud-brick structure of the gate above. Watchtowers at the corners rose one or more meters higher still.[2] Gates were so thick as to contain multiple rooms inside. Furthermore, "gates" could refer not only to the initial structure allowing passage through the barrier of a city wall but also to a sizable open square just inside the structure itself, often preceding a second gate. Stelae positioned in the public square, perhaps extolling the accomplishments of a local king, could measure five meters tall.[3]

---

   2 Daniel A. Frese, "The Civic Forum in Ancient Israel: the Form, Function, and Symbolism of City Gates" (PhD diss., University of California, San Diego, 2012), http://escholarship.org/uc/item/8tp5j3ch, 123.
   3 Frese, "Civic Forum in Ancient Israel," 220.

Myriad activities took place within the inner square of city gates: trade, cultic worship, tax collecting, inspections by soldiers, instruction of youth, and gathering of residents to discuss problems or just to pass the time.[4] Excavations of ancient city gates have uncovered remnants of looms and other tools,[5] suggesting that in upper rooms textile production occurred. Gates were known as the spaces where prophets delivered their messages (Amos, Lady Wisdom) and kings their judgments (2 Sam 19:8). City gates were active, noisy, crowded, busy with all kinds of communal activities. Legal adjudication is the activity most frequently mentioned in biblical and Akkadian texts as occurring in city gates.[6] Complainants delivered their pleas, and town elders decided legal issues brought before them by other members of the community.[7] Such is portrayed in Genesis 34, where Hivite elders decide at their city gates to make peace with Jacob's family through submitting to circumcision. Similarly in Ruth 4, elders at the city gate approve Boaz's request to redeem Elimelech's land and marry Mahlon's widow.

All of these activities form associations that are triggered upon mention of city gates, thereby communicating more than just reference to the physical location. These associations include the *community*, the general public, those who are "inside" and not "outside" the group's boundaries. They include *security*, in light of the protective function of city gates, and *commerce*, due to trade taking place therein, and *law*, due to adjudication. They include also associations of *public debate*.

---

4 See Frese, "Civic Forum in Ancient Israel"; see also Natalie N. May, "Gates and Their Functions in Mesopotamia and Ancient Israel," in *The Fabric of Cities: Aspects of Urbanism, Urban Topography and Society in Mesopotamia, Greece and Rome*, ed. Natalie N. May and Ulrike Steinert (Leiden: Brill, 2014), 77–121; Carey Walsh, "Testing Entry: The Social Functions of City Gates in Biblical Memory," in *Memory and the City*, ed. Diana V. Edelman and Ehud Ben Zvi (Winona Lake, IN: Eisenbrauns, 2014), 43–60.

5 Frese, "Civic Forum in Ancient Israel," 276–77.

6 May, "Gates and Their Functions," 95.

7 Walsh, "Testing Entry," 51.

Verse 23 elevates certain associations over others in what specifically it mentions: "Known at the gates is her husband, in his sitting with the elders of the city." According to this line, the city gates are a social space, where being known takes place, where elders sit together. "Space is a complex social phenomenon," writes Mark George, "not only physical but also constructed by the conceptual systems used to organize it, and the symbolic and mythological meanings societies develop in order to live in space."[8] All this is happening with respect to the city gates in Proverbs 31. According to space theorist Henri Lefebvre, physical, mental, and social aspects of space (also known as perceived, conceived, and lived spaces) occur simultaneously in any location.[9] Identifying these aspects enables understanding the meaning of spaces for a given community, how depictions of spaces as compared with actual use establish communal norms. In verse 23, mention of "gates" reveals a *physical* space as *perceived* to be inhabited by humans. "Being known" and "sitting with the elders" are honoring and honorable activities. As such, they comprise in verse 23 a *mental* space *conceived* as a place of honor and influence for the town's male elders. But are there other ways, unacknowledged, that a space is actually used that have bearing on the identities and opportunities of people occupying that space? What is the *social*, or *lived*, space of the city gates?

To explore this question, let us compare the positioning of the husband in this poem with respect to the city gates with that of his wife. In verse 23, he is set explicitly within the city gates. Any associations attached to a location accrue to the people who are identified and affirmed as belonging there. So the husband, sitting in the gates, acquires all the associations mentioned above, including the honor associated with that location, and he is normalized as participating

---

8 Mark George, "Space and History: Siting Critical Space for Biblical Studies," in *Constructions of Space I: Theory, Geography, and Narrative*, ed. Jon L. Berquist and Claudia V. Camp (New York: T&T Clark, 2007), 29.

9 Lefebvre, *Production of Space*, 38–39, 12. Using the terms translated into English: "spatial practice," "representations of space," and "representational spaces."

in the myriad honor-acquiring activities taking place there. This husband is *known*; he is honored. He sits with the elders. According to Waltke, sitting is "a metonymy for opening his mouth to give authoritative counsel and teaching."[10] The husband depicted this way causes readers to presume he is himself a community leader and judge.[11] His location accrues to himself not only honor and power but also the presumption of public support and of representing and speaking for the community overall.

In contrast to her husband, the *eshet chayil* is not located in the city gates. This omission is curious because, according to how she has been described so far, she must indeed occupy them. She must pass through the gates in obtaining goods from afar (v. 14) and occupy them when trading (vv. 18, 24). The open square of the city gates complex served as a popular spot for trade, especially with foreigners (*kena'ani*) who must come and go through the gates to make contact with buyers and sellers inside. Yoder reports that Persian-era women at Elephantine commonly occupied marketplaces, buying, selling, and bartering.[12] In addition, the *eshet chayil* speaks with wisdom (*khokmah*) and loyalty (*khesed*; v. 26), epitomizes the "fear of Yahweh" (*yir'ath yahweh*; v. 30); she is a woman/wife of *chayil* (vv. 10, 29). These are not terms describing personal virtue. These are terms of communal significance, indicating that she benefits the whole of her people. Yet occupation of the public square or identification with it is not attributed to her. To invoke Lefebvre's tripartite frame: the city gates are *conceived* as occupied by men of honor, yet also revealed as *social, lived* spaces containing, yes, women.

The lack of explicit situating of the *eshet chayil* in the city gates denies her the privileges of its associations: honor, power, and social connection. She is not recognized as being known in the gates, even if she is. She does not gain the status conferred through sitting on the elder's bench, even if she does speak to communal issues, as suggested in verse 29. The *eshet chayil* interacts with many types of people in

---

10 Waltke, *Book of Proverbs*, 530.
11 For example, Rofé, "Valiant Woman," 147.
12 Yoder, *Wisdom as a Woman*, 59.

Proverbs 31: her family, her servants, the poor, and foreign traders. But any social network such as that enjoyed by her husband in his sitting with the elders of the town is not extended to her within the world created in this poem. The *eshet chayil* appears isolated from her peers. In ancient Mediterranean societies the labors of food preparation and textile production typically would be accomplished via groups of women working together.[13] Gatherings in public areas such as the city gates formed one source of a woman's indirect power through developing social allies and allowing information to be exchanged.[14] It stands to reason that conversations (perhaps commiserations) may in fact be crucial to the *eshet chayil*, but they do not warrant mention here. It is the husband's viewpoint that prevails in Proverbs 31, to form the community's understanding of spaces and the identities of people occupying those spaces. "The language of things is as useful for lying as it is for telling the truth," writes Lefebvre.[15]

Her House

The second location mentioned in verses 23–30 is "her house" (*betah*; v. 27). Polyphony of language allows understanding Proverbs 31's four mentions of "her house" (vv. 15, 21, 27) to signal just as much the house *to which the woman belongs* as that the house *belongs in some way to the woman*. Whereas the latter understanding could contribute to an empowered identity for the *eshet chayil* in attributing to her possession or ownership of the house, the former constricts in assigning to the house possession of *her*. Many interpret "her house" in Proverbs 31 as identifying the *eshet chayil*'s proper sphere, contrasting with the city gates, which, as noted, belong to men.[16] Most women in the

---

13 Anne Katrine Gudme, "Inside-Outside: Domestic Living Space in Biblical Memory," in Edelman and Ben Zvi, *Memory and the City*, 69.

14 Carolyn Osiek, "Women, Honor, and Context in Mediterranean Antiquity," *HvTSt* 64, no. 1 (2008): 330.

15 Lefebvre, *Production of Space*, 81.

16 E.g. Lang, Lawrence, Masenya, Waltke.

Hebrew Bible are depicted in relation to domestic, private spaces, and some ancient Mediterranean cultures promoted a male-public/female-private dyad.[17] Note that the husband, positioned explicitly within the gates, is not characterized in relation to the home. This in effect associates each gender with a different space. It separates the husband from association with or expectations concerning the day-to-day activities of the home just as the wife has been separated from the conventional activities that take place in city gates.

We have already observed, however, that although she is not explicitly located either inside or outside the home, the *eshet chayil*'s activities require her to occupy many communal spaces. If we consider these verses according to Lefebvre's triad, the poem expresses both a *mental conception* of space in marking the house as "*her* house" and a *social reality* of space in its implications concerning how the *eshet chayil* actually moves, far beyond the confines of home. An ideology shaping the text here surfaces in the choice to not locate her as explicitly as the husband and to associate the *eshet chayil* with one specific location even though she occupies many.

"Watching over the actions of her house, for laziness does not eat bread" (v. 27). As with the city gates, so also the space of house possesses associations according to how and whether persons are located within it. According to Lefebvre, the memory of house has an "obsessive," "nostalgic" quality, recurring throughout art, poetry, drama, and philosophy. He explains, "The dwelling passes everywhere for a special, still sacred, quasi-religious and in fact almost absolute space."[18] In the Bible, the house usually functions as a place of refuge and safety. It often symbolizes provision and protection, associations that attach to the *eshet chayil* through the poem characterizing the house as "her" house.[19]

---

17 Gudme, "Inside-Outside," 69; Lang, "Hebrew Wife and the Ottoman Wife," 146.

18 Lefebvre, *Production of Space*, 120–21.

19 Gudme, "Inside-Outside," 63, 78.

Some scholars equate "her house" with a similar phrase that occurs in biblical texts, *bet 'em* ("house of the mother.")[20] *Bet 'em* appears less commonly than *bet 'ab* ("house of the father") and seems to correlate with narratives in which the mother figure is central and heroic, for example, Ruth (1:8). In Proverbs 31, the *eshet chayil* is central and heroic, causing Camp to conclude that she fulfills the responsibilities of a *bet 'ab*, "the leader/chieftain of the (ancestral) house."[21] According to this understanding of Proverbs 31, the home is the space where the wife possesses power and honor.

Houses as Gates

An interesting feature of the description of the *eshet chayil* with respect to "her house" is that the language employed actually encourages viewing her and her house as if they are themselves city gates. The initial participle used to describe the *eshet chayil* in verse 27, "watching over" (*tsophiyah*) conjures a watchman scanning for danger at a lookout post.[22] A lookout post was commonly located at the corner towers of a city gate, as indicated in 2 Samuel 18:24: "And David sat between the two gates: and the watchman [*ha-tsopheh*] went up to the roof over the gate unto the wall, and lifted up his eyes, and looked" (KJV). So Tremper Longman renders verse 27a, "She is a lookout post for the doings of her household."[23] This allusion resembles the allusion to city walls in verse 11, where the husband protects himself through hiding in or behind his wife. In both references the wife is a crucial element of fortification.

How ought we to understand this feature of the text, where the female who is not explicitly positioned in the city gates, though she likely does actually occupy them, is depicted as *like* a city gate herself with respect to her house? It could be that the image resists

---

20 Jennie R. Ebeling, *Women's Lives in Biblical Times* (New York: T&T Clark International, 2010), 28.
21 Camp, *Wisdom and the Feminine*, 91.
22 *HALOT*, 1044.
23 Longman, *Proverbs*, 547.

conception of these two spaces as separate and appropriate to only one gender. Perhaps it clarifies that actually a relationship exists between the two, the home and the city gates, the family and the larger community, with the *eshet chayil* forming the pivotal point of connection. We may infer that the *eshet chayil* supports her community through supporting her household and that the community is protected through the battles she fights for "her house."

A second interesting characteristic of the *eshet chayil* with respect to the location, house, is the direction of this woman's gaze. As a watchman, she is not looking outward, as might be expected, across the countryside for an approaching enemy. Instead, she is searching *inside* the gates, judging the actions in her own household. Such focus is indicated in both the first half of verse 27—"watching over the actions of her house"—and the second half of verse 27, which identifies what danger the wife is watching for: "for laziness does not eat bread." This text is usually translated here as some version of "she [the *eshet chayil*] does not eat the bread of laziness." My rendering, following Waltke, Albert Wolters, and JiSeong Kwon, understands the second-person feminine singular pronoun of *lo' to'khal* ("she does not eat") to reference as subject not the *eshet chayil* but "laziness."[24]

Laziness endangers a household. It will not produce bread, in fact, impedes production of bread and all the provisions needed for a household to survive and thrive. It makes sense that a text so frequently promoting economic activity would censure laziness. In this poem, survival depends on full cooperation from all members of a household. Verse 27 injects an undercurrent of tension, as it implies that not all household members pull their weight. It sets these up as

---

24 "Laziness" in Hebrew is also a feminine noun and thus an appropriate antecedent for the verbal conjugation. This reading goes against the Masoretic markings (Waltke, "Role of the 'Valiant Wife,'" 32n36; see also Kwon, "Wisdom Incarnate?"). Wolters: "The immediately following hemistich . . . is usually construed to mean 'and does not eat the bread of idleness,' but it can with equal validity be taken to mean 'and idleness will not eat bread'" ("Ṣôpiyyâ (Prov 31:27) as Hymnic Participle," 583).

traitors, threats against whom the *eshet chayil* guards. Depicting the *eshet chayil* as a watchman at the city gates implies that she will call out these enemies and marshal forces to resist them.

The blending of these two spaces, gates and home, via presentation of the *eshet chayil* fits space theorist Doreen Massey's description of spaces as inherently social and fluid, formed less by boundaries than by "networks of social relations and understandings."[25] The influence of those with the power to move and direct movement in space extends beyond their own named space to other spaces as well. In Proverbs 31, that is true with respect to both the *eshet chayil* and her husband. Her influence extends beyond the home to the gates, and his extends beyond the gates to the home. Though the *eshet chayil* is ascribed power and honor in "her house," it is the male gaze that constructs what goes on there. "Her house" is conceived according to public needs that town elders adjudicate and communicate, as the poem's male (because wife-seeking) speaker describes.

CHARACTERIZATION

This analysis of two locations mentioned in Proverbs 31:23–30 has already revealed much about the characterization of the *eshet chayil* and her *ba'al*. He possesses honor and authority to represent and influence society. He is grouped among the elders, not active in the daily grind of household or entrepreneurial tasks but a recognized leader and arbiter. She is a more nebulous figure, not explicitly located in spaces or among her kind but recognized as benefiting society through commercial accomplishments and her role as guardian over her household. The poem blurs her identity also through its syntax, allowing either that she controls her house or that her house controls her. These elements of characterization based on setting perpetuate the enigma of the *eshet chayil*, sought for but not explicitly located in home, fields, vineyards, or foreign lands.

---

25 Massey, "Power Geometry," 67.

Characterizing the Husband

Beyond these two locations communicating information about the *eshet chayil* and her *baʻal*, many additional details of verses 23-30 also characterize them. To consider first the husband, his activity: he sits (v. 23). Sitting contrasts with the frenetic activity of the *eshet chayil*, who is everywhere, doing everything. Some conclude that the text's silence as to any other activities the husband may be involved in makes him out to be a slacker or not important to the functioning of society.[26] Murphy calls him "inconsequential;" Beatrice Lawrence, a "bystander."[27]

Sitting conveys status, leisure, and wealth. Only the wealthy, the elite, can afford to spend their time sitting; others must toil from dawn to dusk. These are the *ʻani* and *ʼavyon* (vv. 5-9)—and also metaphorically the *eshet chayil*, imaged earlier as a peasant laborer with her skirts tied up, flexing her muscles to cut down crops (v. 17). She is the one who "rises while it is still night" (v. 15), whose "lamp does not go out at night" (v. 18). The wealthy can hire others to labor for them. A text contemporaneous to Proverbs 31, Ben Sirach, considers only men of leisure qualified to study Scripture and exercise authority based on it.[28] Ancient Greeks excluded manual laborers from citizenship based on the belief that such workers would not have time for political activity.[29] Masenya assumes the husband must actually be extremely busy and productive, and that the text does not depict this so as not to detract from praise of the *eshet chayil*.[30] Yet such presumptions risk ruining the effect that depicting the husband as sitting, *only* sitting, actually achieves. Coming as it does after the extensive description of the wife's activity that generates so many material comforts for the husband to enjoy, the husband's sitting identifies yet another way an *eshet chayil* benefits her man.

---

26 Such as McCreesh, who argues, "The husband is left with little or nothing to do!" ("Wisdom as Wife," 27). See also Whybray, *Good Life*, 162.
27 Murphy, *Proverbs*, 247; Lawrence, "Gender Analysis," 343.
28 Ro, "Socio-economic Context," 603.
29 Guillaume, "Wonder Woman's Field," 95.
30 Masenya, *How Worthy*, 105.

The context, though, of the husband sitting in the city gate, among the elders, does imply some other activity than *merely* sitting. As an elder, he must be understood as participating in hearing disputes and resolving them. As an elder, he has the opportunity to advocate for whatever positions he deems best. Such activity could ease the way for the *eshet chayil* in her endeavors: facilitating a sale, for example, determining a purchase price, identifying who among passersby may participate in trade, perhaps playing a role in collecting taxes. In these ways the husband's sitting aids his wife's success. The poem has earlier named several items that the *eshet chayil* draws on for her success: flax (v. 13), land (v. 16), and servants (v. 20). The husband in verse 23 now joins this list.

One other activity attributed to the *eshet chayil*'s husband is speaking: "he praises her" (v. 28). The words that follow in verse 29 are not specifically identified as the husband's direct speech, but such can be inferred due to the setup of the phrase "he praises her" as well as the shift to a second-person singular pronoun, "you," to reference the *eshet chayil*, and the words themselves: "Many daughters do *chayil*, but you, you ascend above them all! Charm is false and beauty a vapor; A woman—fear of Yahweh—she! She will be praised" (vv. 29–30). Here the *baʻal* speaks to compare his wife to other women, deeming her superior. He identifies also just what is so praiseworthy—her doing of *chayil*. A fighting spirit and strategic gains are what this husband declares to be valuable about her. Furthermore, qualities traditionally deemed desirable of women—charm and beauty—the *baʻal* names and rejects as deceitful and fleeting. This praised woman, productive and profitable, epitomizes the "fear of Yahweh." Clearly this husband sees himself as the one to define what is good, what is valuable and deserving of honor, and who measures up to his own established standards. The poem promotes him as such, a voice of authority within the world of the text, in both speech and action shaping the identity of others.

Characterizing the Wife

To consider now additional characterization of the wife in verses 23–30: she is a mother (v. 28). Raising children is not acknowledged as taking up much of her time. Perhaps it is taken for granted, or perhaps these duties fall to her "girls" (v. 15). Primary characterization of the *eshet chayil* is that she, too, like her husband, possesses honor. "Strength and honor are her garments" (v. 25). Verses 23–30 continue earlier verses' listing of honor-accruing activities: textile production, business acumen (v. 24), and giving of wise advice (v. 26).[31] Others in her orbit enact the honor she deserves. "Her sons arise and bless her" (v. 28). This verse resembles the wistful recollection of Job 29:8, when in days before his affliction Job was highly honored: "The young men saw me and withdrew, and the aged rose and stood" (ESV). Concerning the husband's praise of his wife, verse 28 uses the verb *'ashar*, which has been defined as "a word of congratulations that honors a person."[32] Three times in verses 28–31 the verb meaning "to praise" (*halal*) is directed toward the *eshet chayil*.

Mathys identifies multiple allusions in Proverbs 31 to the ancient Phoenicians, including ships, trade, textiles, wisdom, and *kena'ani*. The effect of these is to praise the *eshet chayil* as equal to these sophisticated, accomplished people; "she can keep her head held high." At the same time, Mathys notes, ancient literature portrays Phoenicians negatively as colonizers, exploiters, "deceivers, crooks, swindlers, crafty, cunning fellows."[33] Wicked Jezebel was Phoenician (1 Kgs 16:31). For the *eshet chayil* to be overtly linked with such people, then, reinforces her earlier depiction as crafty and scheming in verses 16 and 19–20. This is a part of what it means to be an *eshet chayil*.

In ancient contexts the best compliment to extend to a woman would be to liken her to a man.[34] Accordingly, verses 23–30 continue earlier verses' portrayal of her as manly through additional warrior language: the watchtower allusion (v. 27), a second mention of *chayil* (v. 29), and the phrase "to ascend above" (v. 29), which in other contexts has to do with engaging battle against an enemy.[35] Another way

---

31 Compare to Prov 3:35: "The wise will inherit honor."
32 Hartley, *Proverbs*, 73.
33 Mathys, "Valiant Housewife," 163–64.
34 Moore and Anderson, "Taking It Like a Man," 269.
35 Wolters, "Proverbs 31:10–31 as Heroic Hymn," 453.

of promoting the *eshet chayil* as manly is by depicting her as not like other women. This first occurs via the comparison in verse 29: "Many daughters do *chayil*, but you, you ascend above them all!" Then, in verse 30, qualities typically attributed to and praised in women are denigrated, with the implication being that these are attributes of the other women referred to in verse 29, attributes that the *eshet chayil* has no need of, since she is a woman of *chayil*, a manly woman (so the Septuagint renders *eshet chayil* into Greek: γυνή ἀνδρεία).

Even as verse 30 compliments the *eshet chayil*, at the same time it also undermines her positive characterization. *Sheqer hakhen vehevel hayophi.* Fox translates this line, "Comeliness is deceit and beauty a vapor."[36] Vayntrub offers, "Grace is a lie and beauty is ephemeral."[37] *Yapheh*, the second quality mentioned, is universally understood to reference a person's physical attractiveness. Its evaluation here is usually translated as "fleeting," but *hevel* can also mean "false."[38] *Khen*, the first quality named, is trickier to conceive. In choosing "comeliness," Fox takes the two halves of line 30a as synonymous. But Waltke, joining several prominent translations, renders *khen* "charm."[39] *Khen* is a word that appears several dozen times in the Hebrew Bible, often within the expression "to find favor [*khen*] in [someone]'s eyes." In biblical texts, *khen* is desired and expected of women: "A woman of *khen* gets honor" (Prov 11:16). Divorce could follow if women failed to display *khen* to their husband's satisfaction (Deut 24:1). Esther is several times associated with *khen* (2:15, 17; 5:2, 8; 7:3; 8:5), celebrated for deploying her beauty and charm to save her people from genocide. This is the quality associated in Proverbs 31:30 with women and deemed false, a lie, deceitful, tricky.[40]

Labeling qualities commonly associated with women negatively has the effect of transferring that negativity onto the people associated with those qualities; it damages women's identities.

---

36 Fox, *Proverbs 10–31*, 889.
37 Vayntrub, "Beauty, Wisdom, and Handiwork," 46.
38 As attached to idols, things that do not really exist; so *HALOT*, 237.
39 Waltke, "Role of the 'Valiant Wife,'" 24.
40 *HALOT*, 1648.

Even if the *eshet chayil* is a *manly* woman, she is still a woman. So how trustworthy can she actually be? The acrostic contains the same mixed messaging as its preceding oracle, where King Lemuel's mother, herself a woman, supposedly wise, warns about other women, suspect in their very nature (v. 3). Even if intended praise, the line draws on and feeds a damaging master narrative about women.

She Is Divine

Although praise for the *eshet chayil* is inconsistent and compromised with respect to gendered attributes, a second image emerging in verses 23–30 better succeeds in honoring her. In these later verses, the *eshet chayil* morphs beyond mere human warrior to resemble Yahweh himself. The "watching over" (v. 27) that she performs resembles descriptions of Yahweh: "In every place are the eyes of Yahweh, watching over the evil and the good" (Prov 15:3). The metaphor of clothing employed to exalt the *eshet chayil* (Prov 31:25) is also used with respect to Yahweh: "Yahweh is king, he is robed in majesty; Yahweh is robed, he girds himself with strength." Where "strength and honor" (v. 25) describes the *eshet chayil*, "majesty and honor" occur in Psalms 96:6, 104:1, and 111:3 to describe Yahweh. Keywords *torah*, *hokmah*, and *khesed*, all attributed to the *eshet chayil*, elsewhere figure significantly in descriptions of Yahweh. Even the husband's and sons' praising of the *eshet chayil* (v. 29) resembles obeisance to a deity. Wolters writes, "God's incomparability, which is so frequent in Israel's hymns, . . . finds its human counterpart in Prov. 31:29." The counterpart to the Psalms proclaiming *halelu-yah* ("praise God") in response to God's creative acts occurs in Proverbs 31's declaring *halelah* or *haleluha* ("praise her"; vv. 28, 31). Here praise recognizes the wonders wrought by the *eshet chayil*.[41]

---

41 Wolters, "Proverbs 31:10–31 as Heroic Hymn," 450–51.

Fear of Yahweh

The subtle equating of the *eshet chayil* to Yahweh leads into the one spot in this poem, and the entire chapter, where Yahweh is explicitly mentioned: "A woman—fear of Yahweh—she! *She* will be praised" (v. 30). This line is usually translated, "A woman *who fears* Yahweh will be praised." In this traditional rendering, fearing Yahweh is considered to be one more item on a list of desirable qualities possessed by the *eshet chayil*. However, the choice to render *yiroth yahweh* in the adjectival sense of "who fears Yahweh" is grammatically questionable. Fox acknowledges that "normally" *yir'ath yahweh*, as it appears in verse 30, is understood to be a construct form, meaning "fear of Yahweh."[42] Yet, he argues, understanding *yir'ath* as "fear of" in verse 30 "does not fit here."[43] Fox does not state why he rejects the standard rendering of *yir'ath yahweh* as "fear of Yahweh." The phrase appears several dozen times elsewhere in the Hebrew Bible. In her monograph on Proverbs, Yoder recognizes *'ishah* ("woman" or "wife") as a noun existing in apposition with its neighbor, the noun phrase, "fear of Yahweh."[44] Rather than an adjectival phrase ("who fears") modifying *'ishah*, she argues, *yir'ath yahweh* should be considered a substantive, establishing an *equivalency* between *'ishah* and *yir'ath yahweh*. This grammatical construction occurs elsewhere involving the specific phrase *yir'ath yahweh*. Psalm 111:10 reads, "The beginning of wisdom [equals/is] the fear of Yahweh." Recognizing this same pattern in Proverbs 31:30 produces "A woman/wife [equals/is] the fear of Yahweh."

To Yoder's argument may be added further diagnosis of the relation of second nouns to first nouns in apposition. According to Waltke and Michael O'Connor, the second noun can (1) provide further information about the first noun, (2) identify the material the first noun is composed of, (3) reveal the quality or character of

---

42 Fox, *Proverbs 10–31*, 899.

43 He designates *yir'ath* "a contracted form of the fem. const. ptpc. equivalent to [*yere'at*] 'fearer of'" (Fox, *Proverbs 10–31*, 899).

44 Yoder, *Proverbs*, 297; see also Mathys, "Valiant Housewife," 162; Alice Ogden Bellis, *Proverbs* (Collegeville, MN: Liturgical Press, 2018), 266.

the first noun, or (4) identify its office.[45] Considering these options as applied to verse 30 yields understanding "fear of Yahweh" to (1) provide further information about "woman," (2) identify the material that woman is composed of, (3) reveal the quality or character of woman, or (4) identify the office of woman. Through this application we see that "fear of Yahweh" in verse 30 need not be understood as merely one of the *eshet chayil*'s many virtues, added to the pile. Rather, this line summarizes what all the previously listed accomplishments indicate. Supplying, scheming, farming, weaving, trading, guarding, and so on, in all these practical labors the *eshet chayil* equals—epitomizes, amounts to—the fear of Yahweh.

This phrase "fear of Yahweh" occurs many times in the Hebrew Bible, and in Proverbs in particular. Jo Ann Davidson identifies it as the *inclusio* delimiting the main theme or motto of the entire book.[46] In Proverbs, "fear of Yahweh" appears in teachings that "offer and establish norms for a rational and purposeful life which rest on the experience and conviction that the good brings with it good fortune and affluence while the bad entails disaster."[47] The phrase has a concrete, practical focus that recognizes what is at stake in personal and communal choices, that these can lead to either wealth or poverty, life or death. Implicit is the belief that God himself will intervene to ensure that consequences match deeds. For the *eshet chayil* to epitomize the fear of Yahweh confirms her value to her community both in light of her own contributions and as a role model for all.

Wisdom and Loyalty

Finally, the *eshet chayil* is characterized as wise and loyal, terms that, as mentioned earlier, hold communal value. "She opens her mouth

---

45 *IBHS*, 229–32.

46 Jo Ann Davidson, "Women Bear God's Image: Considerations from a Neglected Perspective," *AUSS* 54, no. 1 (2016): 35.

47 Horst Balz and Günther Wanke, "Φοβέω, Φοβέομαι Φόβος, Δέος," *TDNT* 9:202.

with wisdom, and the teaching of loyalty is on her tongue" (v. 26). "Opens her mouth" recalls Lemuel's mother's use of this phrase when exhorting her son (vv. 8-9). Does the *eshet chayil* achieve where Lemuel fails? Does she speak for the *'ani* and *'avyon* genuinely and helpfully—or calculatingly? The description of her actions in the chiasm of verses 19-20 indicates the *eshet chayil*'s primary focus is not in caring for the underclass but in promoting herself and her household's interests. Yet she is wise and loyal, according to verse 26. The phrase "with wisdom" can be interpreted in more than one way. It could characterize the quality of the *eshet chayil*'s words, that she speaks wise words, or it could reference a certain type of people, those who are wise, and thereby associate the *eshet chayil* with that group. And who are the wise? Those with privilege to write and read, those in the gates who decide what authoritative documents say and mean, determining as they do what the community will prioritize and practice. Either understanding of "with wisdom" honors her, but the latter conveys the *eshet chayil*'s participation in communal discussions, perhaps a hint of lived experience not acknowledged in the poem's mention of only her husband sitting with the elders in the city gates.

As for the verbal phrase in the second line, "teaching of loyalty" (*torat khesed*) occurs only here among biblical texts. *Torah* can mean "law" or "teaching."[48] If we take it to mean "law," it suggests that in all her actions, the *eshet chayil* is guided by standards of *khesed*. If the sense lies closer to teaching, then *torat khesed* could mean either her teaching about *khesed*—that others can or ought to be *khesed*-like—or her own teaching done in a *khesed*-like manner, that she herself displays *khesed* when she speaks.

But what is *khesed*? Scholars concede difficulty when rendering it into English. English-language Bibles often settle on "kindness," here in verse 26, perhaps in deference to the subject's female gender, assuming, like the rendering of *chayil* in verse 10 or the supposed charity in verse 20, that an honored lady must be associated with

---

48 *HALOT*, 1711.

those qualities that we today attach to the "fairer" or "gentler" sex. But "kindness" lacks the communal commitment inherent to texts that promote *khesed*, such as Ruth, where multiple characters exhibit *khesed* to save the entire Jewish lineage. *HALOT* offers "joint obligation between relatives, friends, host and guest, master and servant; closeness, solidarity, loyalty."[49] Longman translates verse 26 as "Covenantal instruction is on her lips." He explains, "The word [*khesed*] itself does not mean covenant, but it does characterize the type of relationship that exists between covenant partners."[50] Leo Perdue writes of *khesed*, "in this context, a term that probably refers to the bond of solidarity that holds the household together and enables it to transcend individual greed and well-being for the collective good of the entire social unit."[51] In Perdue's definition, "collective good" holds paramount importance. Whether practicing *khesed* herself or teaching it to others, the *eshet chayil* acts for the betterment of her group. Of course, this is how the *eshet chayil* is described by the presumed male speaker. We readers do not hear her speak directly. We do not know what she really thinks but only what others say about her.

Characterizing the Underclass

Such is the characterization of the *eshet chayil* and her *ba'al* in Proverbs 31:23–30. What about the other subjects mentioned in Proverbs 31, in both the oracle and in the first half of the acrostic: the underclass? These were characterized in the oracle as perishing, bitter of soul, speechless, poor and oppressed, wallowing in misery and toil (vv. 5–9). In our examination of verses 10–22 of the acrostic, we located them alluded to in verse 16 as necessary collateral damage in the *eshet chayil*'s fight for survival, and in 19–20 as vital tools put to work to achieve her aims. How is the underclass characterized in verses 23–30?

---

49 *HALOT*, 336–37.
50 Longman, *Proverbs*, 547.
51 Perdue, *Proverbs*, 279.

They are almost not mentioned at all. Only a hint signals awareness of their presence in the land, in this city. That is the reference to laziness in verse 27. Boer notes Proverbs's multiple contrasts of wise and foolish, industrious and lazy, rich and poor—all channel toward a class consciousness in which being rich evidences possession of wisdom, righteousness, and the blessing of God. Conversely, the poor in Proverbs are depicted as being so because they are "wicked, simple, lazy, rotten."[52] Laziness is that vice in Proverbs 31 that could transform blessed elites into God-forsaken peasants. Laziness is rebuked, poverty rejected. The *'ani* and *'avyon* are indirectly characterized here as the "other," the ones to avoid.

TENSIONS AND PLOT

Having explored settings and characterization, let us catalogue any tensions within the text and reactions to these tensions that could constitute a narrative event. As Monika Fludernik observes, "Happy couples are not story worthy."[53] Stories must have an angle, some reason for being told, some problem to solve. In the previous chapter I identified undercurrents in the acrostic of Proverbs 31: the first line's asking "Who can find?" introduces the dilemma of unfulfilled male desire. Tension may be suspected in the absence of direct interaction between the conjectured wife and husband from verses 10–28. The wife is silent—silenced—so we do not know what she thinks of her life, her duties, her relationships. Her omnicompetent and masculinized portrayal raises questions as to what the husband contributes, whether he is valued. Ernst Wendland explains with respect to his Tongan context what many find discomfiting about the Proverbs 31 couple: "Traditional men become insecure if their wives outshine them in any respect (when she might be idiomatically termed *mukaintu mulombwana* 'a woman-man'!), and this can lead

---

52 Boer, "Economic Politics," 536.
53 Fludernik, "Identity/Alterity," 264.

to quarrels in the home or the jealous suspicion that she is showing off to attract other men."[54]

Beyond the marital relationship, readers can detect communal conflict between elites and the underclass via the violent metaphors used to describe land procurement, wealth enhancement, and interaction with the poor. Such communal tensions persist into the poem's second half, less graphically presented but still present via mention of the husband's role sitting with the elders in the gates—often taken as metonymy for adjudicating legal disputes. This is only necessary if there are quarrels to be resolved. They are present also in the wife's monitoring of others in her household, as if loss, discord, or some other threat would occur without these elites imposing order. Remembering verses 10–31 as positioned immediately after the oracle of verses 1–9, connected via proximity and vocabulary, brings Lemuel and his mother's quarrel into this acrostic, too: the mother's critique of her son and its underlying tensions concerning treatment of the underclass. All these tensions challenge the second poem's endeavor to depict a utopian world via its mention of trust (v. 11), goodness (v. 12), and feeling no fear (v. 21).

This list of tensions suffusing Proverbs 31 indicates a rising action within Proverbs 31 understood as drama, and they set up the husband's act in verse 28, when he steps forward to praise his wife. What motivates him to move? What does this act and the particular words that he chooses accomplish? I propose that the commendation he offers in verses 29–30 constitutes this *baʿal*'s attempt to burnish his own honor that has lost luster in light of the honor ascribed to his magnificent wife.

Honor Defense

Bruce Malina has set forth a much-referenced understanding of honor in Mediterranean societies, defining it as a twofold entity that combines (1) a person's self-esteem, assessed according to intersecting

---

54 Wendland, "Communicating the Beauty," 1261.

factors of authority, gender status, and respect; and (2) the esteem attributed to that person by his or her social group. Honor can be either ascribed or acquired. *Ascribed* honor is possessed at birth, for example, owing to gender or family. *Acquired* honor can be gained or lost based on behavioral conformity to established social codes and participation in public spoken performances consisting of challenge and riposte. Job's dialogues with his friends (Job 3–37) and Boaz's outmaneuvering of his kinsman at the city gates (Ruth 4) constitute biblical examples of honor acquired in the public court of reputation through verbal debate. In Proverbs 31, the mention of city gates (v. 23), a communal gathering spot, sets up just such a "public court of reputation," an ancient convention whereby deeds performed in public are assessed by the public.[55]

Zeba Crook writes that a key feature of the ancient Mediterranean honor-shame system was its conception of honor as *limited*, with not enough to spread around to everyone. Therefore, in the public court of reputation, one person's gain in honor must be compensated for by another person's perceived loss.[56] Concern for this happening to the husband in Proverbs 31 seems to underlie some scholars' remarks, as when Thomas McCreesh writes that the *eshet chayil*'s industriousness "correspondingly reduce[s]" the role of the husband to the degree that "ultimately the husband does not have the place of honor in the poem."[57] Biwul, too, laments that the portrayal in Proverbs 31 of the female figure calls for her to be "praised, extolled, honoured, and dignified above [her husband]."[58]

I have noted how both the husband and wife in Proverbs 31 are honored. The husband's ascribed honor is reflected in his label of *ba'al* and through locating him in a space associated with honor, the city gates. His acquired honor exists through the descriptors of activity: *being known* and *sitting with the elders*. The wife is associated with

---

55 Zeba Crook, "Honor, Shame, and Social Status Revisited," *JBL* 128, no. 3 (2009): 593. See also Matthews, "Honor and Shame," 97–112.
56 Crook, "Honor, Shame," 593.
57 McCreesh, "Wisdom as Wife," 28.
58 Biwul, "What Is He Doing," 35.

honor through metaphors likening her to a warrior and to Yahweh, and through attributing to her honorable qualities and behaviors. Although Malina held that women were associated primarily with shame and did not figure into the jockeying for honor that men engaged, evidence has more recently emerged demonstrating that women did in similar manner to men gain and lose honor in the public court of reputation, even in relation to men.[59]

Some might say the husband cannot compete with his own wife for honor because she belongs to him—he is her *baʿal*, her "owner" or "master," after all—and so any honor acquired through her accomplishments would rebound to him. As Davidson writes, "She makes a name for him."[60] But this wife is honored not only for fulfilling traditional feminine duties of running a household, and she is not honored at all for typically feminine traits of beauty and charm.[61] She is honored via overtly *masculine* metaphors for activities bleeding into masculine terrain: acquiring land, trading with foreigners, leading her home. Masculinity, which feeds honor, is also publicly enacted and confirmed via relationships, roles, and societal institutions that promote a status system in which males dominate females and, through contest and comparison, other males.[62] To be a man in this ancient society was to be *not* a woman, to avoid feminization, to affirm the inferiority of women and participate in militarized aggression.[63] To be a man was to possess honor and avoid shame.[64] Yet Proverbs 31 applies to the *eshet chayil*—and *not* her husband—terms traditionally affirming masculinity: *chayil*, *ʿoz*, and so on. Masculinizing the wife in such manner could threaten the husband's own identity as *baʿal*, decreasing his honor in the public court of reputation.

---

59 Crook, "Honor, Shame," 594.
60 Davidson, "Women Bear God's Image," 45; see also Masenya, *How Worthy*, 104.
61 Contrast the earlier sentiment in Prov 11:16: "A gracious [*khen*] woman gets honor, and violent men get riches."
62 Creanga, "Introduction," 6.
63 Moore, "Final Reflections on Biblical Masculinity," 247.
64 Moore, "Final Reflections on Biblical Masculinity," 247.

Such challenge could not go unanswered. According to Crook, in this ancient, collectivistic culture, if the public considered a challenge to have occurred between community members, then such challenge would need to be responded to with riposte, or the one challenged would lose honor and be shamed.[65]

Verbal Riposte

Hence the husband speaks in verse 29: "Many daughters do *chayil*, but you, you ascend above them all!" The line exhibits wit and rhetorical one-upmanship, both qualities of riposte. As to wit: *chayil* forms a pun in referencing both commercial profit-making and military conquest. In terms of rhetorical one-upmanship: the husband both elevates other men's wives by acknowledging that they "do *chayil*" and reduces them by labeling them "daughters" and asserting that his own wife is better than them all. Characterization of his wife as superior projects the husband's own need to rank above his peers. So important is it for the husband to make this point that he even contradicts the praise of his wife extended by the narrator at the outset of the poem, that an *eshet chayil* is rare and hard to find. Here the husband claims there are many women of *chayil* whom his wife exceeds.

Speaking displays power, particularly when done in the city gates. In speaking, the husband reminds the community that he is the one who sees and judges; his wife is seen and judged. He reenacts Adam naming Eve (Gen 3:20), the male asserting control in being the one to label and classify. He includes his wife as among the *banot* ("daughters"), a term some regard as diminutive.[66] Commentators hasten to explain why no offense should be taken to this term: it is a mere synonym for "women," Waltke assures, a linguistic parallel to *baneh* in verse 28, says Raymond Van Leeuwen; it honors her

---

65 Crook, "Honor, Shame," 593.
66 Bergant, *Israel's Wisdom Literature*, 99.

family of origin (Fox).[67] Regardless of these explanations, and despite Waltke's disapproval of conclusions to the contrary as "sour,"[68] the labeling of a woman by a man as daughter without reciprocal labeling of men by women as sons projects a husband's greater power relative to his wife, thus expanding his honor at her expense.

The same is true of verse 30, "Charm is false and beauty a vapor." Fox writes that the speaker here could not be the husband, because "this would be pompous and patronizing."[69] But is it so unlikely for a husband to be pompous and patronizing, one who associates his wife with plunder (v. 11)—or who even can be understood as plundering his wife? As in verse 29, so also in verse 30 the husband asserts an empowered identity and constrains his wife's by being the one to establish the standards by which women will be judged. Verse 30, like verse 29, also resembles a riposte, this time to a prevailing cultural attribution of honor to women based on their pleasing graces and beauty. The husband names the commonly accepted values of charm and beauty but undercuts them as false, a vapor, and then promotes the superior virtue possessed by his wife: fear of Yahweh. Point for him.

"Words can be expressions of the masculine imperative to dominate," writes Stephen Moore.[70] According to Hilary Lipka, several alternatives to the hegemonic ideal of masculinity as strong warrior exist in Proverbs, one being skills in oration, including persuasiveness, wisdom, and honesty in speech.[71] In the Proverbs 31 acrostic, similar qualities are ascribed to the *eshet chayil*: "She opens her mouth in wisdom and the teaching of loyalty is on her tongue" (v. 26). It would be no surprise, then, for a man concerned with honor to demonstrate his own abilities in elocution. In joining the narrator

---

67 Waltke, *Book of Proverbs*, 534; Van Leeuwen, "Book of Proverbs," 263; Fox, *Proverbs 10–31*, 898.
68 Waltke, *Book of Proverbs*, 534.
69 Fox, *Proverbs 10–31*, 898.
70 Moore, "Final Reflections on Biblical Masculinity," 248.
71 Lipka, "Masculinities in Proverbs," 97–98.

and his sons in ascribing honor to the *eshet chayil*, this husband does so in ways that also defend his own reputation.

Multiple Meanings to *sheqer hakhen*

Much more can be explored concerning verse 30's contribution to meaning in this poem. If other ancient assessments of women usually praise beauty and charm (e.g., Esth 1:11; 2:15; Prov 5:19; 11:16), does the derision of these qualities here imply that the *eshet chayil* is *not* attractive or charming, a way of saying, "That's not important, anyway"? I earlier mentioned with respect to characterization that line 30a damages female identity through associating women with the qualities of falsehood and inconstancy. We should also note that verse 30a may constitute a proverb, as per Fontaine's definition, given the "jarring" nature of its seemingly "out-of-context" interjection of negativity embedded within praise.[72] As indicated with the earlier suspected proverb of verse 6 ("Give beer to the perishing, and wine to the bitter of heart"), proverbs are sometimes asserted in conflictual situations or when speakers perceive themselves to be disadvantaged within a status disparity.[73] As a tactic of persuasion, citing a communal proverb inclines an audience to buy into a speaker's argument through bonding over a familiar saying expressing a common belief.[74] In verse 30, then, the speaker may intend a popular proverb concerning women's nature to prime his audience to embrace the acrostic's alternative description of a model woman.

At this point, narrative levels blur: the husband pursues his personal honor-saving agenda while the narrator promotes an honor-enhancing agenda for the community as a whole. Ambiguity of speaker in verse 30 reinforces this duality. The Hebrew text of Proverbs 31 does not contain quotation marks indicating who

---

72 "A proverb is often jarring in that it is '*out of context*'. That is, its *literal* referents in the proverb image used to convey its meaning have no proximate referent in what has just transpired" (Fontaine, "Proof of the Pudding," 185–86).
73 Fontaine, "Proof of the Pudding," 183; Fontaine, *Smooth Words*, 59.
74 Fontaine, *Smooth Words*, 158; Fontaine, "Proof of the Pudding," 188.

speaks when. Neither is there obvious indication of direct speech such as the *vayomer* ("and he said . . .") of other biblical texts. Most interpreters attribute verse 29 to the husband taking over direct speech from the narrator based on the previous line's summarized speech, "he praises her," as well as a shift in pronominal form from the third person of previous verses, "she/her," to the second person, "you." In verse 30, though, the pronoun referencing the *eshet chayil* switches back to the third person, "*she* will be praised." Is the husband still speaking in verse 30, no longer addressing his wife but maybe speaking to himself or shifting his address to a larger audience, perhaps crowds milling about in the city gates, the space he is known to occupy? Or has the narrator now in verse 30 resumed his role? This chapter begins with blurring of speaker, "The words of Lemuel, a king, with which his mother rebuked him" (v. 1). As earlier, so here in verses 29–30, gaps and ambiguities allow more than one speaker to be inferred.

Chapter 1 explained with reference to the writings of Mikhail Bakhtin and Arthur Frank that language is not limited or controllable. Readers or hearers will make connections with present and past contexts, and these associations spark new meanings. Verse 30a's connecting typically female-associated qualities of charm and beauty with words suggesting deception brings to mind the many biblical stories whose plots revolve around women deceiving. Sarah pretends to be a sister, not a wife (Gen 20). Rebekah advises Jacob how to steal his father's blessing (Gen 27); Rachel sits on household gods and claims to have her period (Gen 31). Examples continue throughout the generations. Within this "woman as deceivers" trope, trickery is celebrated because it benefits the ancient community, preserving them, saving them, extending them somehow. In light of these notions pervading the Yehudite psyche, verse 30—"Charm is false and beauty a vapor; A woman—fear of Yahweh—she! *She* will be praised"—not only rejects traditional femininity in favor of "fear of Yahweh"; it likely also *includes* feminine wiles as among the qualities of a God-fearing woman—as long as these are directed against an enemy to benefit Yahweh's people.

Sheqer hakhen. An interesting aspect of the Hebrew word *khen* is that it almost always in biblical texts appears in the context of a relationship in which there is an imbalance of power: one person or group in need of the blessing of another who possesses greater authority, position, or power. As a result, the one in need acts ingratiatingly—that is, exhibits *khen*—toward the one with power, in order to gain some benefit. Joseph and his brothers flatter Pharaoh, and in response the nation enjoys "favor" (*khen*; Exod 12:36), receiving land and food. The handsome David plays the harp before King Saul and is also judged as finding "favor" (*khen*) in King Saul's eyes (1 Sam 16:22), gaining special status in his household. To the one performing *khen*, it does not matter what they truly feel about the person they are appealing to. Their behavior has ulterior motive. Consequently, the entity with power cannot know whether their charming counterpart is sincere. Uncertainty always lurks under *khen*, undermining any bond, as the eventual unraveling of relations in Egypt and in Saul's court reveals. In power disparities, the compliments and pleasing manner that constitute *khen* are always to some degree false. Proverbs 31:30a rings true.

These dynamics exist for Proverbs 31 in its dyad of husband and wife. Although it is claimed that the *baʻal* trusts in his wife (v. 11), and she brings him good, not harm (v. 12), verse 30a forms a Bhaktinian "sideways glance" that acknowledges women still possess autonomy, acting as they will for their own purposes. Men may conceive themselves as training up women in the image they desire, conditioning them, for example, through regular recitation of the Proverbs 31 acrostic. Yet in real lived spaces, women are not so easy to nail down. They cannot be entirely known or controlled. When their independence is revealed, the surprise experienced by their lords feels like betrayal, deserving the judgment of falseness, deceit.

These marital dynamics encapsulate the position of ancient Israel, which knew itself to be weak compared to surrounding empires. Accordingly, prophetic texts image Israel as female to represent that weakness and the need to adopt servile posture as a strategy for gaining favor (e.g., Lam 1, Jer 3, Ezek 16, 23). Israel, like any weaker nation, performed *khen*, pledging loyalty in covenants, giving tributes, bowing and speaking devotion before conquering thrones. It is not real; it is necessary. *Khen* is false, a manipulative ploy, a flattering mist. *Sheqer hakhen vehevel hayophi* is the tactic of the weaker party, a heroic exertion of any *eshet chayil*: Rahab, Jael, Ruth, Esther—*sheqer hakhen* is *khesed* deployed.

COMMUNAL WORK

Having analyzed the settings, characterization, and plot of this poem from its beginning in verse 10 through verse 30—leaving aside only verse 31—let us explore the work that these narrative elements may be doing for a postexilic, Persian-era Yehudite community. What more can we now know concerning the issues and debates to which the *eshet chayil* forms a reply? And what is that reply?

As just noted, this community perceived itself as weak and vulnerable in comparison to the empires that ruled them and neighboring nations. Sometimes this identity appears in biblical texts through hope-infusing themes that acknowledge weakness, for example, the preference of younger sons over the firstborn (Isaac, Jacob, Ephraim, Perez). Other times biblical texts indicate this self-perception through inflated claims of size, for example, numbers of troops and boundaries of borders. According to Ben Zvi, such counterfactual memories aided the postexilic community in processing their present circumstances through expressing "lacks and longings."[75] We can consider Proverbs 31:10–31 to be a type of counterstory resisting the damaging shame identity of being a conquered people. No hint appears of any lord who rules this lord, the focalized one sitting in the gates. Within the world of this text, the *ba'al* and his *eshet chayil* occupy top tier.

At the same time, the poem testifies that occupying positions of dominance and control does not simply happen. The *eshet chayil*

---

75 Ben Zvi, "'Successful, Wise, Worthy Wife,'" 41.

models the effort required of all to achieve it. Her activity in spaces promotes communal values for maximum flourishing within the context of imperial rule.

Pride in Community

The first strategy promoted is simply pride in community. Keywords *eshet chayil*, *hokmah*, *torah*, *khesed*, and *yir'ath Yahweh* all express communal value, with echoes to other sacred writings that condition hearers to prioritize the public good. Two-time mention of city gates, a symbol of community, also reinforces group identity. The nebulous, overlapping positioning of the *eshet chayil* and her husband with respect to the spaces of gates and home suggests a relationship of mutual dependence between these two spheres, encouraging all community members to view their activities at home as supporting their community. So writes Masenya: "Because of the wisdom and power of those operating from the house, the public sphere or 'the gates' flourish."[76] So strong is the value for communal loyalty that even behaviors normally condemned as unethical can be justified to achieve strategic aims. The poem invokes the god of this tribe, Yahweh, not to promote religious rituals or tenets but to affirm any behaviors that strengthen the collective.

Yet, as a dialogic text, the poem expresses ambivalence over the very communal pride it promotes. Whom does this community include? Who is recognized within the gates? The *eshet chayil*? The *'ani* and *'avyon*? She, as noted, is alluded to but not explicitly located. They are acknowledged as used and abused (vv. 16, 19–20) even as verses 5–9 and 26 depict their need for an advocate. The underclass is "othered" in language used to reference them, then seemingly dropped as a focus of attention. So are they a part of this community to be protected, or do they belong outside the gates in preference of others who matter more? City gates form a particularly fitting image for conceiving this dilemma. Their spaces permit mingling of

---

76 Masenya, *How Worthy*, 105.

societal extremes: residents and visitors, wealthy and poor, judges and appellants for justice. Their structure divides insiders from outsiders, yet their opening allows passage for transformation of insider and outsider status. Such liminality encourages assessing where diverse groups are or should be located with respect to the gates and others inside them. Who actually is inside and who is outside the boundaries of this group, the Yehudite Jews?

Social Order

The poem also promotes social order, with the *eshet chayil* acting in her context as resistance to chaos, to anarchy. People who have known generations of battle, destruction, and displacement can be expected to find comfort in the utopian world of Proverbs 31:10–31, where violence is either merely metaphorical or exerted not against them but for them. Ease is evoked in so many images: being full of food, well-clothed, lying in warm beds, lounging in the city gates, peacefully coexisting with Canaanites—all these encourage an audience to believe that such a harmonious world really can exist or at least is worth striving for. That is true even if present reality includes fearing loss of land, autonomy, and resources necessary for survival. The world of Proverbs 31 is on the surface stable, peaceful, and prosperous. These conditions are attained through community members being where they are supposed to be and doing what they ought to do in their designated spaces.

Lefebvre writes that social constructions of space involve "assigning more or less appropriate place to the social relations of reproduction, namely, the biophysiological relations between the sexes, the ages," and other demographic groupings.[77] Priority of elites over underclass occurs in several mentions of the *eshet chayil* acting and of members of the underclass being acted on, whether running a household, obtaining and cultivating land, or producing textiles for trade.

---

77 Henri Lefebvre, "Space, Social Product and Use Value," in *State, Space, World: Selected Essays*, ed. Neil Brenner and Stuart Elden (Minneapolis: University of Minnesota Press, 2009), 186.

A primary means through which Proverbs 31 participates in a social construction of space occurs through gender-associated depiction of gates and home. Though we have established that both husband and wife occupy these two spaces, this poem overtly allocates one sphere for each. Its representative male belongs in the city gates, as asserted in verse 23. Its model female, though nebulously positioned, belongs to the home, as indicated via four-time reference to "her house." A mutually reinforcing identity loop develops based on the gender assigned to a space and the activities taking place there. Men only being associated with the gates produces an expectation and belief that men belong in public spaces, occupy and own public spaces in ways that women do not. As males and not females become expected to occupy spaces of authority and honor that befit their identities, spaces such as the elders' bench, they are "naturally" looked to for the behaviors associated with these spaces. They are ascribed the honor of these spaces regardless of how they actually behave. Consequently, it is males in this ordering of society who have more power due to their assigned location and the behaviors taking place therein, which allow them to impose their will.

Massey labels this condition "power geometry." Power geometry pertains not only to how people act in a given space but also to who determines how people act and how the different groups relate to each other with regard to exercising power or being subject to it. Massey writes, "There are groups who, although doing a lot of physical moving, are not 'in charge' of the process in the same way."[78] This fits the depiction of the *eshet chayil* in Proverbs 31. "Space indeed speaks, but it does not tell all," writes Lefebvre. "Above all, it prohibits." The *eshet chayil* cannot sit in the city gates. Verses 23–30 fit Lefebvre's observation of lived spaces as "a tacit agreement, a non-aggression pact" in which relationships are normalized into an unwritten rule that "there is to be no fighting over who should occupy a particular spot."[79]

---

78 Massey, "Power Geometry," 62.
79 Lefebvre, *Production of Space*, 142, 56.

As Proverbs 31's audience identifies with its gendered characters, they absorb expectations concerning their own gendered role in society, where they should be and how they should act in relation to others. Gender construction is a complicated process, according to Creanga, involving "social norms, expectations, ideologies, and biases ingrained in each culture regarding what is an 'acceptable' or 'unacceptable' man or woman."[80] Although the verb in verse 10 commencing this poem is "to find" (*matsa'*), the extensive description that follows of the wife's qualities and benefits to the husband suggest that perhaps the text is not motivating its male audience toward merely looking for a wife or hoping one will appear. Rather, it is conditioning men as part of their identity as males to understand their duty to train up the type of wife who will satisfy them and enhance the entire community. A contemporaneous text, *Oeconomicus*, portrays an Athenian husband instructing his younger wife in household management.[81] The way Ben Zvi phrases the theme of Proverbs 31 reveals (perhaps unwittingly) just such a purpose: "The judicious management of a wife was likely to lead to increased social power."[82] His phrase can be taken two ways—as referring either to the manner in which a wife manages a household or to the manner in which a husband manages his wife.

Though we have identified a second work of this poem as promoting social order, involving gendered spaces in which males possess more power than females, the ambivalence of positioning the *eshet chayil* and the emphasis in crediting her as valuable indicates that it would be too simplistic to ascribe a strict hierarchy of male over female to the world created by this text. According to Carol Meyers, the power relations reflected in Proverbs 31 resemble actual conditions of ancient Israel. Using the term "heterarchy," Meyers argues that power between men and women was continually being negotiated to shape society. Male dominance existed in such areas as the military, property ownership, and control of female sexuality, but it

---

80 Creanga, "Introduction," 5.
81 Lang, "Hebrew Wife and the Ottoman Wife."
82 Ben Zvi, "'Successful, Wise, Worthy Wife,'" 33.

was not universally hierarchical or static.[83] Women, too, are vital to communal flourishing; this poem's male narrator and originating community struggle to acknowledge this.

Values That Benefit Community

Finally, the poem promotes the importance of trade and hard work in producing wealth even as it reveals ambivalence about such pursuits. There is some difference of opinion among scholars as to how robust was the economy of Persian-era Yehud. The discovery of weights and measures shows some level of participation in trade.[84] "Palestine" was not isolated, writes Yoder, and in fact experienced "unprecedented growth in international commerce" commensurate to a cosmopolitan marketplace.[85] Yet according to Marvin Lloyd Miller, the Persian Empire did not target the provinces of Yehud and Samaria for development or trade, tapping instead its agricultural region primarily to extract taxes. Even so, he notes, communities located along major trade routes could specialize in crafts and nonagricultural goods so as to enhance their income.[86] Textiles functioned as "liquid wealth, for they could be readily converted to cash."[87] The textile industry produced not only clothing and bedding such as mentioned in Proverbs 31 but also rugs, curtains, containers, tents, wall hangings, and more.[88] Such items vastly expanded beyond what could be attained through farming a household's wealth and standard of living.[89]

---

83 Carol Meyers, *Rediscovering Eve: Ancient Israelite Women in Context* (New York: Oxford University Press, 2012), 198, 193.

84 Adams, *Social and Economic Life*, 101.

85 Yoder, "Woman of Substance," 441.

86 Marvin L. Miller, "Cultivating Curiosity: Methods and Models for Understanding Ancient Economies," in *The Economy of Ancient Judah in Its Historical Context*, ed. Marvin Lloyd Miller et al. (Winona Lake, IN: Eisenbrauns, 2015), 14.

87 Sarah Pomeroy, *Xenophon, Oeconomicus: A Social and Historical Commentary, with a New Translation by Sarah B. Pomeroy* (Oxford: Oxford University Press, 1994), 62, 6–66, cited in Lang, "Women's Work," 193.

88 Ebeling, *Women's Lives in Biblical Times*, 56.

89 Adams, *Social and Economic Life*, 41.

In chapter 3 we noted Ben Zvi's speculation that perhaps Proverbs 31's depiction of the wife and not the husband engaging in trade can be attributed to the negative view of trade among elite classes, sparing this husband the dishonor of associating with trade even while enjoying its benefits. This dynamic may also explain why the *eshet chayil*'s engaging trade is not specifically located in the city gates, even though that is where it likely would have occurred. Because the city gates are *conceived* as the space of honor and associated with men, keeping unfocused the activities of trade in the gates spares any hit to the honor of this prestigious husband that such activity by his wife in his space of honor would incur to him. The text's construction of space forms a boundary that protects some through erasing the lived experience of others.

Nonetheless, in considering the gendered promotion of trade, we ought to note the implications of Proverbs 31's deliberately *masculine* depiction of the *eshet chayil*. Esther Fuchs comments, "When women act like men, the audience laughs, and the message is that men had better wake up to their patriarchal and national responsibilities."[90] The *eshet chayil*'s liminality of gender invites an audience to expand their notions of acceptable behavior for elite men as well as women. Everyone can get in on this game.

In trade and any other occupation, hard work is required, modeled by the *eshet chayil*, encouraged through warning against laziness (v. 27). Two additional motivators framing the poem also encourage hard work. These are the reference to the *eshet chayil* being more valuable than jewels (v. 10) and to her being "the fear of Yahweh" (v. 30). Both jewels and women are to men objects of desire, commonly motivating exertion in order to acquire. Many biblical texts also commend "the fear of Yahweh" as worthy of pursuit (e.g., Pss 128:1, 4; 145:19; 147:11). Some scholarly commentary has expressed concern as to the abruptness of this first mention of Yahweh in Proverbs 31, its seeming incompatibility with the practical skills and worldly

---

90 Esther Fuchs, "Laughing with/at/as Women: How Should We Read Biblical Humor?," in *Are We Amused?: Humour about Women in the Biblical Worlds*, ed. Athalya Brenner (London: T&T Clark International, 2003), 132.

achievements celebrated throughout the poem. Ben Zvi posits that mention of Yahweh might be an obligatory late emendation.[91] Yet Yahweh is alluded to in earlier verses (vv. 25–27), and the phrase "fear of Yahweh" triggers a host of associations with prominent themes in Proverbs 31, including power (2 Chr 1:14), wisdom (Prov 15:37), knowledge (1:7), security (19:23), and wealth (22:4).

Equating the *eshet chayil* with the fear of Yahweh in Proverbs 31:30 teaches that men ought to seek such a woman with the same devotion they know they should be seeking the fear of Yahweh. Conversely, they ought also to seek and practice fear of Yahweh—defined in this poem as acting out of loyalty to community—with the same fervor that they now desire their fantasy woman. The leisure enjoyed by the husband at the gates does not easily, let alone *naturally*, occur. Everyone must vigorously pursue it.

All this exertion intends to bolster this community's acquisition of wealth. Land, silver, household goods, access to power: wealth is the protective barrier against any threat that would pound on the gates. This husband and wife in their successful accumulation and in the honor ascribed to them are ideals to imitate. Pursuit of wealth is not unconflicted, however. The poem acknowledges some have lost out in these upper-class strivings. Lurking beneath the celebration exists the question of how the harm to others aligns with the value of *khesed* to community. At what price the acquisition of wealth? And who pays?

CONCLUSION

In our previous chapter, we ended our study of Proverbs 31:10–22 not knowing whether geographical, social, and ethical boundaries unclear midway through the poem would clarify in future verses, and whether those that were already clear would be reinforced or modified. Our study of verses 23–30 indicates within this drama considerable boundary establishment in the explicit situating of the husband in city gates, with its associations and implications. It

---

91 Ben Zvi, "'Successful, Wise, Worthy Wife,'" 32.

reveals also geographical, social, and ethical boundary crossing in the liminality of the wife located both inside and outside the gates, depicted as both masculine and feminine, the gates as both excluding and including, and the home as both separate from and enmeshed with the public spaces of the gates. These conceptions surface and attempt resolutions to issues related to optimal communal strength. If all of life is a battle, these are tactics for winning.

We ended study of verses 10–22 also aware of tensions, even injury, existing between the celebrated *eshet chayil* and her *ba'al*, and more starkly between the *eshet chayil* and the underclass she uses and abuses. We wondered what would happen to these relatable characters: a wife-seeking man, hard-toiling woman, exploited workers. Now our present study of verses 23–30 reveals some plot progression: focus on or concern for the underclass fades away while the *eshet chayil*, still constrained from direct speech, vastly expands in stature within the community. In response, the *ba'al* eventually, finally, acts. He speaks to defend his honor, offering a verbal riposte that asserts his prominence, reinforcing his socially sanctioned position as establisher of standards, judge of others, imposer on the public his view of how things are or ought to be.

So what happens next? How are his words received? Will his audience recognize his honor-defending assertion and assent? Or will they dissent?

We have reached as yet only the *pen*ultimate verse of this acrostic poem. There is still one more to go: verse 31, beginning with the letter *tav*. This final letter completes the acrostic, finalizing its expression, fulfilling the holistic nature of acrostic form. Unlike the oracle of verses 1–9, in the acrostic, the speaker does receive a spoken reply. That is in verse 31.

Proverbs 31:31

31 Give to her from the fruit of her hands,
   and let them [/they will] praise her in the gates, her works.

CHAPTER FIVE

Class and Conflict at the City Gates
Proverbs 31:31

Here it is at last: verse *tav*: final verse of Proverbs 31. Assumptions as to genre influence interpretation, acting like a key deciphering a riddle. So scholars typically interpret verse 31 according to a presumed genre of encomium, or heroic poetry.[1] As such, it is deemed to complete a litany of praise, the second line mentioning *halleluha* ("praise her"), after all. So Waltke writes, "As a fitting climax to his eulogy, the poet and sage shifts from recording the wise family's spontaneous accolades (vv. 28–29) to obliging all in the gate to extol her."[2]

Yet we have earlier identified narrative features in Proverbs 31's two poems: in verses 1–9, a quarrel between royal mother and son evokes Persian-era tensions between classes in Yehud; and in verses 10–31, a husband and wife promoted as euphoric betray tensions with each other and, again, between societal elites and the underclass. In this present chapter I explore how verse 31 contributes to such drama: Does it advance a particular plotline? Resolve disputes? What else beyond simple praise could be happening in verse 31?

---

1 Fox, *Proverbs 10–31*, 903; Wolters, "Proverbs 31:10–31 as Heroic Hymn."
2 Waltke, *Book of Proverbs*, 536.

As with so many earlier lines of the poem, this verse contains ambiguities, gaps, and contradictions. Whereas a traditional hermeneutic advances one meaning only for an utterance, we here continue to follow Bakhtin's preference for polyphony—unmerged voices sounding differing claims—believing such approach improves on understanding the "full meaning of the word."[3] Just as an author of a polyphonic text will strive "to expose and develop all the semantic possibilities embedded in a given point of view,"[4] so will we as interpreting readers.

Our subjects for examination in this chapter include this one verse's vocabulary and syntax, and the implications of these, depending on various supposed contexts, for understanding the poem's characters, setting, and plot. Who speaks? To whom? What do they say, and why? In such exploration we recognize communal chatter befitting any public square or ancient city gate. We hear diverse voices with diverse interests advocate differing locations for the *eshet chayil*.

MULTIPLICITIES OF MEANING: VOCABULARY

Let us begin by identifying the multiple options for meaning suggested in the vocabulary of this verse.

Tenu Lah

Tenu is disputed as to the verbal root from which it derives. Masoretic markings render its consonants into an inflection of *nathan*,[5] meaning "to give," and so the line is often translated, "Give to her of the fruit of her hands." But others disagree with the Masoretes' judgment and argue that the first word actually derives from *tanah*,

---

3 Mikhail Bakhtin, "Dostoevsky's Dialogue," *Soviet Literature* 2 (1971): 139.
4 Bakhtin, *Problems of Dostoevsky's Poetics*, 69.
5 Murphy, *Proverbs*, 244; also Waltke, *Book of Proverbs*, 514.

meaning "to sing or extol."[6] Deborah's song in Judges 5, a warrior hymn celebrating a female's achievement, also contains *tenu:* "Let them rehearse the righteousness of Yahweh" (v. 11; see also Judg 11:40). When *tenu* in verse 31 is taken as deriving from *tanah*, then it has been translated, "Extol her for the fruit of her hands" or "Celebrate what her hands achieve."[7] Such a rendering fits Mark Sneed's categorization of much wisdom literature as rhetorically "epideictic," involving not a call to action but instead praising or blaming a person, event, or idea.[8] It also perpetuates the earlier depiction of the *eshet chayil* as worthy of worship, like a deity, like Yahweh. However, Fox argues that *tanah* does not actually mean "sing" or "extol" but, more closely, "recount," "repeat," or "rehearse," and, furthermore, *tanah* followed immediately by *lah* (as in v. 31) does not make sense, as it amounts to "Recount to her from the fruit."[9] Based on an occurrence of *tenu* in Psalm 28:4, Fox explains its meaning in verse 31 as "give her what she deserves."[10]

Tenu, then, as *nathan* ("give") reveals verse 31 as differing from Sneed's description of epideictic wisdom literature, which does not involve a call to action. Another type of ancient public argumentation, *deliberative rhetorical*, may better suit to describe verse 31. Future oriented, occurring in public assemblies, deliberative rhetoric "focuses on expediency and attempts to persuade an audience to engage in a particular action." Sneed claims, "There is no deliberative rhetoric in the wisdom literature because it does not attempt to call people to take action for a particular cause."[11] Proverbs 31:31

---

6 Murphy, *Proverbs*, 244; Waltke, *Book of Proverbs*, 514; Wolters, "Proverbs 31:10-31 as Heroic Hymn," 449; Clifford, *Proverbs*, 277; Waltke, "Role of the 'Valiant Wife,'" 24.

7 Waltke, "Role of the 'Valiant Wife,'" 24; Murphy, *Proverbs*, 244. Vayntrub offers "Laud" ("Beauty, Wisdom, and Handiwork," 46).

8 Sneed, *Social World of the Sages*, 250.

9 Fox, *Proverbs 10-31*, 899. *HALOT* agrees, offering "recount" as the most certain meaning (1759-61).

10 Fox, *Proverbs 10-31*, 899.

11 Sneed, *Social World of the Sages*, 247-48.

interpreted in light of contextual narrative features complicates this characterization of biblical wisdom literature.

When performed orally, *tenu* would sound like either "extol/rehearse" or "give." Dialogic interpretation permits acknowledging multiple meanings contributing to the communal work of the text. As "extol/rehearse," *tenu* summarizes the poem's dominant theme: that the *eshet chayil* drives communal prosperity and ought to be honored as such. As "give," *tenu* confirms the poem's subtler undertones, those implied in the poem's opening line, "*Eshet chayil*, who can find?" (v. 10). Evoking loss and desire, this introductory query implies that all is not so sublime in the seemingly utopian world of the text. The command in verse 31—"Give!"—confirms as much through proposing a change to the status quo.

From the Fruit of her Hands

Verse 31's second phrase, "from the fruit of her hands," also arouses interest. A similar expression that occurs more commonly in biblical texts is "from the fruit of her womb" (Gen 30:2; Deut 7:13; 28:4, 11, 18, 53; 30:9; Isa 13:18; Ps 127:3). The variation in Proverbs 31:31 reinforces one last time this wife's masculinity. She is more Adam than Eve, identified not with procreative abilities ("she [Eve] was the mother of all living," Gen 3:20) but with other types of labor ("the Lord God sent him [Adam] out from the garden of Eden to work the ground from which he was taken," Gen 3:23). She is associated with what her hands form and send out into the world rather than her womb.

An almost identical phrase has already occurred earlier, in verse 16: "From the fruit of her hand, she plants a vineyard." These two occurrences use different words for "hand"—*kaph* (v. 16), which seems to refer more precisely to the palm, and *yad* (v. 31)—but this variation does not appear to be significant. Vayntrub associates the phrase with the woman's deeds.[12] In chapter 3, I explained it as referencing the profits of her industry, used for such activities as to

---

12 Vayntrub, "Beauty, Wisdom, and Handiwork," 54.

purchase seed and tools, and perhaps pay laborers. I identified it also as contributing to the erasure of the underclass, who likely actually do the planting of fields but who are not acknowledged in preference of promoting the *eshet chayil*.

Here in verse 31, as in verse 16, it also makes sense to think of "the fruit of her hands" as a reference to profits, of which (taking *tenu* as "give") some portion should be given to the *eshet chayil*. Philippe Guillaume explains the logic of this interpretation as, "Because what wives earn belongs to their husbands, husbands would be wise to reward their successful wives for their tireless labours. In this way, a wife will have even more incentive to increase his capital."[13] Redeploying the verse 16 metaphor in verse 31, rather than using an abstract term such as "profits," triggers within the audience recall of its earlier use and context. Verse 16 credits the wife with such substantial achievements as securing fields and establishing vineyards. The metaphor in verse 31 thus incentivizes its audience by enabling it to envision the tangible gains that await if those addressed will accede to the speaker's urging. Not acknowledging peasant hands that literally work the fields, instead attributing these gains to "her hands," concludes the poem with a tacit endorsement of the aggressive wealth-management tactics earlier described so graphically as striking, ensnaring, and pushing into position the ʿ*ani* and ʾ*avyon* (vv. 19–20).

Significantly, those addressed in this verse are not directed to give over *all* their financial assets, not even all that the *eshet chayil* produces. They are only asked to give *mipri* ("*from/of* the fruit"). As Ellen Davis and others translate, "Give her *a share* in the fruit of her hands."[14] Fox likens the *eshet chayil* in Proverbs 31 to an employee in her husband's firm, with all profits going to him. For Fox, then, verse 31 envisions the husband disbursing a bonus based on

---

13 Guillaume, "Wonder Woman's Field," 95.

14 Ellen Davis, *Proverbs, Ecclesiastes, and the Song of Songs* (Louisville: Westminster John Knox, 2000), 151. Also Gafney, "Who Can Find a Militant Feminist?," 26 (emphasis added).

exemplary performance.[15] Clearly, while the speaker directs his audience to give some measure of honor and material resources to wives, he also expects husbands to retain the main part for themselves. Such action and the assumptions that lie behind it preserve masculine priority and power.

Halleluha

Bakhtin admired the novelistic word that "registers with extreme subtlety the tiniest shifts and oscillations of the social atmosphere."[16] *Halleluha*, in Proverbs 31, constitutes just such a subtle registration of the social atmosphere. Like the verb in the previous line, *tenu*, it can be taken as an expression of will—an intervention that advocates for action. But the inflected person has changed, from the direct second-person plural, "(you all) give," to a third-person plural jussive/imperfect: "Let them praise" or "They will praise." Who now is the them/they desired or anticipated as praising? Conventions of parallelism may encourage assuming the same subject doing this action as acted in the previous line, so those who give (or extol) should also be those who praise, and some interpreters render the line in this way. Longman offers: "Give to her from the fruit of her hands, and praise her deeds in the gates."[17] But reading to the end of the line reveals that the subject of this verb, "to praise," is located at the very end of the verse, past the city gates: "her works."

This separation between verb and subject causes readers to momentarily fill in the gap with their own conjectured subjects performing this praise. Possibilities include the public generally or husbands particularly. Such anticipated subjects praising makes sense in view of preceding context, so it comes as a surprise to find at verse end that in fact neither of these groups is directed to praise but instead "her works."

---

15 Fox, *Proverbs 10–31*, 914.
16 Bakhtin, "Discourse in the Novel," 300.
17 Longman, *Proverbs*, 548.

Is this a displacement? Though husbands really ought to praise an *eshet chayil*, in light of the benefit they receive, assigning "her works" as doing so instead spares men the loss of honor that would come from praising those who, according to cultural conceptions of gender and honor, ought to occupy a lower position in the communal honor-shame spectrum. Viewing this line as a displacement forms of it a continuation of the verbal riposte of verses 29–30 that defends male honor and preserves privilege while seemingly affirming the *eshet chayil*. Husbands maintain dignity through merely sitting, while "her works" praise her instead. The Septuagint rendering of verse 31 goes even further to guard male honor, rendering verse 31 as "And in the gates may *her husband* be praised."[18]

Over a dozen times in the psalter, songs of praise to Yahweh end with the exclamation *Hallelu-yah!* ("Praise Yah!") (as in Pss 104–6, 113, 115–17, 135, 146–50). Proverbs 31:10–31 abounds with praise for the *eshet chayil*, even using the verb *halal* (vv. 28, 30, 31). Earlier verses liken the *eshet chayil* to Yahweh, so we may expect this poem to continue its imitation and close with a climactic *hallelu-ha* ("Praise her")! But it does not. *Hallelu-ha* is not the final cry. This phrase does appear but buried mid-verse. Why? Would continuing the psalmic pattern to end with *hallelu-ha* have gone too far in equating the *eshet chayil* to Yahweh? Again the poem limits even as it praises. This woman's worth may indeed exceed jewels (v. 10) but is not above all, not above Yahweh, and not above the object of praise that does close out the poem: "her works."

In the Gates

Mention of gates in verse 31 recalls their earlier mention in verse 23, repetition signaling emphasis. The gates matter, especially as these two mentions of gates occur in midpoint and final verses, both significant locations. In Ruth, "gates" serves as a metonymy for the

---

18 Prov 31:31 in *Septuaginta: With Morphology*, Logos electronic ed. (Stuttgart: Deutsche Bibelgesellschaft, 1979) (my translation).

community when Boaz, making a momentous decision, tells Ruth, "All the gate of my people know that you are an *eshet chayil*" (3:11). "All the gate"—where people congregate, make important business and legal decisions, and share information—is an image of Boaz's community. His people rely on him as a man of social standing— an *'ish gibbor* (Ruth 2:1)—to make wise decisions that preserve or enhance their communal strength. He is accountable to them for his reputation as a man of honor.[19] This same assumption of mutual dependence can be understood to be signaled in Proverbs 31:31 when the location for praising is identified as "in the gates." Not just husbands or immediate family but entire communities have a stake in the behavior and treatment of the *eshet chayil*. Furthermore, the entire community contributes to the *eshet chayil*'s identity, opportunities, and welfare.

Fields and vineyards (v. 16), houses (vv. 15, 21, 27), foreign lands (vv. 14, 24), city gates (vv. 23, 31): locations matter in this poem—who is where, doing what. We earlier noted how definitively the husband is located in this poem: he is "known in the gates, where he sits" (v. 23). Such overt placement contrasts with the ambiguous positioning of the *eshet chayil* in any of her associated spaces, city gates in particular, because her activities as they are described indicate she must be there. This representation of space in comparison to inferred lived spaces is one work of the poem, to construct conceptions of space that form identity: who is expected to occupy certain spaces and to behave in certain ways with respect to what is in those spaces, including objects and other people. In Proverbs 31, the gates—the public forum, the space of speech and authority—are overtly represented, at least through verse 30, as the husband's and not the wife's domain.

So what of verse 31? Does this second mention of gates affect the gendered identities spatially constructed in the poem? "Let them [they will] praise her in the gates, her works." This wording leaves ambiguous who or what is located in the city gates. Are "her works" in

---

19 Ruth immediately follows Proverbs in the Hebrew Bible. Boaz's comment connects "the gate" with the phrase *eshet chayil*—as does Prov 31.

the gates, praising her there, or is *she* in the gates, being praised—or both? The poem could be more clear. Not to be clear is a choice among other options. Continued lack of overt location of the *eshet chayil*, on the one hand, continues her disadvantage, her being harder to find as compared to her husband and consequently harder to associate with the power and agency that city gates symbolize.

On the other hand, the lack of explicit location in verse 31 also opens up possibilities. "Praise her in the gates." She could in fact, according to this line, be present in the gates. We may infer an ellipsis, understanding the line as "Let them praise her [*who is*] in the gates." This choice to fill a gap with definitive location forms of verse 31 what space theorist Tim Cresswell describes as "transgressive acts": unsanctioned, nontraditional actions within a given space committed by marginalized groups in violation of the norms of behavior expected to occur in that space.[20] Such "deviance" brings into focus what the norms of society actually are by revealing what has been violated through the transgressive act.[21] This latest interpretive option then answers the question posed in verse 10: "A woman of *chayil*, who can find?" She can be seen in city gates by any who are willing to recognize her there.

As transgressive act, verse 31's mention of city gates contrasts with their mention in verse 23. "Known at the gates is her husband, in his sitting with the elders of the city." Verse 23 presented a conceived mental representation of how some—those empowered to speak for the community, those who identify with the husband of the *eshet chayil*—would like that space to be used: as space where, "naturally," males dominate and control. In any community, habits of behavior in space come to be seen as normal or natural, "unstated and taken for granted" expectations for behavior supporting the existing power structure.[22] Elders sitting in the gates serve as an example of this. They are the ones who act to make decisions concerning communal issues. The marginalized—whether women or peasants—do not.

---

20 Cresswell, *In Place/Out of Place*, 9–11.
21 Cresswell, *In Place/Out of Place*, 24.
22 Cresswell, *In Place/Out of Place*, 3.

But verse 31 calls for a better alignment between the poem's earlier representation of space and its *lived* space, an acknowledgment of what is communally perceived as real needing to be set alongside the conceived ideal. The gates in actuality *are* a space of female labor, production, instruction, and influence. They should be a place of communal support and affirmation of women—and all who labor. Verse 31 advocates for the *eshet chayil* both a better physical location and a better social position. Such assertion by the speaker on behalf of those actually doing the labor within a space Lefebvre identifies as essential toward changing the world for the better. It explodes "imposed space" and frees up a "collective and practical [space], controlled by the base, that is, democratic."[23]

In light of verse 31's gaps and ambiguities, the *eshet chayil* both is and is not recognized as belonging inside the gates; her location remains a subject of debate. It is fitting that in this poem gates would be the image linked with such liminal state. Gates as physical objects mark inside and outside. When moving through them, a person's identity shifts, becoming at some midway point neither and both insider/outsider. Carey Walsh writes, "Liminality is the condition of uncertainty involved in a status transition. It is a threshold moment of the vulnerable, suspended state between a past status and one not yet secured. The gate, then, marks a psychic threshold of sorts, the in-between state inherent in status change."[24] Several biblical scenes depict evaluation of community members as to their status occurring in ancient city gates. Absalom's appearance at the gate displaced his father, David, and elevated Absalom (2 Sam 15). Walsh notes examples of female identity assessment taking place in city gates:[25] Rahab's residence in the city wall aligns with her liminal status as a citizen yet a prostitute (Josh 2). Ruth's assimilation into Boaz's family takes place in the city gates and is declared by "the elders and all the people at the gate" (Ruth 4:11). In light of this pattern, it is reasonable

---

23 Lefebvre, "Space: Social Product and Use Value," 193.
24 Walsh, "Testing Entry," 50.
25 Walsh, "Testing Entry," 54.

to perceive similar activity taking place in Proverbs 31:31's mention of gates with respect to a woman.

Her Works

Final words are weighty. With nothing further to absorb, a reader or hearer lingers over final phrases. These then impact recall of what came before. Authors carefully choose which words should form their ending. In Proverbs 31 it is "her works." Like the earlier metaphor of the fruit of her hands, this phrase reminds an implied male audience of what is in it for them in their treatment of the *eshet chayil* and, by extension, all their women. As celebrated earlier in the poem, "her works" includes their own safety, prosperity, prestige, family coherence, and other gains. Ending the poem with "her works"—and not with mention of the *eshet chayil* or a final call for praise (*halleluha*)—clarifies the focus of celebration within the poem. Her works are its true devotion and praise.

We should mark also that these important works are in the end confirmed as *her* works. This is one final constructor of the *eshet chayil*'s identity. Though she is identified also as having a husband and home, the *eshet chayil* is producer of all these many works; that is who she is. While this phrasing, as before, obscures others' contribution in these accomplishments, it also prevents others' usurping credit for them. These are *not* the *ba'al*'s works or the community's works but "her works."

As noted above, many commentators ignore the grammatical construction of verse 31b that assigns "her works" as the subject praising the woman. Instead they recast the line as one in which an individual or group praises the *eshet chayil*'s works—or praises her *for* her works.[26] Such interpretation requires significant emendation.

---

26 McKane (*Proverbs*, 670) and Longman (*Proverbs*, 548) do the former. Hartley (*Proverbs*, 334) and Waltke (*Book of Proverbs*, 536) do the latter. Yoder: "The poet's parting appeal is that everyone, including and perhaps especially those at the city gates (31:23), 'give her' (e.g., Pss. 28:4; 68:34 [Heb. v. 35]) credit and recognition for her labors" (*Proverbs*, 297).

It may be motivated by expectations based upon presumed genre, that within a supposed hymn of praise, people praising is what *should* be happening. But no, it is the works themselves that praise the *eshet chayil*. Wolters identifies these as likely the woven belts and other textiles she produces.[27] Created things praising their creator continues the poem's imaging of the *eshet chayil* as divine. In Psalms, that is what Yahweh's works of creation do: "Praise him, sun and moon, praise him all you shining stars" (Ps 148:3). The word for "works" in verse 31, *maʿaseh*, most often elsewhere in biblical texts refers to Yahweh's creation, as in Psalm 111: "Great are the works of the Lord, sought by all who delight in them" (v. 2). For Yoder, one of the works that the poem celebrates is the husband's "rank," so deduced because his positioning in the city gates occurs within the catalogue of the *eshet chayil*'s accomplishments.[28] According to this interpretation, then, the assertion that "her works" will (or should) praise her constitutes a call for the husband, as himself a "work," to praise his "creator," the one who has made him what he is: his wife.

MULTIPLICITIES OF MEANING: PARALLELISM AND INTONATION

This scrutiny of verse 31's vocabulary reveals already numerous multiplicities of meaning representing diverse interests within the ancient Yehudite community. Two other features of verse 31, when fully attended to, expand interpretative options: parallelism and intonation. Regarding parallelism, the verbs and nouns of verse 31's two lines occupy roughly the same position within each line. This pattern encourages interpreting the lines according to conventions of parallelism. *Antithetical* parallelism is not usually difficult to identify and interpret, but distinguishing between *synonymous* and

---

27 Wolters, "Proverbs 31:10–31 as Heroic Hymn," 450.
28 Yoder, *Wisdom as a Woman*, 89; similarly Waltke, *Book of Proverbs*, 529.

synthetic/progressive parallelism can represent a challenge.[29] When antithetical parallelism is not obvious, commentators tend to assume a parallel as synonymous. Synonymous parallelism enables decoding a tricky phrase in one line through appropriating the meaning of its counterpart in the parallel line. Regarding verse 31, for example, William McKane references his interpretation of the second line ("deeds should be publicly acknowledged and acclaimed") as "confirming" his interpretation of the first line: "give her credit for her achievements."[30] Thus both lines would have to do with praise.

Yet readers do not a priori know that the second line *is* synonymous to the first, and simply assuming that it is interrupts the interpretive process, preventing exploration of equally viable meanings that considering synthetic/progressive parallelism could suggest. Two lines of a parallel construction can actually modify each other in infinite ways.[31] In *synthetic* or *progressive* parallelism, the second line is understood to complete or extend the idea expressed in the first. Enticing possibilities arise if Proverbs 31:31 is viewed as such. What if line b in verse 31 does not simply repeat the same idea as line a but extends or completes it? Such possibility invites inferring a second ellipsis, rendering the verse as "Give to her from the fruit of her hands, and [then] they will praise her in the gates, her works." According to this understanding, the verse asserts a relationship of cause and effect, that (line a) *if* the woman is properly rewarded, (line b) *then* the community, husbands in particular, will get to enjoy even more of "the fruit of her hands" (profits) when she reinvests them, as verse 16 describes her as doing. Line b as *consequence* of line a is a very different meaning from understanding line b as just one more expression of praise. It also more closely fits an understanding

---

29 *Synonymous parallelism* reinforces a concept via both lines of a couplet saying basically the same thing. *Antithetical parallelism* uses opposite images to reinforce the same point in both lines. In *synthetic* or *progressive* parallelism, the second line completes or extends the idea proffered in the first. See Sneed, *Social World of the Sages*, 223–24.

30 McKane, *Proverbs*, 670.

31 Sneed, *Social World of the Sages*, 224.

of verse 31 as deliberative rhetorical, motivating toward a certain course of action.

As for intonations, we should bear in mind that Proverbs 31 developed in a time of interdependence between orality and script.[32] Although the visual significance of the acrostic form and chiasma show an origin in script, homophones, alliterations, repetitions,[33] and allusions to orality (in vv. 1, 8, 9, 26, 28, 31) indicate also a context of public oral performance. The inflections and intonations of oral performance can shift meanings as compared to silent reading of the written word. Regarding verse 31, the word "*Give!*" if emphasized more strongly than surrounding words, can convey, "Stop holding back!" And "To *her!*" could communicate "not to *him*; he has enough already!" Including meanings based on possibilities of intonation supplies yet another means for us to participate in the egalitarian approach to narrative that Bakhtin admired in Dostoevsky, that he "brought together ideas and worldviews, which in real life were absolutely estranged and deaf to one another, and forced them to quarrel."[34] The words of verse 31 are not only about the *eshet chayil*. They also include her context, people in her orbit, who may or may not be praiseworthy. Verse 31's word of praise to the *eshet chayil* can communicate pointed rebuke to these others, inside or outside Proverbs 31's story world. Perhaps verse 31 should be taken as partner to the exhortation and rebuke of verse 8: "Open your mouth for the speechless, on behalf of all who are perishing." Imagining intonations enables exploring the utterance of verse 31 as such.

IMPLICATIONS FOR CHARACTERIZATION

Recognizing these multiple possible meanings in verse 31 affects our understanding of characterization in the acrostic. If we take the

---

32 Miller, "Performance of Oral Tradition," 181.
33 The words *mah, chayil, bayit, sha'arim, ba'al, 'ani,* and *'avyon*. Alliterations occur in vv. 11, 20, 26, 27, as noted by Wendland, "Communicating the Beauty," 1245.
34 Bakhtin, *Problems of Dostoevsky's Poetics*, 91.

verse as instructing husbands to reward their wives or give them more control of household resources, it adds to the portrayal of the *eshet chayil* as capable and strong while reinforcing her husband's dominance. In affirming the wife as worthy of praise in the city gates, it reinforces the *eshet chayil* as someone for the community to claim as their own. She represents them, belongs to them and with them.

This verse also forefronts two additional "characters": the audience and speaker. Notice that the first word, *tenu*, is a plural second-person imperative. There is no direct address in the previous verse, so its occurrence here comes as a surprise. According to Bakhtin, every expression is not simply focused on its topic but "is accompanied by a continual sideways glance at another person."[35] In verse 31, the second-person inflection drops the literary convention that obscures speaker and audience. It makes clear that these two are present and do contribute to the meaning of an utterance. But who is the implied "you (all)" of *tenu*? Direct address occurs earlier, in verse 29, singularly inflected. Based on "he praises her" of verse 28, it is presumably spoken by the husband to the *eshet chayil*. Whom should we imagine as the plural audience addressed in verse 31? Is it the crowd perpetually milling at the gates? Or, more particularly, those ten men known to occupy the elders' bench of city gates (Ruth 4:2)? These are possibilities that exist at the level of the story world. At another narrative level, the addressees could be scribal apprentices or other community members whom we can infer as listening to public performance of this poem. Telescoping even further out, the audience could include us ourselves, readers of the text, incorporated through direct address as characters expected to participate in the poem's narrative event.

Who, also, is the speaker? Richard Clifford supposes it is the husband and sons of verse 28 who here address the "public assembly."[36] Verse 31 does not specify who speaks these lines, so we may imagine several possibilities. One character we may consider unlikely to be speaking in verse 31 is the *eshet chayil*, since the line reads, "Give to

---

35 Bakhtin, *Problems of Dostoevsky's Poetics*, 32.
36 Clifford, *Proverbs*, 277.

her." Verse 31, then, consistent with previous verses, denies this wife one final opportunity to speak. Perhaps it is the husband, turning from addressing his wife to now instruct his peers, finishing up his verbal riposte through another self-promotion in being the one to speak, to articulate what is praiseworthy, asserting who should act, and how, and who should receive the actions of others.

In light of identified tensions between husband and wife, the speaker of verse 31 could also be a nameless community member responding to the verbal riposte he has observed, taking on a mediating role, advising the *eshet chayil*'s husband as to what he owes his wife. Or perhaps a community member, impressed by the husband's praise, speaks to urge others to imitate him and treat their wives with a similar generosity. Some honor-seeking challenger may oppose the husband's prior speech by implying that men must do *better* than the *eshet chayil*'s husband. They must give not just *words* of praise but *material* support. In Ruth, the women of Bethlehem supply an example of advocacy in city gates. "The women of the neighborhood gave him a name, saying, 'A son has been born to Naomi'" (4:17). Proverbs 31:31 could constitute a similar interjection on a woman's behalf.

Even the *eshet chayil*, it turns out after all, cannot be completely discounted as speaker, considering verse 31's abruptness of shifting subject and direction of address. After all the rumination of previous verses, reflecting the "arrogant eye" that centers male interests and point of view, perhaps verse 31 supplies a sample of the wise (*hokmah*) and loyal (*khesed*) teaching for which the *eshet chayil* is known (v. 26). Anticipating her portrayal being used to pressure and shame less accomplished women, perhaps she breaks in here to advocate better conditions for worn-out sisters. Doing so would make real the advice of Lemuel's mother, to speak on behalf of the speechless (v. 8). It would also counter that same mother's warning of women as a threat through insisting on their worth.

Interpreters need not remain strictly within the story world of the *eshet chayil*, either. Could the speaker be Lemuel, following his mother's advice in verses 8–9 to "open your mouth"? Could it be Lemuel's mother, forming an *inclusio* of the chapter via her voice? She earlier speaks with imperative commands: "Do not give to women" (v. 3), "Give beer to the perishing" (v. 6), "Open your mouth," and "Judge" (vv. 8, 9). In the oracle, she advocates for social welfare via a decidedly self-interested, top-down approach, concerned for her son's kingly role. As speaker in verse 31, she shows development in her thinking, advocating a more specific remedy for those who lack credit—reputational and material—to increase their opportunity and agency. (Recommending just a portion of profits ceded to those who labor indicates still a ways to go in her advocacy.)

Verse 31 is not only the final verse of a poem and chapter but also of Proverbs as a whole. Perhaps it is therefore spoken by the one introduced as author at the book's beginning: "Solomon, son of David, king of Israel" (Prov 1:1). Telescoping further out, the speaker of verse 31 could be no one named within the text but an unknown scribe, abandoning neutrality, addressing readers of the poem directly, telling his desired lesson for us to learn, what we ought to do as a result of hearing his poem.

IMPLICATIONS FOR SETTING AND PLOT

In addition to affecting characterization, tracing multiple meanings in verse 31 also affects our understanding of Proverbs 31:10–31's narrative-like features of setting and plot. Situating praise in the gates encourages conceiving any action that occurs within the poem as taking place in that location, the city gate. This is because the poem throughout expresses praise, so the gates is where, according to verse 31, this poem occurs. Her sons arise to bless her, and her husband acts to praise her; these also occur in the city gates. Hearers of this praise, including us, within the world created by the text, occupy the city gates. We are a part of its throng. We matter to what is happening here.

Shaming Speech

The city gates as setting encourages conceiving verse 31 as a dramatic shaming speech. Lady Wisdom, who calls out folly (Prov 1–9), is located there. According to Matthews, a group-oriented, honor-conscious society such as postexilic Yehud expected every member of a household to uphold the honor of that household. Should lapse occur, all household members were expected to exert pressure to prevent recurrence. Verse 27 has already informed as to the *eshet chayil*'s monitoring her household for the shameful behavior of laziness. Shaming speech eliciting public embarrassment served as principal method for defending honor, one in which women commonly engaged.[37] Frequently, such speech would resemble a "wisdom argument" calling on "traditional practice, social codes, and covenantal allegiance." The public setting would fuel the effectiveness of the rebuke in drawing support and reinforcement from its audience.[38]

Also writing about shame in ancient societies, Lyn Bechtel identifies three main functions of public shaming: discouraging undesirable behavior, preserving through negative pressure social cohesion, and manipulating social status through dominating others.[39] We have seen such functions enacted in Lemuel's mother's rebuke. Verse 31, building off the praise in previous verses, can also be understood to execute these functions, discouraging negative behavior of exploiting without reward, promoting social cohesion in reminding of all they have to gain through proper treatment of their wives, and manipulating social status through elevating women but not too much. If aimed at a male, possibly younger, impressionable audience, the lines could imply, "And you, what do *you* contribute? You also ought to do what *you* can." It can mean, "Don't you be squandering what she has worked so hard to produce"—a throwback to verse 3's "Do not waste your *chayil*."

---

37 Matthews, "Honor and Shame," 98–99; Matthews, "Female Voices," 11.
38 Matthews, "Honor and Shame," 99–100.
39 Lyn M. Bechtel, "Shame as a Sanction of Social Control in Biblical Israel: Judicial, Political, and Social Shaming," *JSOT* 49 (1991): 53.

Adjudication

A second possibility for understanding the city gates as setting is as enacting a scene of jurisprudence. Zeba Crook lists three examples of Hellenistic women successfully arguing legal defenses before magistrates in public. Others through male representatives brought charges against males for criminal or civil offenses.[40] These incidents enable us to imagine verse 31 as somehow concerning a legal dispute, to be decided by the elders at the gate.

Verse 31's opening phrase, *tenu lah*, has overtones of such. First Kings 3 tells of two mothers arguing over parental rights to one baby, and it uses this same phrase. It first occurs when one mother pleads with King Solomon to save her son—"Please, my lord, give to her [*tenu lah*] the living baby! Don't kill him!" (v. 26). It appears a second time when Solomon renders judgment in this pleading mother's favor: "Give to her [*tenu lah*] the living child" (v. 27). Perhaps in Proverbs 31:31, *tenu lah*—"give to her"—can be similarly understood as legal appeal or judgment rendered in response to appeal.

All sorts of legal actions occurred in the space of ancient city gates: transfers of land or other property, marriages, divorces, punishment of lawbreakers, appeals for retributive justice due to injury, judgments thereof, and more.[41] Such practices may form the basis for the law of Deuteronomy 21, parents instructed to bring a rebellious son to the gates for correction, and of Deuteronomy 25, wherein a woman may seek satisfaction at city gates if a brother-in-law refuses levirate marriage. In *Law, Power, and Justice in Ancient Israel*, Douglas Knight notes that the laws that operated in historical reality were not the same as laws recorded in biblical texts. The latter, not always practiced, served ideological purposes such as regulating power relations, legitimizing cultic activity, and so on. For most of Israel's history, oral tradition sufficed as legal code. Written codes such as those in biblical texts emerged only in the Persian era as a result of Persian policy

---

40 Crook, "Honor, Shame," 606.
41 See Douglas A. Knight, *Law, Power, and Justice in Ancient Israel* (Louisville: Westminster John Knox, 2011).

that sought them. The Persian Empire granted significant autonomy to its districts, allowing local governments to establish and enforce laws as long as these local governments maintained order, loyalty to the empire, and payment of taxes and tribute.[42]

Issues of concern could vary greatly between villages and cities. Whereas village life mostly involved agricultural pursuits, cities possessed greater diversity of occupation and other activities. Thus legal issues in cities could be more complex, often concerning property ownership and commercial transactions. Urban dwellers possessed considerably more wealth and power than rural residents, who frequently served city elites. This disparity formed a significant source of tension and distress. City dwellers depended on villagers and possessed the means to make villagers behave in ways that served the interests of a city's elite at the expense of villagers' own rural communities. One such means the city dwellers possessed included occupying positions of leadership that allowed them to set, interpret, and decide legal matters.[43] These conditions of Persian-era Yehud resemble those described in Proverbs 31: land seizures (v. 16), elites coercing the poor into service (v. 20), and the husband's occupation of the elders' bench (v. 23).

Legal Appeal

In light of such social context, let us consider how verse 31 might serve as a legal appeal. "Give to her from the fruit of her hands, and let them praise her in the gates, her works." Perhaps the speaker of verse 31 is the type of advocate for whom suffering Job longed, someone to testify on his behalf in circumstances where it seems no one is listening, pleading his case before a judge (Job 16:19–21). The speaker could be a Boaz-like figure as from Ruth, one who negotiates on behalf of widows or others portrayed as being in need (Ruth 4). It is interesting that in both Job and Ruth, the main characters are

---

42 Knight, *Law, Power, and Justice*, 11, 78, 27.
43 Knight, *Law, Power, and Justice*, 176, 222–23.

depicted as victims even though they belong to the elite class of their society and retain much privilege. They are wealthy and leisured (Job); they own land (Naomi, Ruth, Boaz). The *eshet chayil*, with servants and fancy clothes, also belongs to this privileged class. Verse 31 as an appeal lobbies for an elite version of justice: a recognized position in society and the necessary resources to thrive. In such scenario, connecting verse 31 to verse 30 produces a new understanding of the meaning of "*khen* is false and beauty a vapor." As discussed in chapter 4, these are the assets traditionally recognized as those that women rely on to gain what they need. Verse 31 can be understood to argue that if the *eshet chayil* could have economic freedom and communal standing, she would not need to resort to such tactics. Reinvesting "the fruit of her hands" is the true source of prosperity, rendering *khen* ("charm") and beauty, indeed, worthless illusions and vapors. Job, Boaz, Naomi, Ruth, *eshet chayil*: they all represent the scripture-writing *golah* of Yehud, and verse 31 advocates for them.

Land possession hovers in verse 31 via the echo of verse 16 in "the fruit of her hands." In the Persian era, land played a big part of the social change affecting all segments of society. Residents of cities acquired large landholdings formerly occupied by villagers,[44] who now were wanted to farm this land for luxury goods desired by empire and not to meet their own subsistence needs. According to Boer, resolving the "determinative contradiction" between the desires of palatine estates and the subsistence survival needs of village communes is a primary focus of many biblical texts.[45] We can infer such activity happening here in Proverbs 31.

In this communal conversation, the *eshet chayil* becomes doubly liminal. We earlier noted her gendered ambiguous positioning, unofficially occupying but not overtly located within the public space of the city gates. She is liminal, too, in representing both the elite and the underclass, victimizer and victim. As a successful member

---

44 Knight, *Law, Power, and Justice*, 202.
45 Boer, "Economic Politics," 537.

of the elite class, her participation in exploiting peasants is clear (vv. 16, 19–20). As a female, she is the "other" to text-producing males, societal leaders, so she can also effectively represent other "others," the exploited poor and the "oppressed" *golah*. The community's laborer par excellence, she embodies all those who labor and lack rest, recognition, or material rewards. Line a of verse 31 communicates that the *eshet chayil* is not receiving what the speaker considers her due; she is a victim of injustice. Verse 31 appeals on behalf of the *eshet chayil*, powerful wife of a landed lord, who herself enjoys the pleasures of food, fine clothing, security, and honor. And it appeals for the *eshet chayil*, the laborer, who ceaselessly toils to accrue all these comforts for the pleasure of others.

Even as verse 30 denounces *khen*, verse 31 actually enacts it, the strategic, clever, sometimes deceptive appeal to another's ego in order to advance one's own interests. The rationale for recommended change in verse 31 consists *not* primarily of how the advocated action would benefit the *eshet chayil*. Perhaps that was deemed too risky to those who might feel threatened by her honor or power, thus actually discouraging reform. Rather, the way that the appeal of verse 31 is phrased focuses on how the proposed alteration will benefit those appealed to. Those in position to give are the ones who will increase wealth as a result of their actions. Verse 31's *khen* may be usefully compared to Tamar's plea to her brother Amnon in 2 Samuel 13. Although at first pointing out the harm to herself ("Where could I get rid of my disgrace?" v. 13), Tamar quickly abandons this line of reasoning and focuses instead on her attacker's own interests: "What about you? You would be like one of the wicked fools in Israel. Please speak to the king; he will not keep me from being married to you" (2 Sam 13:13). As stated in verse 30, *khen is* deceptive—and valued and necessary to people with limited resources and power. The presence of *khen* in the final verse of Proverbs 31 shows communal adroitness in deploying it whenever needed to survive and thrive.

Judgment Rendered

Another way of understanding verse 31 in relation to legal procedure, instead of as an appeal, is as judgment rendered *following* appeal. We may hear the elders of the city gates speaking verse 31 as a response to the implicit appeal in verses 10–30's praising of the *eshet chayil*, her accomplishments and worth. It may be the entire community, sometimes invoked to add legitimacy (Ruth 4), who speaks here. "Yes," this verse communicates, "our women/these laborers *should* have a share of their profits, our wealth, and yes, this practice will continue to see us blessed." Lemuel's mother was concerned about her son rendering unjust judgment through immoral behavior. Could verse 31 be Lemuel's effort to show her fears unfounded?

According to Knight, ancient oral law developed through decisions about specific situations that then served as precedent for future incidents. Proverbs 31:31 may be viewed as an instance of emerging oral law. Premodern legal systems assessed guilt *collectively* much more readily than law courts do today. Many dispute resolutions focused on community-strengthening remedies such as restitution rather than punishment alone.[46] We can see these priorities in verse 31 if understood as judgment. The instruction, *tenu lah*, targets a plural audience, thereby involving the entire community. It seeks a material allotment to the *eshet chayil* following the implicit argument in verses 10–30 of what she contributes and deserves. "Laws are products of power," writes Knight. "They stemmed from those who sought to control their worlds."[47] The rationale of benefit to the entire community of the recommended course of action maintains order through keeping everyone satisfied enough in their respective roles and rewards not to rebel against the status quo. Verse 31 as verdict spoken by elders at the gate retains control of the ruling class over those who labor and serve.

---

46 Knight, *Law, Power, and Justice*, 35, 48, 34.
47 Knight, *Law, Power, and Justice*, 89.

CONCLUSION

We have explored how verse 31 of Proverbs 31 may be understood not only as climactic expression of praise for one exceptional woman but also as a dramatic act expressing many desires present within the Persian-era Yehudite community. "Open your mouth," urged Lemuel's mother (vv. 8–9). Here in verse 31, someone actually does, calling for action, addressing characters inside and outside this text's narrative world. What actually is called for can be understood in multiple ways: to shrewdly invest for greatest return, to more equitably allocate resources, to reassess and relocate those whose societal placement restricts or excludes—and many more meanings inhabit this text. Some messages preserve elites in their positions of power, while others resist this poetic world's damaging master narrative about women, that they are a threat, to be guarded against, that they are solitary and silenced in service, not themselves in any need of care. To the extent the *eshet chayil* represents all who labor, these messages in verse 31 challenge their depraved existence (vv. 6–9) as well. Writes Biwul of Proverbs 31:31: "To praise one's wife . . . in public in such a society would mean to initiate a shift in paradigm from what is normative."[48]

Tantalizingly, this poem does not reveal how verse 31's addressees respond. Do they give what is called for? Should we? The poem gifts readers an open ending, similar to Jonah, which ends with a question: "Should I not have pity on Nineveh, that great city?" (4:11).[49] Both biblical texts grapple with identity and communal obligations: who belongs to the group and how those deemed "other" should be treated. In both, lack of definitive answer at the end allows multiple options for response. Assent? Reject? Delay?

Bakhtin would have it this way, not expecting nor desiring closure in a polyphonic work.[50] He valued depictions of internally unfinal-

---

[48] Biwul, "What Is He Doing," 55.

[49] For discussion of Jonah's open ending, see Gunn and Fewell, *Narrative in the Hebrew Bible*, 129–46.

[50] Newsom, "Bakhtin, the Bible," 294.

ized heroes.[51] Proverbs 31 evokes this type of threshold moment in scenes at the gates that convey clashes between family members, sexes, and classes. These need not resolve into monologic agreement but may remain in dialogue—or quarrel—with each other. Such an unfinalized ending circles back to the chapter's beginning, which introduced its oracle as a quarrel and an ambiguity of voicings. Acknowledging multiplicity may feel uncomfortable in lacking resolution, but it more accurately reflects how knowledge emerges, not through finite pronouncements but through ongoing dialogue with others and one's inner thoughts.[52] Verse 31 crystallizes the chapter's function as site of ongoing contestation, with social, political, and economic interests asserting themselves to define and debate the best activities and identities for diverse people in their shared space.

---

51 Bakhtin, *Problems of Dostoevsky's Poetics*, 53.
52 Bakhtin, "Dostoevsky's Dialogue," 128.

CHAPTER SIX

The Implications of Wisdom's Cry

A search for Proverbs 31 in the blogosphere reveals countless devoted Bible readers eager to explain how women can emulate the *eshet chayil*—and numerous confessions of failure. All these readings assume the proverbial woman is one to imitate. But what if she is not? What if she is both victim and vanquisher, roles that no one should seek? The *eshet chayil*'s identity—and ours—forms not in isolation but in correspondence with other people according to their needs. Our reading of Proverbs 31 highlights the community surrounding the *eshet chayil*, revealing how this text's projections serve for working out communal anxieties, needs, and strategies to survive and thrive.

OUR METHOD

We accomplished this through applying Bakhtinian insights as to the dialogic nature of utterances, recognizing that texts can teem with multiple meanings when attention is paid to gaps, ambiguities, polyphonies, echoes, and other dialogic elements. A monologic reading ignores multiplicities, favors one meaning alone. But attending to the rhetorical purpose of dialogic components such as the sideways glance, interruption, juxtaposition of quotations, change in address, double-voicedness, questions, and intertextuality shifts readers from passively receiving a communication to actively engaging to form it. It empowers them to investigate agendas driving what is said and how it is said, to consider also what has not been said but should be and why silence exists instead. Portions of Proverbs 31 particularly conducive to dialogic analysis are its setup as a mother-son quarrel (v. 1), likely interjection of communal proverbs (vv. 6–7, 30), chiasm binding the *eshet chayil* to textile production and treatment of the poor (vv. 19–20), suggestions of a publicly performed honor riposte (vv. 28–30), and legal appeal or judgment (v. 31). These mini-scenes exist and contribute to meaning just as much as do expressions of ethical principles or descriptions of admirable behavior that drive traditional reception of verses 10–31 as job description for an ideal wife.

We accomplished this reading also through noting narrative elements of Proverbs 31, including characters, settings, focalization, tensions, suspense, action, and plot. Genre classifications of Proverbs 31 as poetry, wisdom literature, oracle, encomium may explain why interpreters largely overlook its narrativity. Yet the appeal of Proverbs 31's two poems lies largely in their narrative elements, whether readers are aware of this or not. "Story = character + predicament + attempted extrication,"[1] writes Jonathan Gottschall. Through narratives, people understand their world.[2] Life is complex. Our senses gather endless streams of experiential data that would overwhelm our brains to the point of paralysis without some system for filtering information. To manage all this incoming data, our brains foreground, background, or discard entirely various details of our life experiences. Stories imitate and support this process, supplying, as it were, prepackaged collections of information necessary to establish limits and give shape to our individual lives.[3] They grab our interest through presenting characters we identify with and root for in

---

[1] Jonathan Gottschall, *The Storytelling Animal: How Stories Make Us Human* (Boston: Houghton Mifflin Harcourt, 2012), 53.

[2] David Herman, "Stories as a Tool for Thinking," in Herman, *Narrative Theory and the Cognitive Sciences*, 185.

[3] Frank, *Letting Stories Breathe*, 47.

their troubles. Readers form causal links between perceived narrated episodes in order to make sense of a story. Lemuel and his mother, the *eshet chayil* and her husband have anxieties and needs, just as we do. Their drama maximizes our imaginative engagement with the text and the lessons we learn from them.

Our reading also incorporated socionarratology, which asks what work is being done in a given community through its narratives. Presuming a postexilic, Yehudite context, we ask, What are the questions to which Proverbs 31 forms a reply? What threat? What need? How does Proverbs 31 shape identities and other perceptions for people pondering it?

OUR INTERPRETATION

Interpreting Proverbs 31 through these lenses reveals the chapter's primary characters as morally complex and compromised. Several mentions within the text signify their elite status in society: having titles, wealth, comforts, servants, opportunities, movement, security, honor, success at business, and participation in adjudication. King Lemuel and his mother, the *eshet chayil* and her master—and all Yehudite Yahweh worshippers whom these four represent: while focalized in Proverbs 31 as heroes of their own story, dialogic interjections in this very text also reveal them as the villains of others' tales. These others are the "sons of affliction/poverty/misery" (vv. 5, 9, 20), "perishing . . . bitter of soul" (vv. 6, 8), "in poverty . . . toiling" (v. 7), "unable to speak" (v. 8), "living in want/oppressed" (vv. 9, 20). Those deprived of their land, lacking even subsistence needs, coerced into laboring and producing what others then consume, suffer under the power flaunted by elites who prioritize looking after themselves. Commentator Bruce Waltke cautions of verse 15 that "the 'preying' metaphor must not be pressed to signify unethical activity; this woman fears the LORD (v. 30)."[4] But in our fresh reading we do

---

4 Waltke, *Book of Proverbs*, 525.

press its jarring details. We see in Proverbs 31 acknowledgment of the damage elite Yahweh-fearers have done.

Proverbs 31 acknowledges questionable behavior and also critiques it through calls for justice. Lemuel's mother's preference that beer and wine be served to the poor instead of at royal banquets can be understood as protesting rulers' callousness and suggesting need for social change. Even though Lemuel's mother benefits from the status quo arrangement of society and fails to identify any specific changes to aid the poor, her general advice still rings out: "Open your mouth for the speechless, on behalf of all who are perishing. Open your mouth—judge rightly! Plead the case of the poor and oppressed" (vv. 8–9). A second voice, also at the conclusion of its poem, in verse 31 calls for change: "Give to her from the fruit of her hands, and they will praise her in the gates, her works." Mention of the city gates brings to mind other biblical cries for justice also situated in city gates, such as those of Lady Wisdom in earlier chapters (Prov 1, 8, 9). Proverbs 31 mentions the underclass repeatedly, and combined with reference to city gates we can hear an echo of Proverbs 22:22–23: "Do not rob the poor because he is poor, nor oppress the afflicted at the gate; for the Lord will plead their cause, and plunder the life of those who plunder them." In light of such intertextual connections we may add Lady Wisdom or Yahweh himself to the list of possible speakers in verse 31.

Acknowledging, critiquing—and yet another communal voice chimes in. The text also *justifies* the elites' treatment of the poor in its focalization, a spin that makes Lemuel and his mother, the *eshet chayil* and her husband seem so dignified, responsible, devoted. The context for repeated mentions of the poor in verses 5–9 concerns royal privileges and duties, so the poor, though mentioned, are still not central: these women who destroy kings, who might suck them dry of their *chayil* (v. 3), the female servants (v. 15), vineyard laborers, and workers of fields (v. 16). The poem does not elaborate on what life is like for them. Nameless, unimportant women referenced in verses 3, 15, and 29 fit Iris Marion Young's characterization of women's exploitation as "energies and power are expended, often unnoticed and unacknowledged, usually to benefit men by releasing them for more important and creative work, enhancing their status or the environment around them, or providing them with sexual or emotional service."[5] But reading through our lenses named above brings these women into focus as we come to understand how the text reinforces hierarchy of gender and class.

One dialogic way of looking at Proverbs 31 justifying elite exploitation is to understand its second poem as Lemuel's response to his mother's rebuke. She wants her son to reign, to preserve his *chayil*: power, wealth, lineage (v. 3). And she wants justice for the poor. But can she have it both ways? Her dilemma is the *golah*'s dilemma. The fantasy of verses 10–30 supplies the reply that if Lemuel is to prosper as his mother desires, he will need land and workers. To get these, his wife, the manager, representative, symbol of his household, must possess the devious qualities alluded to in verse 30, stereotypical qualities likely stimulating his mother's earlier warning against women (v. 3). As Lemuel's retort, the acrostic means something like, "Okay, well: I need land (v. 16); I need workers (v. 20)—I need . . . I need . . ." Verse 31 culminates Lemuel's reply by saying, in effect: if you want so much for me, we will need someone onto whom I can project the dirty work requisite for thriving in this land. Someone closely identified with me but not actually me, a proverbial woman, the *eshet chayil*. "Give to *her* from the fruit of her 'hands'" means to free her up in all her wealth-generating activity—including coercion of the "hands"—the peasant class who actually work the land. *Then* you will be happy, Mother, as we all thrive.

Any community will include members possessing multiple conflicting, contradictory perspectives on vital issues, and that is what we see reflected here in Proverbs 31. Communities are not static. They change as diverse individuals and groups strive for their best advantage. The Proverbs 31 mini-world depicts this process of social negotiation affecting how various people and groups are conceived: their abilities, opportunities, identities.

---

5 Young, *Justice and the Politics of Difference*, 51.

In three spots Proverbs 31 depicts elites' familiarity with jurisprudence: Lemuel's mother using legal terminology and referencing legal procedures (vv. 5–9), *ba'al* implied as sitting as a judge in the city gates (v. 23), and legal terminology and the court setting of the gates included in the final call to action (v. 31). In *Law, Power, and Justice in Ancient Israel*, Knight observes that resolving conflict is only one purpose of law; another is to advance the interests of one party over another.[6] Whoever has authority within the legal system has the power to shape the ordering of society in ways not available to those who are not part of that structure. Lemuel's mother in her advocacy conditions her son into this dominant role. The Proverbs 31 acrostic does the same. Contrary to Fox's rebuttal of feminist scholarship on Proverbs 31, wherein he insists about the chapter "Nor is power at issue,"[7] power is in fact repeatedly asserted and reinforced in Proverbs 31. Lemuel's mother warns against a threat to her son's power. She urges him to deploy his power on behalf of the poor. The *eshet chayil*'s physical strength and entrepreneurial activity celebrate exercises of power, and her husband's compliment in verse 29 expressly ascribes to her power (*chayil*) over others. More appropriate as an emphasis in Proverbs 31, therefore, is Jean-Daniel Macchi's observation concerning Hebrew Bible texts in general, "Since people live in societies, the question of the exercise of power arises."[8]

Other meanings that emerge from our interpretive approach include understanding the utopian features of Proverbs 31 as counterfactual depictions of problems that exist in the world behind the text. Proverbs 31 celebrates productivity, trade, and profit. According to Ben Zvi, utopian descriptions ignore those features of society that are working well in favor of encouraging more of what is not

---

6 Knight, *Law, Power, and Justice*, 36.
7 Fox, *Proverbs 10–31*, 913.
8 Jean-Daniel Macchi, "Denial, Deception, or Force: How to Deal with Powerful Others in the Book of Esther," in *Imagining the Other and Constructing Israelite Identity in the Early Second Temple Period*, ed. Ehud Ben Zvi and Diana Vikander Edelman (London: Bloomsbury T&T Clark, 2014), 219.

happening enough.[9] Textual peace and prosperity resist the real stresses of daily life brought about by Persian rule and temple authority, onerous taxes, sickness, famine, and so on. The active, powerful, effective women with *chayil* (v. 29) may intend to inspire a sense of agency that community members currently lack, and a *baʻal* taking his place among elders at the city gates may oppose social conditions where men do not have the status or authority they would wish, either in public or in their homes.

So Proverbs 31 works to shore up a certain social order. As Knight asserts, every society, through a variety of punishments and rewards, conditions members into norms of behavior and belief.[10] Proverbs 31 does this through shamings and praisings. Lemuel's mother shames her son for intemperate behavior and urges sober rule (in two senses: both serious and uninebriated). This world normalizes the poor's depending on the rich for provision and accepting their judgments as just. Verses 10–31 praise industry and communal loyalty while shaming laziness. Focalization in this seeming utopia conditions husbands into their patriarchal role and wives to support their "masters" through service to their households. Such counterfactual expression resembles a concern explicitly named in Esther, when Queen Vashti is punished as an object lesson teaching all wives to respect their husbands' authority (Esth 1).

Proverbs 31 constrains its women through Lemuel's mother's warning depicting them as takers, problems, threats (v. 3), and through the oracle's picture of women's ceaseless activity channeled to serve their husbands. Yet the call for action in verse 31 shows an ongoing struggle to identify a sweet spot of controlled agency for women: "Give to her *from* the fruit of her hands." In the beginning of the chapter, the mother warns, "Do not give to women," with male *chayil* the treasure so carefully guarded. But at the end, someone orders, "Give to her from the fruit of *her* hands." After all the celebration of what her hands achieve, we may understand the

---

9 Ben Zvi, "'Successful, Wise, Worthy Wife,'" 41.
10 Knight, *Law, Power, and Justice*, 31.

fruit of her hands as in essence her *chayil*. Perhaps some number of this town's males, sitting and talking together within the gates, are contemplating that their *chayil* actually is women's *chayil*, it is where theirs comes from, what they depend on.

Proverbs 31 also promotes *khesed*, communal loyalty. This value appears in mention of *khesed* as what the *eshet chayil* teaches (v. 26), and also via two-time reference to the gates, which symbolize community. The chapter as a whole constitutes an exercise of *khen* on behalf of *khesed*, like Esther's strategic charm offense to save her people, like Jael's (Judg 4–5). Verses 1–9 deploy the emotional pull of a mother's rebuke to position a male audience into defensive posture regarding their behavior, and then verses 10–30 entice them with visions of an ideal life, replete with pleasure, security, and honor. These two emotion-laden scenes soften the audience to respond affirmatively to the exhortation to action in verse 31. Like all performances of *khen*, the request is harder to resist following appeals to relational connectedness and vanity.

Priority for *khesed* also is apparent in what is praised as good and derided as bad. Trade, wealth, profit, productivity: these strengthen the community. Laziness threatens. Notably, no markers distinguish endogamy as preferable to exogamy. Aramaisms in Lemuel and his mother's vocabulary hint of foreignness. Such may suggest, in line with the Bible's other *eshet chayil*, Ruth the Moabite, that crossing ethnic boundaries is no problem at all when aligned with *khesed* for Israel.

WHY THIS READING MATTERS

We need the fresh reading of Proverbs 31 supplied here in *The Proverbial Woman: Class, Gender, and Power in Hebrew Poetry* because this text, like its two strong women, deserves mixed assessment as to its impact on human lives. Laboring poor permeate this text, growing and harvesting land that is not theirs, maintaining wealthy elites in their positions of privilege. Yet focalization shifts attention away from them; they are largely ignored. Just as focalization and characterization marginalizes the underclass in Proverbs 31, so interpretation and application of this text marginalizes the poor in real societies. The comparative lack of commentary about them in Proverbs 31 perpetuates their plight.

Yes, Proverbs 31 can inspire virtue: self-control, concern for the poor, devotion to family, appreciation for wives, for hard work, charity, kindness, wisdom—some qualities not even actually named within the text. Interpretations can highlight the *eshet chayil*'s strength and initiative. But Proverbs 31 also can foster vice. Its first poem attracts comparatively little attention, but the second, the acrostic: a "cattle prod for husbands," cautions blogger Stephen Altrogge.[11]

Throughout the world, over many centuries, readers have taken the *eshet chayil* as God's role model for women. Understood as such, this text pressures them to perform to an impossible standard, faults them when they fail. Mother's Day sermons inspired by Proverbs 31 make women feel "guilty and inadequate."[12] "It is a vicious way to live, as we try to reconcile who we are with who we believe we should be," writes Bailey Jo Welch.[13] Conditioning women to orient their lives around service to their families inhibits them from developing their own independent interests or believing that they deserve support from others, too. Some cultures justify women being worked "like a donkey" through reference to this text, laments Kenyan Anglican priest Domnic Misolo.[14]

Masenya points out that the pressure to perform in Proverbs 31 is one-sided. "There is nothing wrong if a wife does good to her

---

11 Stephen Altrogge, "Do I Want My Wife to Be a Proverbs 31 Woman? Sorta, Kinda, Maybe," The Blazing Center, February 18, 2015, https://theblazing center.com/2015/02/do-i-want-my-wife-to-be-a- proverbs-31-woman-sorta-kinda -maybe.html.

12 Karen L. Shaw, "Wisdom Incarnate: Preaching Proverbs 31," *The Journal of the Evangelical Homiletics Society* 14 (2014): 44.

13 Bailey Jo Welch, "'She's Literally Fictional': What the Church Won't Tell You about the Proverbs 31 Woman," FaithIt, September 28, 2017, https://faithit .com/church-got-wrong-proverbs-31-woman-bailey-jo-welch/.

14 Personal communication.

husband; the problem arises, however, when the goodness is only expected of one party."[15] With no corresponding poem praising attributes of a good *husband* (not merely a man), males get a pass. Women sacrifice and suffer to benefit their families, while men adopt domination as their right. Ezra Chitando writes, "In the name of submitting to culture, tradition and religion, [men] claim that it is the duty of women to look after the sick."[16] A wife of noble character must, above all, respect her husband, writes author of the website Woman of Noble Character (the website name a notable allusion to Prov 31). Being a Proverbs 31 wife means "putting God first and your husband second and everything, yes, even your children, after that.... A virtuous wife is what her husband (not any other husband, but HER husband) needs. God created woman to be man's *helper*."[17] A husband is the head of the household. "He does get the last word," writes the host and author of avirtuouswoman.org.[18]

Such champions of modern-day Proverbs 31 womanhood teach that men should not take advantage of their leadership role to abuse their wives. But disparate power dynamics make abuse more likely to happen and more difficult to resist.[19] And who defines abuse? If a husband as head of the household is viewed as final decision maker, consulting only other men (as per Prov 31:23), does a woman's opinion count? How to weight it against the testimony of her *ba'al*

---

15 Masenya, *How Worthy*, 154.

16 Chitando, "'Good Wife,'" 153.

17 Susan J. Nelson, "13 Characteristics of a Wife of Noble Character in Today's World," Woman of Noble Character, https://www.womanofnoblecharacter.com/a-wife-of-noble-character/.

18 Melissa Ringstaff, "Happily Submissive," A Virtuous Woman, October 12, 2009, https://avirtuouswoman.org/happily-submissive/?unapproved=135257&moderation-hash=2a3709bdfb79917e6ece42f9a3110c8c#comment-135257.

19 A claim beyond the scope of this project but much discussed on the website for Christians for Biblical Equality, cbeinternational.org. For example, Maureen Farrell Garcia, "Understanding the Link between Theology and Abuse: A Defense of Ruth Tucker's *Black and White Bible, Black and Blue Wife*," CBE International, January 30, 2017, https://www.cbeinternational.org/resource/understanding-link-between-theology-and-abuse-defense-ruth-tuckers-black-and-white-bible-black/.

("husband/master")? This teaching implies that women should put up with anything *but* abuse. It imposes a burden on women to assess whether each particular unwelcome behavior from their man sinks to the level of abuse they are permitted to resist (if they can) or whether, as a lesser offense, it must be tolerated, classified instead as thoughtlessness, ignorance, forgivable sin, test from God or the devil, perhaps treatment deserved due to her own failure to please. Men, because of their empowered identity (physically and positionally stronger), do not need to think about their circumstances in this way, but many Proverbs 31 women do every single day.

Another problem with common interpretations of this text is a perceived separation between the public sphere, associated with males, and the domestic sphere, associated with females. Masenya notes that this resembles and reinforces conditions in many African communities, where important issues of justice are discussed and settled in male spaces without presence or input of women.[20] While Proverbs 31 may be understood to affirm some female exercise of leadership, where it really counts in terms of societal power and authority: there they are excluded.

Kang invokes Michel Foucault's concept of the panopticon—a watchtower's unrelenting spotlight illuminating prisoners—to describe how Proverbs 31 conditions women into docility. The *eshet chayil* "is constantly under the gaze of the narrator, her husband, her children and YHWH. This gaze permeates her every behavior throughout her domestic and public spheres." Scrutiny motivates conformity of speech and behavior in order to avoid judgment and punishment. Even "praising her works and contributions, this too becomes a discourse of God-talk that constructs a system of power over women, especially those who want to be faithful and wise."[21]

In light of such lessons extracted from Proverbs 31, of course, *of course*, this reading is needed. One test of the ethics of narrative is to ask not what it explicitly states as good or bad but what

---

20 Masenya, *How Worthy*, 155.
21 Kang, "Re-reading a 'Virtuous Woman,'" 142.

sort of person it shapes.[22] Fomenting identities that deny roles and relationships, inhibit opportunity and agency: Is this text worthy of women? Of the poor? If we do not want more people reading Proverbs 31 to conceive women's identity in terms of men, in terms of their value as workhorses, silent and submissive, then let us drown such meanings in other meanings. *The Proverbial Woman* notes cracks in constructions of identities, their inconsistencies and contradictions. It recognizes how insecure is the *eshet chayil*'s position even amid so much praise. This reading sees the *eshet chayil*'s liminality, both oppressor and oppressed. It hears protest for her and against her, and the cry to relocate this paradigmatic woman to a spot of more sure footing alongside more dominant groups. Flooding a damaging master narrative with competing interpretations dilutes its impact. Letting stories fully breathe through meanings suggested in their gaps, contradictions, ambiguities, and polyphonies "improve[s] the quality of companionship between people and stories."[23]

BUT DOES IT REPAIR?

We have gathered ingredients for a communal counterstory, one that, in accordance with Lindemann Nelson's description, allows "oppressed people to refuse the identities imposed on them by their oppressors and re-identify themselves in more respectworthy terms." Master narratives targeted by counterstories "are those that are generated by oppressive forces within an abusive power system and which impose on a subgroup an identity that marks its members as morally defective."[24] In chapter 2, our reading highlighted Proverbs 31:1–9's characterizing women as a threat, subjugated to men, and depicting the underclass as hopelessly dependent, destined to suffer. We acknowledged then that recognizing such damaged identities

---

22 Arthur Frank, *The Wounded Storyteller: Body, Illness, and Ethics* (Chicago: University of Chicago Press, 1995), 157.
23 Frank, *Wounded Storyteller*, 19.
24 Lindemann Nelson, *Damaged Identities, Narrative Repair*, 22, 157.

and resisting, through our dialogic, socionarratological reading, the master narratives that form them offers some benefit to injured groups. But recognition and resistance do not in and of themselves repair. Repairing damaged identities requires replacing the "arrogant eye" with a "loving eye,"[25] developing and circulating a counterstory with sufficient heft to shift social understanding of these damaged groups. With limited raw material for such a project embedded in verses 1–9, we turned in subsequent chapters to Proverbs 31's second poem, the acrostic of verses 10–31. There, a busy, successful wife, labeled an *eshet chayil*, and her husband (*ba'al*—"master") outdo one another in honor, differ in their respective associations with spaces, gain increasing wealth and power through strategically crafty behavior. We uncovered how this narrative-like poem, too, damages identities, normalizing portrayal of the underclass as marginalized, disempowered, exploited, and women also as subjugated, controlled, required to sacrifice their own well-being for others' benefit.

But she is supposed to be powerful, the *eshet chayil*, a trait emphasized in verses 10–31 a dozen times or more. The poem's narrator praises her as skillful trader, garment maker, landowner, household manager, teacher. Ambivalence surrounds her inclusion in the gates, communal seat of authority, yet she does greatly influence her home and some public domains. Verse 30 rejects pejorative stereotypes of femininity as unworthy of the *eshet chayil* in favor of a positive equation: "Woman—fear of Yahweh!" This one deserves to be praised.

"Identity and agency are both interpersonal notions. Who I am, morally speaking, is in some measure a matter of who others say I am and this has a direct bearing on how freely I am able to exercise my moral agency. Moreover, how others perceive me also influences how I perceive myself, and that too has a direct bearing on my freedom to act,"[26] writes Lindemann Nelson. Such insights as to the role others play in personal identity encourage viewing the above-noted positive characteristics of the *eshet chayil* as evidence of a loving

---

25 Lindemann Nelson, *Damaged Identities, Narrative Repair*, 174.
26 Lindemann Nelson, *Damaged Identities, Narrative Repair*, 34.

eye, and they mark verse 31 as particularly suited to constituting an identity-constructing line. In verse 31 a speaker addresses a plural public: "[You all] give." This intervention occurs in the community-symbolizing setting of city gates. The action advocated concerns the *eshet chayil*, established in chapter 5 as representing both women and the laboring poor.

According to Lindemann Nelson, a credible counterstory possesses three features: (1) it restoratively explains members of the damaged subgroup according to values or issues important to the larger group, (2) it incorporates action as evidence to support the identity claims and/or as anticipated future action consistent with the identity claims, and (3) it has enough heft to be adopted both by members of the oppressed subgroup and the dominant group.[27] "Give to her from the fruit of her hands, and they will praise her in the gates, her works." Through allusion, this line exhibits at least the first two of these criteria. It connects the *eshet chayil* to profits, products, and to the positive benefits she brings. In so doing it explains her in relation to communal values and concerns. The phrase "the fruit of her hands" alludes to impressive past activity, the seizing of fields and clearing them for vineyards. "They will praise" (or "let them praise") has a future orientation that promises good things in accordance with the repaired identity promoted here. The speaker's counterstory in verse 31 shifts the proverbial woman from being conceived as a tool put to use at communal toil to being the forger and user of all communal tools, a marked identity upgrade for her. Some voice here is advocating a narrative repair.

But what of its heft? While one lone speaker may create a counterstory, community is needed to legitimate it.[28] Verse 31 is positioned at the very end of its poem, a location signaling emphasis and significance; it gets a lot of attention. Mention of gates, the second mention in this poem, as a symbol of the community at large adds weight also in reminding hearers of what is at stake in the ask that

---

27 Lindemann Nelson, *Damaged Identities, Narrative Repair*, 92.
28 Lindemann Nelson, *Damaged Identities, Narrative Repair*, 175.

is extended. Such details indicate effort to make of this exhortation a compelling argument for change.

And do these ingredients of counterstory succeed in repair? Does our reading here?

The answer depends on readers' preference and choice. Multiple voices in Proverbs 31 express diverse points of view, some constructing identities that degrade, others resisting and offering repair. Each reader can choose with whom to align. *Eshet chayil*, a truly powerful woman: we have found her; now what shall we do with her? An unfinalized and open dialogue is "hostile to any sort of *conclusive conclusion:* all endings are merely new beginnings."[29] The poem's lack of reply to verse 31's cry invites each reader to decide. As Bakhtin writes in appreciation of Dostoyevsky's dialogic novels, "Nothing conclusive has yet taken place in the world, the ultimate word of the world and about the world has not yet been spoken, the world is open and free."[30]

CONCLUSION

It is easy to imagine objections to *The Proverbial Woman*, its method, conclusions, and invitation to readers to join in making meaning of texts. This work may receive protests of subjectivity, bias, *agenda*. Some will dismiss it as mere eisegesis. But we all bring interests to the texts we read, and we all interpret accordingly. I am urging here communal sensibility. The Bible is a far more community-oriented, conversational text than often recognized. In one biblical narrative, a set of commandments, written in stone, descends from Mount Sinai to the people below (Exod 32). But that is not the Bible. The Bible is a collection of texts developed over time, differing one from another in content, context, style, even language. When read in light of one another, such varying texts enable deeper, fuller contemplation of

---

29 Bakhtin, *Problems of Dostoevsky's Poetics*, 165.
30 Bakhtin, *Problems of Dostoevsky's Poetics*, 166.

topics addressed, topics that concern all the people of God. While, yes, we can bind texts together and strain from their contents "one epic narrative".[31] Is that the *best* we can do? Might not there be something lost in that interpretive approach? We all do choose an approach; this one notices as meaningful a text's gaps, ambiguities, contradictions, polyphonies, and other dialogic elements.

"*Eshet chayil*, who can find?" The analysis we have engaged here in *The Proverbial Woman* can advance us all into people of *chayil*: empowered, resourceful, effective. We understand now how a communal master narrative such as Proverbs 31 shapes identities, for help and for harm. Equipped and endorsed to replace damaged identities with narrative repair, we need not merely listen, mute, to this text (or any). It need not be treated as monologic instruction, as Lemuel may at first appear to do, and as many would presume fitting for an *eshet chayil*. The cacophony of voices revealed through dialogic interpretation frees any in community to occupy spaces of debate and decision, to open our mouths and to speak out concerning what we see and what we need.

---

31 As, for example, The Bible Project video, "What Is Bible Project," September 13, 2018, https://youtu.be/vFwNZNyDu9k?si=F6ufAjY85Rf1tLy5.

Bibliography

Adams, Samuel L. *Social and Economic Life in Second Temple Judea*. Louisville: Westminster John Knox, 2014.
Altrogge, Stephen. "Do I Want My Wife to Be a Proverbs 31 Woman? Sorta, Kinda, Maybe." The Blazing Center, February 18, 2015. https://theblazingcenter.com/2015/02/do-i-want-my-wife-to-be-a-proverbs-31-woman-sorta-kinda-maybe.html.
Bakhtin, Mikhail. "Discourse in the Novel." In *The Dialogic Imagination: Four Essays*, edited by Michael Holquist, translated by Caryl Emerson and Michael Holquist, 259–422. Austin: University of Texas Press, 1981.
———. "Dostoyevsky's Dialogue." *Soviet Literature* 2 (1971): 127–40.
———. "The Problem of Speech Genres." In *Speech Genres and Other Late Essays*, edited by Caryl Emerson and Michael Holquist, translated by Vern W. McGee, 60–102. Austin: University of Texas Press, 1987.
———. *Problems of Dostoevsky's Poetics*. Edited and translated by Caryl Emerson. Minneapolis: University of Minnesota Press, 1984.
Bal, Mieke. *Narratology: Introduction to the Theory of Narrative*. Toronto: University of Toronto Press, 2009.
Balz, Horst, and Günther Wanke. "Φοβέω, Φοβέομαι Φόβος, Δέος." *TDNT* 9:189–203.
Barrett, Lisa Feldman. *How Emotions Are Made: The Secret Life of the Brain*. New York: Houghton Mifflin, 2017.
Bechtel, Lyn M. "Shame as a Sanction of Social Control in Biblical Israel: Judicial, Political, and Social Shaming." *JSOT* 49 (1991): 47–76.
Bellis, Alice Ogden. "Proverbs in Recent Research." *CurBR* 20, no. 2 (2022): 133–64.
———. *Proverbs*. Collegeville, MN: Liturgical Press, 2018.
Ben Zvi, Ehud. "The 'Successful, Wise, Worthy Wife' of Proverbs 31:10–31 as a Source for Reconstructing Aspects of Thought and Economy in the Late Persian / Early Hellenistic Period." In *The Economy of Ancient Judah in Its Historical Context*, edited by Marvin Lloyd Miller et al., 27–50. Winona Lake, IN: Eisenbrauns, 2015.
———. "Total Exile, Empty Land and the General Intellectual Discourse in Yehud." In *The Concept of Exile in Ancient Israel and Its Historical Contexts*,

edited by Ehud Ben Zvi and Christoph Levin, 155–68. Berlin: de Gruyter, 2010.

Bergant, Diane. *Israel's Wisdom Literature: A Liberation-Critical Reading*. Minneapolis: Fortress, 1997.

Berquist, Jon L. "Critical Spatiality and the Construction of the Ancient World." In *"Imagining" Biblical Worlds: Studies in Spatial, Social and Historical Constructs in Honor of James W. Flanagan*, edited by David M. Gunn and Paula M. McNutt, 14–29. Sheffield: Sheffield Academic, 2002.

Biwul, Joel. "Reading the Virtuous Woman of Proverbs 31 as a Reflection of the Attributes of the Traditional Miship Woman of Tanzania." *OTE* 26, no. 2 (2013): 275–97.

———. "What Is He Doing at the Gate? Understanding Proverbs 31:23 and Its Implications for Responsible Manhood in the Context of African Societies." *OTE* 29, no. 1 (2016): 33–60.

Blumenthal, David R. "Images of Women in the Hebrew Bible." In *Marriage, Sex and Family in Judaism*, edited by M. Broyde, 15–60. Lanham, MD: Rowman & Littlefield, 2005.

Boer, Roland. *Bakhtin and Genre Theory in Biblical Studies*. Atlanta: Society of Biblical Literature, 2007.

———. "The Economic Politics of Biblical Narrative." In *The Oxford Handbook of Biblical Narrative*, edited by Danna Nolan Fewell, 529–39. Oxford: Oxford University Press, 2016.

———. "The Sacred Economy of Ancient Israel." *SJOT* 21, no. 1 (2007): 29–48.

Brenner, Athalya. "Figurations of Women in Wisdom Literature." In *A Feminist Companion to Wisdom Literature*, edited by Athalya Brenner, 50–56. Sheffield: Sheffield Academic, 1995.

Brenner, Athalya, and Fokkelien van Dijk-Hemmes. *On Gendering Texts: Female and Male Voices in the Hebrew Bible*. Leiden: Brill, 1993.

Brown, Jeannine K. *Scripture as Communication: Introducing Biblical Hermeneutics*. Grand Rapids: Baker Academic, 2007.

Camp, Claudia V. *Wisdom and the Feminine in the Book of Proverbs*. Decatur, GA: Almond, 1985.

Chase, Amy J. "Feeling Womb-ey: The Presence and Significance of Emotion in Proverbs 31:1–9." *Bible and Critical Theory* 18, no. 2 (2022). www.bibleandcriticaltheory.com/issues/vol-18-no-2-2022/vol-18-no-2-2022-amy-j-chase/.

Chitando, Ezra. "'The Good Wife': A Phenomenological Re-reading of Proverbs 31:10–31 in the Context of HIV/AIDS In Zimbabwe." *Scriptura* 86 (2004): 151–59.

Claassens, L. Juliana. "The Woman of Substance and Human Flourishing: Proverbs 31:10–31 and Martha Nussbaum's Capabilities Approach." *JFSR* 32, no. 1 (2016): 5–19.

Clifford, Richard J. *Proverbs: A Commentary*. Louisville: Westminster John Knox, 1999.

Clines, David. "David the Man: The Construction of Masculinity in the Hebrew Bible." In *Interested Parties: The Ideology of Writers and Readers of the Hebrew Bible*, 212–41. Sheffield: Sheffield Academic, 1995.

Creanga, Ovidiu. "Introduction." In *Biblical Masculinities Foregrounded*, edited by Ovidiu Creanga and Peter-Ben Smit, 3–14. Sheffield: Sheffield Phoenix, 2014.

Crenshaw, James L. "A Mother's Instruction to Her Son (Proverbs 31:1–9)." *PRSt* 15, no. 4 (1988): 9–22.

———. "Poverty and Punishment in the Book of Proverbs." *QR* 9, no. 3 (1989): 30–43.

Crespo, Maria, and Violeta Fernandez-Lansac. "Memory and Narrative of Traumatic Events: A Literature Review." *Psychological Trauma: Theory, Research, Practice, and Policy* 8, no. 2 (2016): 149–56.

Cresswell, Tim. *In Place/Out of Place: Geography, Ideology, and Transgression*. Minneapolis: University of Minnesota Press, 1996.

Crook, Margaret Brackenbury. "The Marriageable Maiden of Proverbs 31:10–31." *JNES* 13, no. 3 (1954): 137–40.

Crook, Zeba A. "Honor, Shame, and Social Status Revisited." *JBL* 128, no. 3 (2009): 591–611.

Davidson, Jo Ann. "Women Bear God's Image: Considerations from a Neglected Perspective." *AUSS* 54, no. 1 (2016): 31–49.

Davis, Ellen F. *Proverbs, Ecclesiastes, and the Song of Songs*. Louisville: Westminster John Knox, 2000.

Dobbs-Allsopp, F. W. *On Biblical Poetry*. Oxford: Oxford University Press, 2015.

Ebeling, Jennie R. *Women's Lives in Biblical Times*. New York: T&T Clark International, 2010.

Eskenazi, Tamara Cohn. "The Lives of Women in Postexilic Era." In *The Writings and Later Wisdom Books*, edited by Christl M. Maier and Nuria Calduch-Benages, 11–32. Atlanta: SBL Press, 2014.

Fewell, Danna Nolan. "The Work of Biblical Narrative." In *The Oxford Handbook of Biblical Narrative*, edited by Danna Nolan Fewell, 3–26. Oxford: Oxford University Press, 2016.

Fludernik, Monika. "Identity/Alterity." In *The Cambridge Companion to Narrative*, edited by David Herman, 260–73. Cambridge: Cambridge University Press, 2007.

———. *An Introduction to Narratology*. London: Routledge, 2009.

Fontaine, Carole R. "The Proof of the Pudding: Proverbs and Gender in the Performance Arena." *JSOT* 29, no. 2 (December 2004): 179–204.

———. "Proverbs." In *The Women's Bible Commentary*, edited by Carol A. Newsom and Sharon H. Ringe, 145–52. Louisville: Westminster John Knox, 1998.

———. *Smooth Words: Women, Proverbs, and Performance in Biblical Wisdom*. London: Sheffield Academic, 2002.

BIBLIOGRAPHY

Foster, Benjamin R., and Karen Polinger Foster. *Civilizations of Ancient Iraq.* Princeton: Princeton University Press, 2011.

Fox, Michael V. *Proverbs 10–31: A New Translation with Introduction and Commentary.* New Haven, CT: Yale University Press, 2009.

Frank, Arthur W. *Letting Stories Breathe: A Socio-narratology.* Chicago: University of Chicago Press, 2010.

———. *The Wounded Storyteller: Body, Illness, and Ethics.* Chicago: University of Chicago Press, 1995.

Freedman, David Noel. "Preface." In *Chiasmus in Antiquity: Structures, Analyses, Exegesis,* edited by John W. Welch, 7–8. Hildesheim: Gerstenberg, 1981.

Frese, Daniel A. "The Civic Forum in Ancient Israel: The Form, Function, and Symbolism of City Gates." PhD diss., University of California, San Diego, 2012. http://escholarship.org/uc/item/8tp5j3ch.

Fuchs, Esther. "Laughing with/at/as Women: How Should We Read Biblical Humor?" In *Are We Amused? Humour about Women in the Biblical Worlds,* edited by Athalya Brenner, 127–36. London: T&T Clark International, 2003.

———. *Sexual Politics in the Biblical Narrative: Reading the Hebrew Bible as a Woman.* JSOTSSup 310. Sheffield: Sheffield Academic, 2000.

Gafney, Wilda C. M. "Who Can Find a Militant Feminist? A Marginal(ized) Reading of Proverbs 31:1–31." *The AME Zion Quarterly Review* 112, no. 2 (2000): 25–31.

Garcia, Maureen Farrell. "Understanding the Link between Theology and Abuse: A Defense of Ruth Tucker's *Black and White Bible, Black and Blue Wife.*" CBE International, January 30, 2017. https://www.cbeinternational.org/resource/understanding-link-between-theology-and-abuse-defense-ruth-tuckers-black-and-white-bible-black/.

Geiger, Michaela. "Creating Space through Imagination and Action: Space and the Body in Deuteronomy 6:4–9." In *Constructions of Space IV: Further Developments in Examining Ancient Israel's Social Space,* edited by Mark K. George, 44–60. London: Bloomsbury T&T Clark, 2013.

George, Mark. "Space and History: Siting Critical Space for Biblical Studies." In *Constructions of Space I: Theory, Geography, and Narrative,* edited by Jon L. Berquist and Claudia V. Camp, 15–31. New York: T&T Clark, 2007.

Gerrig, Richard J., and Giovanna Egidi. "Cognitive Psychological Foundations of Narrative Experiences." In *Narrative Theory and the Cognitive Sciences,* edited by David Herman, 33–55. Stanford, CA: CSLI Publications, 2003.

Goh, Elaine. "An Intertextual Reading of Ruth and Proverbs 31:10–31, with a Chinese Woman's Perspective." In *Reading Ruth in Asia,* edited by Jione Havea and Peter H. W. Lau, 73–87. Atlanta: SBL Press, 2016.

Goh, Samuel. "Ruth as a Superior Woman of חיל?: A Comparison between Ruth and the 'Capable' Woman in Proverbs 31.10–31." *JSOT* 38, no. 4 (2014): 487–500.

Goldingay, John. *The First Testament: A New Translation.* Downers Grove, IL: InterVarsity, 2018.

BIBLIOGRAPHY

Gottschall, Jonathan. *The Storytelling Animal: How Stories Make Us Human.* Boston: Houghton Mifflin Harcourt, 2012.

Green, Barbara. *Mikhail Bakhtin and Biblical Scholarship: An Introduction.* Atlanta: Society of Biblical Literature, 2005.

Gudme, Anne Katrine. "Inside-Outside: Domestic Living Space in Biblical Memory." In *Memory and the City in Ancient Israel*, edited by Diana Vikander Edelman and Ehud Ben Zvi, 61–78. Winona Lake, IN: Eisenbrauns, 2014.

Guillaume, Philippe. "Wonder Woman's Field in Proverbs 31: Taken, Not Bought! Economic Considerations on Proverbs 31:16." In *Ugarit-Forschungen: Internationales Jahrbuch für die Altertumskunde Syrien-Palästinas*, edited by Manfried Dietrich and Ingo Kottsieper, 85–102. Munster: Ugarit-Verlag, 2016.

Gunn, David M., and Danna Nolan Fewell. *Narrative in the Hebrew Bible.* Oxford: Oxford University Press, 1993.

Hartley, John E. *Proverbs: A Commentary in the Wesleyan Tradition.* Kansas City, MO: Beacon Hill, 2016.

Healey, John F, trans. *The Targum of Proverbs, Translated, with a Critical Introduction, Apparatus, and Notes.* Collegeville, MN: Liturgical Press, 1991.

Herman, David. "Stories as a Tool for Thinking." In *Narrative Theory and the Cognitive Sciences*, edited by David Herman, 163–92. Stanford, CA: CSLI Publications, 2003.

———. *Story Logic: Problems and Possibilities of Narrative.* Lincoln: University of Nebraska Press, 2002.

Herman, Luc, and Bart Vervaeck. "Ideology." In *The Cambridge Companion to Narrative*, edited by David Herman, 217–30. Cambridge: Cambridge University Press, 2007.

Jansen, Ilze. "Proverbs 31:10–31: A Contextual Reading." *Verbum et Ecclesia* 41, no. 1 (2020): 1–9.

Kang, Sun-Ah. "Re-reading a 'Virtuous Woman' (*eshet chayil*) in Proverbs 31:10–31." In *Landscapes of Korean and Korean American Biblical Interpretation*, edited by John Ahn, 133–43. Atlanta: SBL Press, 2019.

Kassis, Riad Aziz. *The Book of Proverbs and Arabic Proverbial Works.* Leiden: Brill, 1999.

Kessler, Rainer. *The Social History of Ancient Israel.* Translated by Linda M. Maloney. Minneapolis: Fortress, 2008.

Kimche, J. J. "A Husband of Valor: Who Can Find? The Husband's Role in Proverbs 31:10–31." *JBQ* 49, no. 3 (2021): 143–57.

Kimilike, Legion Peter. "Poverty Context in Proverbs 31:1–9: A Bena Tanzanian Analysis for Transformational Leadership Training." *OTE* 31, no. 1 (2018): 135–63.

Kirk-Duggan, Cheryl A. "Rethinking the 'Virtuous' Woman (Proverbs 31): A Mother in Need of Holiday." In *Mother Goose, Mother Jones, Mommie Dearest*, edited by Cheryl A. Kirk-Duggan and Tina Pippen, 97–112. Leiden: Brill, 2009.

Klein, Kitty. "Narrative Construction, Cognitive Processing, and Health." In *Narrative Theory and the Cognitive Sciences*, edited by David Herman, 56–84. Stanford, CA: CSLI Publications, 2003.

Knight, Douglas A. *Law, Power, and Justice in Ancient Israel*. Louisville: Westminster John Knox, 2011.

Kwon, JiSeong. "Wisdom Incarnate? Identity and Role of אשת־חיל ('the Valiant Woman') in Proverbs 31:10–31." *Journal for the Evangelical Study of the Old Testament* 1, no. 2 (2012): 167–88.

Labahn, Antje. "'Wealthy Women' in Antiquity: The 'Capable Woman' of Proverbs 31:10–31 and Mibtahiah from Elephantine." *IDS* 48, no. 1 (2014): 1–9.

Lang, Bernhard. "The Hebrew Wife and the Ottoman Wife: An Anthropological Essay on Proverbs 31:10–31." In *Anthropology and Biblical Studies: Avenues of Approach*, edited by Louise J. Lawrence and Mairo I. Aguilar, 140–57. Leiden: Brill, 2004.

———. "Women's Work, Household and Property in Two Mediterranean Societies: A Comparative Essay on Proverbs xxxi 10–31." *VT* 54, no. 2 (2004): 188–207.

Lavoie, Jean-Jacques. "Vin et Bière En Proverbes 31,4–7." *SR* 44, no. 1 (March 2015): 33–54.

Lawrence, Beatrice. "Gender Analysis: Gender and Method in Biblical Studies." In *Method Matters: Essays on the Interpretation of the Hebrew Bible in Honor of David L. Petersen*, edited by Joel M. LeMon and Kent H. Richards, 333–48. Atlanta: Society of Biblical Literature, 2009.

Lefebvre, Henri. *The Production of Space*. Oxford: Blackwell, 1991.

———. "Space, Social Product and Use Value." In *State, Space, World: Selected Essays*, edited by Neil Brenner and Stuart Elden, 185–95. Minneapolis: University of Minnesota Press, 2009.

Leith, Mary Joan Winn. "New Perspectives on the Return from Exile and Persian-Period Yehud." In *The Oxford Handbook of the Historical Books of the Hebrew Bible*, online ed., edited by Brad Kelle and Brent Strawn, 147–69. Oxford Academic, November 10, 2020. https://academic.oup.com/edited-volume/34226.

Lensky, Gerhard. *Power and Privilege: A Theory of Social Stratification*. New York: McGraw-Hill, 1966.

Lichtenstein, Murray H. "Chiasm and Symmetry in Proverbs 31." *CBQ* 44 (1982): 202–11.

———. "Psalm 68:7 Revisited," *JANES* 4 (1972): 97–112.

Lindemann Nelson, Hilde. *Damaged Identities, Narrative Repair*. Ithaca, NY: Cornell University Press, 2001.

Lipka, Hilary. "Masculinities in Proverbs: An Alternative to the Hegemonic Ideal." In *Biblical Masculinities Foregrounded*, edited by Ovidiu Creagna and Peter-Ben Smit, 86–106. Sheffield: Sheffield Phoenix, 2014.

Liverani, Mario. *Israel's History and the History of Israel*. Translated by Chiara Peri and Philip R. Davies. London: Equinox, 2003.

Lodge, David. *After Bakhtin*. London: Routledge, 1990.
Longman, Tremper V., III. *Proverbs*. Grand Rapids, MI: Baker, 2006.
Low, Katherine B. "Implications Surrounding Girding the Loins in Light of Gender, Body, and Power." *JSOT* 36, no. 1 (2011): 3–30.
Macchi, Jean-Daniel. "Denial, Deception, or Force: How to Deal with Powerful Others in the Book of Esther." In *Imagining the Other and Constructing Israelite Identity in the Early Second Temple Period*, edited by Ehud Ben Zvi and Diana Vikander Edelman, 219–29. London: Bloomsbury T&T Clark, 2014.
Marbury, Herbert. "The Strange Woman in Persian Yehud: A Reading of Proverbs 7." In *Approaching Yehud: New Approaches to the Study of the Persian Period*, edited by Jon Berquist, 167–82. Leiden: Brill, 2008.
Masenya, Madipoane J. "Brief Notes: Response to Biwul." *OTE* 29, no. 2 (2016): 360–69.
———. *How Worthy Is the Woman of Worth? Rereading Proverbs 31:10–31 in African-South Africa*. New York: Peter Lang, 2004.
Massey, Doreen. *For Space*. London: SAGE, 2005.
———. "Power-Geometry and a Progressive Sense of Place." In *Mapping the Futures: Local Cultures, Global Change*, edited by Jon Bird et al., 59–69. London: Routledge, 1993.
———. *Space, Place and Gender*. Cambridge: Polity, 1994.
Mathys, Hans-Peter. "The Valiant Housewife of Proverbs 31:10–31: A Phoenician Business Woman." In *Foreign Women—Women in Foreign Lands*, edited by Angelika Berlejung and Marianne Grohmann, 157–74. Tubingen: Mohr Siebeck, 2019.
Matthews, Victor H. "Female Voices: Upholding the Honor of the Household." *BTB* 24, no. 1 (1994): 8–15.
———. "Honor and Shame in Gender-Related Legal Situations in the Hebrew Bible." In *Gender and Law in the Hebrew Bible and the Ancient Near East*, edited by Victor Matthews et al., 97–112. Sheffield: Sheffield Academic, 1998.
May, Natalie N. "Gates and Their Functions in Mesopotamia and Ancient Israel." In *The Fabric of Cities: Aspects of Urbanism, Urban Topography and Society in Mesopotamia, Greece and Rome*, edited by Natalie N. May and Ulrike Steinert, 77–121. Leiden: Brill, 2014.
McCreesh, Thomas P. "Wisdom as Wife: Proverbs 31:10–31." *RB* 92, no. 1 (1985): 25–46.
McKane, William. *Proverbs: A New Approach*. Philadelphia: Westminster, 1970.
Meyers, Carol. *Rediscovering Eve: Ancient Israelite Women in Context*. Oxford: Oxford University Press, 2012.
Mildorf, Jarmila. Review of *Letting Stories Breathe: Socio-narratology. Biography* 34, no. 4 (2011): 833–37.
Miller, Cynthia L. "Silence as a Response in Biblical Hebrew Narrative: Strategies of Speakers and Narrators." *JNSL* 32, no. 1 (2006): 23–43.
Miller, Marvin L. "Cultivating Curiosity: Methods and Models for Understanding Ancient Economies." In *The Economy of Ancient Judah in Its Historical*

Context, edited by Marvin Lloyd Miller et al., 3–23. Winona Lake, IN: Eisenbrauns, 2015.

Miller, Robert D. "The Performance of Oral Tradition in Ancient Israel." In *Contextualizing Israel's Sacred Writings*, edited by Brian Schmidt, 175–96. Atlanta: SBL Press, 2015.

Mirguet, Francoise. "What Is an 'Emotion' in the Hebrew Bible?" *BibInt* 24, nos. 4–5 (2016): 442–65.

Moore, Stephen. "Final Reflections on Biblical Masculinity." In *Men and Masculinity in the Hebrew Bible and Beyond*, edited by Ovidiu Creanga, 240–55. Sheffield: Sheffield Phoenix, 2010.

Moore, Stephen D., and Janice Capel Anderson. "Taking It Like a Man: Masculinity in 4 Maccabees." *JBL* 117, no. 2 (Summer 1998): 249–73.

Morris, Pam. "Introduction." In *The Bakhtin Reader*, edited by Pam Morris, 1–24. London: Edward Arnold, 1994.

Mosher, Harold F., Jr. "Towards a Poetics of Descriptized Narration." *Poetics Today* 12, no. 3 (1991): 425–45.

Murphy, Roland E. *Proverbs*. WBC 22. Nashville: Thomas Nelson, 1998.

———. *The Tree of Life: An Exploration of Biblical Wisdom Literature*. Grand Rapids: Eerdmans, 2002.

Nelson, Susan J. "13 Characteristics of a Wife of Noble Character in Today's World." Woman of Noble Character. https://www.womanofnoblecharacter.com/a-wife-of-noble-character/.

Newsom, Carol A. "Bakhtin, the Bible, and Dialogic Truth." *JR* 76, no. 2 (1996): 290–306.

Nwaoru, Emmanuel. "Image of the Woman of Substance in Proverbs 31:10–31 and African Context." *BN* 127 (2005): 41–66.

Nzimande, Makhosazana Keith. "Postcolonial Interpretation in Post-apartheid South Africa: The Gibirah in the Hebrew Bible in the Light of Queen Jezebel and the Queen Mother of Lemuel." PhD diss., Bright Divinity School, 2005.

Osiek, Carolyn. "Women, Honor, and Context in Mediterranean Antiquity." *HvTSt* 64, no. 1 (2008): 323–37.

Pastor, Jack. *Land and Economy in Ancient Palestine*. London: Routledge, 1997.

Perdue, Leo G. *Proverbs*. Louisville: Westminster John Knox, 2000.

Reinhartz, Adele. *Why Ask My Name? Anonymity and Identity in Biblical Narrative*. New York: Oxford University Press, 1998.

Rendsburg, Gary A. "Bilingual Wordplay in the Bible." *VT* 38, no. 3 (1988): 267–74.

Riess, Jana K. "The Woman of Worth: Impressions of Proverbs 31:10–31." *Dialogue* 30, no. 1 (1997): 141–51.

Rimmon-Kenan, Shlomith. *Narrative Fiction: Contemporary Poetics*. London: Methuen, 1983.

Ringstaff, Melissa. "Happily Submissive." A Virtuous Woman, October 12, 2009. https://avirtuouswoman.org/happily-submissive/?unapproved=135257&moderation-hash=2a3709bdfb79917e6ece42f9a3110c8c#comment-135257.

Ro, Johannes Un-Sok. "Socio-economic Context of Post-exilic Community and Literacy." *ZAW* 120, no. 4 (2008): 597–611.

Rofé, Alexander. "The Valiant Woman, *gynē sunetē* and the Redaction of the Book of Proverbs." In *Vergegenwartigun des Alten Testaments*, edited by Christoph Bultmann, Walter Dietrich, and Christoph Levin, 145–55. Gottingen: Vandenhoeck & Ruprecht, 2002.

Rollston, Christopher A. "Scribal Curriculum in the First Temple Period: Epigraphic Hebrew and Biblical Evidence." In *Contextualizing Israel's Sacred Writing: Ancient Literacy, Orality, and Literary Production*, edited by Brian Schmidt, 71–101. Atlanta: SBL Press, 2015.

Ryan, Marie-Laure. "Toward a Definition of Narrative." In *The Cambridge Companion to Narrative*, edited by David Herman, 22–38. Cambridge: Cambridge University Press, 2007.

Scheffler, Eben. "Poverty in the Book of Proverbs: Looking from Above?" *Scriptura* 111 (2012): 480–96.

Septuaginta: With Morphology. Logos electronic ed. Stuttgart: Deutsche Bibelgesellschaft, 1979.

Shaw, Karen L. "Wisdom Incarnate: Preaching Proverbs 31." *The Journal of the Evangelical Homiletics Society* 14 (2014): 44–53.

Sneed, Mark. *The Social World of the Sages*. Minneapolis: Fortress, 2015.

Soza, Joel. "Linking the חיל אשת ('Woman of Strength') of Proverbs and Ruth in the Leningrad Codex." *ATJ* 45 (2013): 21–27.

Stiebert, Johanna. "The People's Bible, Imbokodo and the King's Mother's Teaching of Proverbs 31." *BibInt* 20, no. 3 (2012): 244–79.

Van Leeuwen, Raymond. "The Book of Proverbs." *NIB* 5:17–264.

Vayntrub, Jacqueline. "Beauty, Wisdom, and Handiwork in Proverbs 31:10–31." *HTR* 113, no.1 (2020): 45–62.

Vice, Sue. *Introducing Bakhtin*. Manchester: Manchester University Press, 1997.

Walsh, Carey. "Testing Entry: The Social Functions of City Gates in Biblical Memory." In *Memory and the City*, edited by Diana V. Edelman and Ehud Ben Zvi, 43–60. Winona Lake, IN: Eisenbrauns, 2014.

Waltke, Bruce. *The Book of Proverbs: Chapters 15–31*. Grand Rapids: Eerdmans, 2005.

———. "The Role of the 'Valiant Wife' in the Marketplace." *Crux* 35, no. 3 (1999): 23–34.

Welch, Bailey Jo. "'She's Literally Fictional': What the Church Won't Tell You about the Proverbs 31 Woman." FaithIt, September 28, 2017. https://faithit.com/church-got-wrong-proverbs-31-woman-bailey-jo-welch/.

Wendland, Ernst. "Communicating the Beauty of a Wise and 'Worthy Wife' (Prov 31:10–31): From Hebrew Acrostic Hymn to a Tonga Traditional Praise Poem." *OTE* 19, no. 3 (2006): 1239–74.

"What Is Bible Project." Bible Project. September 13, 2018. https://youtu.be/vFwNZNyDu9k?si=F6ufAjY85Rf1tLy5.

Whybray, Norman. *The Composition of the Book of Proverbs.* Sheffield: JSOT Press, 2009.
———. *The Good Life in the Old Testament.* London: T&T Clark, 2002.
Wolters, Albert. "Proverbs 31:10–31 as Heroic Hymn: A Form-Critical Analysis." *VT* 38, no. 4 (1988): 446–57.
———. "Ṣôpiyyâ (Prov 31:27) as Hymnic Participle and Play on Sophia." *JBL* 104, no. 4 (December 1985): 577–87.
Yoder, Christine. *Proverbs.* Nashville: Abingdon, 2009.
———. *Wisdom as a Woman of Substance: A Socioeconomic Reading of Proverbs 1–9 and 31:10–31.* Berlin: de Gruyter, 2001.
———. "The Woman of Substance (*'št-Ḥyl*): A Socioeconomic Reading of Proverbs 31:10–31." *JBL* 122, no. 3 (2003): 427–47.
Young, Iris Marion. *Justice and the Politics of Difference.* Princeton: Princeton University Press, 1990.
Zucker, David J. "Esther: Subverting the 'Capable Wife.'" *BTB* 48, no. 4 (2018): 171–78.

Subject Index

absent interlocutor, 58
acrostic, 19, 20, 82, 95, 132, 148
affect, 1, 2, 3
agency, 8, 33, 40, 41, 43, 52, 69, 143, 151, 167, 172 173
alcohol, 40, 41, 44, 49, 50, 51, 60
alliterations, 20, 148
ambiguity, 12, 13, 26, 34, 36, 43, 48, 49, 65, 68, 81, 92, 97, 122, 136, 144, 159, 176
ancient community, 12, 16, 19, 20, 62, 101, 119, 121, 122, 128, 146, 157
Aramaisms, 41, 168
arrogant eye, 3, 50, 61, 75, 150, 173
audience, 27, 38, 39, 47, 65, 76, 121, 126, 130, 145, 149, 152, 157, 168
author, 12, 15, 18, 19, 25, 36, 136, 145, 151, 170
authorial intent, 13
authority, 11, 14, 43, 45, 59, 76, 105, 106, 107, 117, 123, 127, 142, 166, 167, 171, 173

ba'al, 9, 75, 91, 92, 95, 97, 105, 106, 107, 116, 117, 118, 123, 124, 132, 166, 167, 173
Babylon, 54, 55
Bakhtin, 4, 24, 25, 27, 34, 35, 36, 39, 57, 122, 136, 140, 148, 149, 158, 161, 175
body, 3, 8, 20, 45, 75, 76, 95

Canaanites (*kena'ani*), 68, 100, 126
charity, 81, 85, 86, 113, 169
chayil, 42, 44, 46, 62, 66, 76, 168
characterization, 18, 21, 41, 71, 77, 93, 105, 107, 108, 109, 114, 148
charm, 107, 109, 118, 120, 121, 122
chiasm, 80, 81, 83, 84, 88, 89, 95, 113, 148, 162
cities, 154, 155
class, 13, 22, 23, 24, 34, 42, 48, 50, 52, 56, 67, 69, 74, 75, 87, 130, 131, 132, 135, 156, 165, 168, 169, 171, 172
conflict, 17, 41, 56, 59, 66, 92, 116, 121, 135, 166
context, 12
  literary, 4, 5, 35, 37, 38, 71, 72, 83, 85, 107, 114, 123, 125, 126, 136, 139, 140, 148, 164, 175
  of readers, 2, 8, 9, 13, 50, 115, 122,
  Persian-era, 20, 53, 55, 56, 87, 88, 90, 108, 154, 163
contradictions, 27, 59
counterfactual history, 124, 167
counterstory, 29, 61, 62, 172, 173, 174, 175
court of reputation, 117, 118
Cyrus, 53, 55

deceit, 107, 109, 123
dialogism, 25, 26, 27, 60, 65
dialogue, 26, 27, 39, 57, 175

SUBJECT INDEX

economy, 129
Elephantine, 7, 100
ellipsis, 143, 147
elites, 54, 55, 56, 57, 61, 66, 69, 80, 86, 87, 88, 91, 92, 96, 106, 115, 126, 154, 155, 156, 158, 163, 164, 165, 166, 168
emotion, 1, 2, 14, 21, 33, 37, 38, 39, 45, 52, 61, 77, 165, 168
empire, 16, 34, 53, 54, 56, 66, 68, 70, 80, 88, 90, 93, 123, 124, 129, 154, 155
erasure, 79, 139
exploitation, 50, 80, 164

farming, 74, 88, 112, 129
Fear of Yahweh (*yiroth yahweh*), 15, 100, 107, 111, 112, 120, 122, 130, 131, 163, 164, 173
focalization, 19, 40, 50, 51, 76, 164, 167, 168, 169
foreigners, 100, 118
foreign lands, 21, 24, 68, 105, 142
foreignness, 41, 168

gaps, 12, 17, 27, 29, 34, 65, 81, 97, 122, 136, 144, 161, 172, 176
gates, 19, 21, 24, 95, 96, 97, 100, 101, 113, 122, 124, 127, 130, 131, 135, 140, 141, 146, 150, 151, 152, 167
 associations with community, 98, 117, 125, 142, 147, 149, 168
 associations with jurisprudence, 75, 98, 116, 153, 157, 164, 166
 forming identity, 67, 75, 99, 100, 102, 103, 104, 105, 117, 119, 142, 143, 144, 173, 174
 as liminal space, 126, 132, 144, 145, 155, 159
gebirah, 43
gender, 7, 8, 12, 13, 22, 23, 24, 36, 38, 43, 62, 67, 77, 91, 97, 102, 104, 110, 113, 117, 127, 128, 130, 141, 142, 155, 165

genre, 5, 11, 13, 14, 34, 38, 135, 146, 162
golah, 69, 87, 90, 96, 155, 156, 165

hands, 6, 75, 79, 80, 82, 83, 84, 85, 86, 89, 139, 165, 167
harm, 4, 15, 23, 30, 50, 53, 67, 90, 123, 131, 156, 176
heft, 3, 62, 173, 174
heroic hymn, 5, 83, 135, 137
home (household), 9, 40, 54, 67, 69, 74, 75, 87, 90, 101, 102, 103, 104, 105, 125, 126, 127, 128, 129, 132, 152, 165, 170, 173
honor, 40, 69, 72, 78, 99, 100, 103, 105, 107, 108, 113, 116, 117, 118, 119, 120, 121, 127, 130, 131, 132, 138, 140, 141, 142, 150, 152, 173
humor, 20
husband, 8, 9, 11, 12, 14, 15, 45, 47, 67, 68, 69, 70, 73, 75, 76, 77, 90, 91, 95, 99, 100, 101, 103, 105, 106, 107, 108, 115, 116, 117, 118, 119, 120, 121, 122, 130, 131, 139, 140, 141, 142, 143, 146, 147, 149, 150, 154, 163, 167, 169, 170

identity, 9, 22, 36, 45, 55, 70, 71, 76, 77, 105, 118, 120, 125, 127, 142, 158, 171, 172, 173
 construction/shaping of, 3, 4, 5, 11, 29, 43, 44, 76, 80, 107, 128, 144, 145, 161, 174
 damaged, 33, 41, 49, 52, 61, 62, 78, 96, 121, 124, 172, 173, 174, 176
ideology, 11, 19, 23, 25, 28, 55, 57, 87, 102, 128, 153, 179
instruction, 5, 14, 19, 34, 35, 39, 60, 78, 91, 96, 109, 114, 144, 157, 173, 176
interpretation, 1, 2, 5, 10, 12, 13, 14, 15, 17, 24, 27, 29, 36, 38, 58, 81, 135, 138, 163, 172
intertextuality, 26, 164
Israel, 34, 84, 123, 128, 168

SUBJECT INDEX

judge, 44, 100, 132, 154, 166
judgment, 13, 43, 49, 52, 56, 60, 66, 98, 104, 119, 120, 123, 153, 157, 162, 167
justice, 49, 153, 155, 164, 165, 171

khesed, 113, 114, 125, 131, 150, 168

labor, 50, 69, 70, 79, 80, 83, 88, 96, 101, 112, 138, 144, 145, 151, 156, 158, 163, 164, 168, 174
Lady Wisdom, 51, 98, 152, 164
land, 24, 54, 55, 56, 74, 78, 79, 87, 88, 89, 90, 91, 96, 98, 116, 118, 123, 126, 131, 153, 154, 155, 163, 165, 168
laziness, 6, 70, 102, 104, 115, 130, 167, 168
leisure, 7, 69, 106, 131
Lemuel, 12, 40, 41, 42, 52, 56
Lemuel's mother, 33, 37, 40, 42, 43, 44, 45, 52
liminality, 126, 130, 132, 144, 155, 172
location, 21, 23, 30, 66, 67, 70, 71, 87, 97, 98, 99, 100, 101, 102, 104, 105, 106, 127, 136, 143, 144, 151, 174
loving eye, 61, 173

meaning, 2, 5, 13, 16, 24, 25, 27, 28, 36, 41, 57, 65, 122, 136, 148, 162, 166, 172, 175
memory, 6, 36, 37, 40, 102, 124
metaphor, 10, 14, 37, 79, 80, 106, 110, 116, 118, 126, 139, 145, 163
monologism, 25, 29, 36, 39, 65, 159, 161, 176
mother, 9, 45, 51, 103, 138, 153, 169

name, 2, 43, 46, 107, 120
narrative, 4, 11, 12, 16, 17, 18, 21, 23, 28, 29, 34, 37, 90, 93, 135, 148, 158, 162, 175

event, 89, 90, 115, 149
identity shaping, 3, 5
levels, 19, 20, 121
master, 3, 29, 33, 41, 55, 61, 62, 110, 158, 172, 173, 176
repair, 61, 62, 172, 173, 174, 176
narratee, 19, 20
narrativity, 17, 90
narrator, 8, 15, 18, 19, 20, 25, 50, 75, 76, 80, 121, 122, 129, 173

Oeconomicus, 67, 91, 128
oracle, 5, 37
orality, 148

parallelism, 46, 48, 60, 72, 83, 84, 146, 147
performance, 12, 19, 20, 21, 59, 117, 140, 148, 149, 179
Persian Empire, 16, 53, 54, 56, 66, 68, 70, 124, 129, 154, 155
plot, 11, 89, 93, 115, 132, 151
plunder (*shalal*), 73, 74, 80, 89, 90, 120, 164
polyphony, 42, 65, 101, 136
productivity, 69, 80, 96, 166, 168
profit, 27, 70, 74, 79, 80, 84, 89, 107, 119, 138, 139, 147, 151, 157, 166, 168, 174
prophecy, 37, 62, 98, 123

questions, 13, 18, 23, 24, 25, 27, 33, 34, 53, 58, 65, 66, 71, 76, 131, 143, 162

readers, 1, 2, 3, 4, 12, 15, 16, 19, 27, 28, 29, 30, 33, 34, 37, 38, 41, 48, 50, 51, 56, 58, 59, 66, 67, 68, 72, 77, 86, 89, 90, 91, 92, 93, 95, 96, 97, 100, 116, 122, 136, 140, 145, 147, 149, 151, 161, 162, 163, 169, 175
rebuke, 21, 33, 37, 38, 40, 43, 45, 52, 115, 122, 148, 152, 165, 168

189

SUBJECT INDEX

repetition, 20, 33, 38, 39, 40, 52, 60, 95, 141, 148
reply, 24, 58, 65, 124, 132, 163, 165, 175
riposte, 117, 119, 120, 132, 141, 150, 162

scribe, 12, 19, 55, 69, 151
setting, 21, 22, 67, 70, 96, 97, 151, 152, 153
shaming speech, 21, 40, 152
silence, 16, 36, 39, 53, 58, 66, 106, 115, 158, 162
social order, 87, 126, 127, 128, 154, 167
socionarratology, 28, 163
space, 16, 21, 22, 23, 24, 45, 67, 68, 69, 70, 71, 98, 99, 100, 101, 102, 103, 104, 105, 117, 122, 123, 125, 126, 127, 128, 130, 132, 142, 143, 144, 153, 155, 159, 171, 173, 176
speaker, 15, 20, 27, 35, 36, 38, 39, 43, 50, 51
suspense, 89, 93

tension, 104, 115, 116, 135, 154
trade, 7, 13, 21, 53, 68, 69, 74, 88, 98, 100, 101, 107, 108, 126, 129, 130, 166, 168, 173

underclass, 53, 54, 55, 57, 61, 62, 66, 78, 79, 80, 81, 82, 86, 88, 89, 92, 93, 96, 97, 113, 114, 116, 125, 126, 132, 135, 139, 155, 164, 169, 172, 173
unfinalizability, 39, 158, 159, 175
utopia, 90, 91, 92, 116, 126, 138, 166, 167
utterance, 4, 25, 26, 29, 34, 39, 57, 136, 148, 149, 161

warrior, 9, 71, 73, 74, 75, 79, 81, 83, 84, 89, 96, 108, 110, 118, 120, 137
wealth, 4, 7, 13, 24, 42, 46, 47, 53, 54, 56, 62, 66, 67, 71, 72, 73, 74, 79, 80, 81, 83, 84, 85, 89, 96, 106, 112, 116, 126, 129, 131, 139, 154, 155, 156, 157, 163, 165, 168, 173
wisdom literature, 5, 6, 14, 34, 41, 137
work, 16, 22, 129, 130, 169, 172, 175. *See also* labor
  of elites, 61, 70, 84, 89, 145, 152
  of laborers, 45, 68, 77, 78, 80, 87, 88, 106, 132, 139, 165
  of Proverbs 31, 53, 66, 96, 114, 124, 128, 138, 142, 146, 167

Yahweh, 73, 79, 85, 110, 111, 118, 131, 141, 146

Scripture Index

Genesis
book of 57
2–3 2
3:20 2, 119, 138
3:22 83
3:23 138
9:2 82
11:6 79
16:6 82
16:12 82
20 122
23:13 79
24:30 35
27 34, 122
30:2 138
31 122
34 98
37:30 39

Exodus
9:29 85
9:33 85
12:36 123
17:7 35, 37
23:5 37
32 175

Numbers
11:24 35

Deuteronomy
7:13 138
15:7–9 85

19:19 79
21 153
21:11 73
21:18 38
24:1 109
25 153
28:4 138
28:11 138
28:18 138
28:52 73
28:53 138
30:9 138

Joshua
2 144
8:3 73
10:7 74

Judges
4–5 168
5:11 137
5:26 83
5:30 73
11:40 137

1 Samuel
1 38
16:22 123
30:2 73

2 Samuel
12:1–4 37
13:13 156

SCRIPTURE INDEX

14	37
15:11	144
18:24	103
19:4	39
19:8	98
23:8	73

1 Kings

1	34
3:26–27	153
8:22	85
8:38	85
8:54	85
10:2	72
11:19	43
12:11	38
15:9–14	59
15:13	43
16:31	108

2 Kings

10:13	43
18:5	73
18:19–22	73
18:24	73
18:30	73
19:10	73

Isaiah

13:1	37
13:18	138
14:28	37
15:1	37
17:1	37
19:1	37
19:8	85
21:1	37
21:11	37
21:13	37
22:1	37
23:1	37
25:11	85
30:1	37
65:2	85

Jeremiah

3	123
4:28	79
4:31	85
13:18	43
29:2	43
51:12	79

Ezekiel

12:10	37
12:13	85
16	123
17:20	85
19:8	85
23	123
32:3	85

Hosea

5:1	85
7:12	85

Jonah

4:11	158

Nahum

1:1	37

Habakkuk

1:1	37

Zechariah

1:6	79
8:14	79
8:15	79
9:1	37
12:1	37

Malachi

1:1	37

Ezra

1	54
9:5	85
10	56

SCRIPTURE INDEX

Nehemiah
5	55
5:1–5	92
5:17	54
13:28	54

2 Chronicles
6:12	85
6:13	85
6:29	85
9:1	72
10:14	38
15:16	43
22:2–4	59

Psalms
28:4	137
44:20	85
68:7	83
96:6	110
104–6	141
104:1	110
111:2	146
111:3	110
111:10	111
113	141
115–17	141
127:3	138
128:1	130
128:4	130
135	141
143:6	85
145:19	130
146-50	141
147	130
147:11	130
148:3	11, 146

Proverbs
1–9	152
1	164
1:1	151
1:7	131
2:16	48
5:3–4	47
5:8–10	47
5:19	121
7:5	48
8	164
9	164
11:16	109, 121
12:4	72
15:3	110
15:37	131
19:17	86
19:23	131
22:4	131
22:22–23	164
30:1	35
30:20	46
31:1–9	33–62, 96, 116, 132, 168, 172, 173
31:1	33, 35, 38, 41, 43, 44, 148, 162
31:2–4	41
31:2–3	41
31:2	14, 27, 38, 45, 52, 58, 60
31:3–4	44
31:3	16, 41, 42, 46, 47, 48, 49, 52, 62, 66, 72, 110, 151, 164, 165, 167
31:4–9	44
31:4–7	39
31:4–5	56
31:4	45, 52, 60
31:5–9	46, 48, 49, 86, 106, 114, 125, 164, 166
31:5	43, 49, 52, 59, 60, 163
31:6–9	158
31:6–7	50, 162
31:6	39, 59, 60, 121, 151
31:7	49, 163
31:8–9	39, 44, 60, 66, 113, 151, 158, 164
31:8	49, 148, 150, 163
31:9	49, 52, 60, 148, 163
31:10–22	65–93, 114, 131, 132

SCRIPTURE INDEX

31:10	1, 27, 65, 67, 71, 72, 76, 96, 100, 113, 130, 138, 141, 143	31:30	5, 15, 30, 100, 109, 111–12, 120, 121, 122, 123, 130, 131, 141, 142, 155, 156, 162, 163, 173
31:11	70, 73, 75, 82, 90, 91, 95, 96, 116, 120, 123		
31:12	15, 70, 73, 75, 76, 89, 116, 123	31:31	27, 67, 75, 96, 110, 132, 135–59, 162, 164, 165, 166, 167, 174
31:13	15, 68, 74, 75, 77, 88, 107		
31:14	67, 68, 74, 100		
31:15	14, 15, 67, 69, 74, 77, 78, 85, 88, 101, 106, 108, 142, 163, 164	*Job*	
		1:1	41
		3–37	117
31:16	67, 68, 74, 75, 78, 79, 88, 107, 108, 114, 125, 138, 139, 142, 154, 155, 156, 164, 165	11:13	85
		16:19–21	154
		29	69
31:17	74, 76, 82, 106	29:8	108
31:18	15, 74, 77, 88, 100, 106		
31:19–21	74	*Ruth*	
31:19–20	75, 80–86, 88, 108, 113, 114, 125, 139, 156, 162	1:8	103
		2:1	142
31:19	72	3:11	72, 142
31:20–21	92	4	98, 117, 154, 157
31:20	15, 89, 107, 113, 154, 163, 165	4:2	149
		4:11	144
31:21–22	74	4:17	150
31:21	15, 69, 70, 77, 88, 101, 116		
31:22	15, 68, 88, 91	*Lamentations*	
31:23–30	95–132	1	123
31:23	68, 69, 70, 75, 76, 95, 96, 97, 99, 106, 107, 117, 127, 142, 143, 154, 166, 170	1:10	85
		1:13	85
		1:17	85
31:24	15, 68, 74, 100, 108, 142	2:17	79
31:25–27	131	4:4	85
31:25	108, 110		
31:26	15, 66, 76, 100, 108, 113–14, 120, 125, 148, 150, 168	*Esther*	
		1	167
		1:11	121
31:27	5, 15, 69, 82, 101–5, 108, 110, 115, 130, 152	2:15	109, 121
		2:17	109
31:28–30	162	5:2	109
31:28–29	70, 135	5:8	109
31:28	75, 107, 108, 110, 116, 119, 141, 149	7:3	109
		8:5	109
31:29–30	107, 110, 116, 122, 141	*Sirach*	
31:29	95, 100, 107, 108, 109, 119, 120, 122, 148, 149, 164, 167	38:24	69